THE
GREENE COUNTY
CATSKILLS
A HISTORY

FIELD HORNE

FOR THE GREENE COUNTY
HISTORICAL SOCIETY

BLACK · DOME

BLACK DOME PRESS CORP.
RR 1, Box 422
Hensonville, NY 12439
Tel: (518) 734-6357
Fax: (518) 734-5802

Published by
Black Dome Press Corp.
RR1, Box 422
Hensonville, New York 12439
(518) 734-6357

For the Greene County Historical Society, Inc.
Bronck House Museum
Coxsackie, New York 12051

First Edition, 1994

Library of Congress Card Catalog Number 94-071411

ISBN 1-883789-02-8

Design by Carol Clement, Artemisia, Inc.

Printed in the USA

DEDICATION

*W*hile it may be true that in every community organization the combined effort of all members determines success, it is also true that in most community endeavors there is one person whose guiding spirit sets a pace and character essential to that success. The name Raymond Beecher is almost synonymous with Greene County history. As member of the Board of Trustees of the Greene County Historical Society (and past president), former curator of the Bronck Museum, Coxsackie Town Historian, for over thirty years the Vedder Memorial Librarian, Greene County Historian, author and educator, Raymond Beecher has truly been tireless in his pursuit of the preservation of our community's heritage. It is to Raymond Beecher that we dedicate this book with our gratitude and highest esteem.

The Board of Trustees
The Greene County Historical Society

INTRODUCTION

One of the first responsibilities I assumed when I came to Albany in 1975 as Secretary of State was that of Keeper of the Great Seal of New York. Though it wasn't the most time-consuming of my duties, I got to know the Great Seal pretty well. The designers of our seal, which was adopted in 1778, turned to the Catskills for appropriate images of the State's wealth and promise. At the center of the icon is the sun shining down on a somewhat idealized Catskill mountain and two other peaks lying further west; in the middle distance a stretch of the Hudson enlivened by two cargo vessels under sail; in the foreground, fertile agricultural lands. In the minds of our forebears, these images captured the symbolic importance to the State of its natural resources, and their relationship to our economic well-being. It is no coincidence that, as noted in this interesting book, there was a Catskills area newspaper in the 1790's named *The Rising Sun.*

Nothing is new under the sun. The symbolism is still potent, the relationship still direct and the role of the Hudson and the Catskills in New York's affairs more vibrant than ever.

The Catskills and Greene County region is important for the part it plays in New York's enormous recreation and tourism industry; for its agriculture and forest products; for its water resources, which provide the purest and most dependable supply of water enjoyed by any big city in the world; for its cultural values as the cradle of American landscape painting and of the nation's wilderness recreation ethic; but most of all for its people—its diverse, independent residents, proud defenders of their mountains, valleys and hamlets and the life they pursue there.

The nation's first native "school" of painting arose with landscapist Thomas Cole, who in the 1820's achieved enormous success with naturalistic and romantic canvasses depicting an untamed and unspoiled wilderness. Cole's images of the Hudson Valley and Catskills (and those of his followers Frederic Church, John F. Kensett, Asher Durand and others) introduced the notion not of a wilderness inimical to man, made available by providence merely to be conquered and exploited (the 17th and 18th Century view), but rather a uniquely American Eden in all its pristine glory: landscapes to refresh us, humble us and inspire in us wonder at God's creation.

Popular writers such as New Yorkers Washington Irving, James Fenimore Cooper, William Cullen Bryant and Nathaniel P. Willis expanded on this theme in their poetry, fiction and non-fiction (as did, on a more philosophical level, New Englanders such as Thoreau and Emerson). These artists and writers perceived in America's rapidly expanding drive to industrialize and exploit natural resources a mounting threat to the spiritual values embodied in the landscapes they celebrated. Ironically, it was the "industrial," intrusive steamboat and railroad that made the Hudson Valley and Catskills accessible to ten of thousands of city-dwellers who, having been lured by the paintings and writings, wished to experience in person the river and the wilderness—

thereby hastening the degradation of these landscapes. Out of this evolved the wilderness park and conservation movement (in which Frederick Law Olmstead played a role), culminating with State and Federal government-administered programs of land preservation and public recreation. It has been said that one of America's preeminent contributions to world civilization has been our pioneering public and private commitment to land conservation on a large scale.

The phenomenal growth of wilderness recreation has helped to fuel tourism, which in New York is described by many as the State's second largest industry, after agri-business. Meanwhile, the parallel wilderness preservation movement gave rise to the establishment of the Catskill Forest Preserve and Park. The Catskill Mountain House in Greene County provided the locale for many events symbolizing these varied threads in our nation's cultural life. While the historic old Mountain House is now only a memory, it is a memory kept bright by this book—as is so much else of value in the diverse heritage of Greene County. Taking the place of the old hotel is an exceptionally popular State campground, recreational day-use area and trailhead, their spectacular forest setting protected in perpetuity by a provision of the State Constitution and enjoyed by more than 100,000 vistors annually.

Half a generation after the Luminists and the Transcendentalists, another New York writer made the natural world of the Catskills famous throughout the land. "O my native hills!" John Burroughs exclaimed in old age. "Will they ever mean to anyone else what they have meant to me?" It is for all of us together, in our time, to respond with a resounding "yes!" Field Horne's fascinating history of Greene County, along with a steadily growing number of other fine books documenting the storied past and cultural diversity of this region, will surely help succeeding generations meet a grand old man's heartfelt challenge to posterity of clarifying and deepening in the reader an abiding sense of place—Greene County!

Mario M. Cuomo
Governor of New York

FOREWORD

*O*ver the past several years there have been suggestions for the updating of Beers' (1884) *History of Greene County, N.Y.* The Greene County Historical Society finally came to the conclusion that an entirely new comprehensive volume would serve a more scholarly purpose. The Society's interest in carrying out its educational mandate as spelled out in its permanent charter coincided with the goal of Black Dome Press, which is to publish volumes relating to the Catskill region and the mid-Hudson area. A series of meetings finally developed a three-way working arrangement among the Society, the publisher, and the author, Field Horne. Horne's proven "track record" with other publications was helpful in getting the Society's Board to invest a substantial sum of capital in the project. Chairman of the Board J. Theodore Hilscher was particularly helpful with finalizing arrangements.

The confidence given to Field Horne has not been misplaced; he now may add another successful volume to his record of authorship. He has proven especially adept at utilizing the holdings of research facilities such as the New York State Library and the Vedder Memorial Library operated by the Green County Historical Society. Mr. Horne has organized selected material into three major units: Prehistoric and Colonial, the Nineteenth Century of growth, and finally the Twentieth Century of major change. Within each of the units is a wide selection of subject material reflecting the economic and social conditions which have served to weave the Greene County fabric.

Visual illustrations reinforce printed words. The excellent selection and generous donation of photographs from public and private holdings is an added plus to the volume. In addition to the quality of illustrations, I commend the author's use of verbatim quotations from several generations of visitors and local residents. The extensive listing of sources consulted, both published and unpublished, should be a boon to others contemplating local history publications.

The richness of Greene County's history, one strongly influenced by the Hudson River on the east and the northern Catskill range of mountains in the more westerly section, has long been a challenge to historians. Beers' history is now more than a century in vintage. The first county historian, Jessie V.V. Vedder, set the cut off date for her 1927 county history at 1800. Gallt's *Dear Old Greene County* was never intended to be a complete history but rather an assemblage of segmented material. The goal of the American Revolution Bicentennial publication that came out in 1976 was to provide an overview rather than a detailed examination. Numerous authors such as William F. Helmer, Alf Evers and Roland Van Zandt have written competently on more specialized aspects, i.e., the railroads, the Catskill Mountains, and the Mountain House itself. All of these, as well as other efforts, should be recognized as contributing to the preservation and interpretation of local history.

In the last few decades researchers have had a wide range of primary and secondary resource material available as public and private holdings have grown. In some cases this has led to a more careful evaluation of earlier writings, resulting in more sophisticated conclusions. It has also allowed a more multi-disciplinary approach to examining prehistoric cultures. Thus, archaeology plays an important role in the newer approaches to understanding the importance of Coxsackie township's Mineberg (Flint Mine Hill). Similarly, the Dutch period, lasting about half a century, benefits from the work of the New Netherland Project, which has enabled scholars to have access to a wide range of translated Dutch manuscripts.

Paralleling these research trends is the growing scholarly interest in the more mundane aspects of daily living. Periodic publications such as the Greene County Historical Society's *Quarterly Journal* and the Mountain Top Historical Society's *The Hemlock* are outgrowths of this developing interest. Genealogy has also played a role, particularly as family researchers from other sections of the country seek out biographical information relating to their Greene County forebears; they are frequently contributors as well as users of resource material. Immigration into Greene County has enriched its history. One only needs to read Joe Pavlak's publications on Cementon to comprehend this point.

Each generation seems to approach Greene County history in the light of its own interests. Some are full-time residents while others maintain second homes in the county. These residents have encouraged an interest in the architectural history of properties which has brought into being the Greene County Historical Register, an effort which seeks to develop an understanding of the wealth of building styles which enrich this more rural area. The New York State history curriculum in our primary and secondary school systems, plus the independent studies programs found on the higher levels are all encouraging signs. Public and organizational research libraries are giving more attention to the utilization of local history collections in all the various formats.

We do not live in a static society; change is inevitable. Field Horne has captured that essence of timeliness. His volume will, in the years ahead, become a major reference source for Greene County history, one finding its established place on the bookshelves of public and private local history collections.

Raymond Beecher
Greene County Historian

ACKNOWLEDGEMENTS

*T*his book drew upon the research and resources, the time and talents, of many people; without their patience, expertise, and willingness to contribute, my efforts as author would have been much diminished. Foremost among them were the Greene County Historical Society and Raymond Beecher, repositories both of much that is known of Greene County's past. All of the trustees of the Greene County Historical Society deserve great credit for their vision, unfailing support and tireless footwork in tracking down material, but particular mention must be made of the enormous contributions of Ted Hilscher and Robert Stackman.

Expert assistance came from many quarters; Justine Hommel, the Mountain Top Historical Society and the Haines Falls Free Library provided a wealth of information unobtainable without their generous participation and careful preservation of the artifacts in their trust. A similar debt of gratitude is owed to Shelby Kriele of the Bronck House Museum, Pat Millen of the Zadock Pratt Museum, Vernona Fleurent of the Durham Center Museum, and Greenville Town Historian Donald Teator.

Special thanks are warmly extended to all the individuals who granted access to their private collections and independent research: Joseph Pavlak helped us with Cementon, Betty Jean Poole with Athens, Robert Uzzilia with Cairo, Larry Tompkins with the Mountaintop and Robert Carl with the valley towns. William E. Higgins, Professional Land Surveyor, of Windham expertly crafted the patent map specially for this publication. Patricia H. Davis carefully, and with great skill, edited the text.

The staff in Manuscripts and Special Collections at the New York State Library was always ready to help me track down material, and special thanks to Billie Aul of that division for her superb index.

Any history is a collaborative effort. To the above collaborators on this history, and to all the many others whose contributions were of benefit—indeed, in many cases essential—but which space unfortunately does not permit me to enumerate and acknowledge in full, my sincerest gratitude.

Field Horne
1994

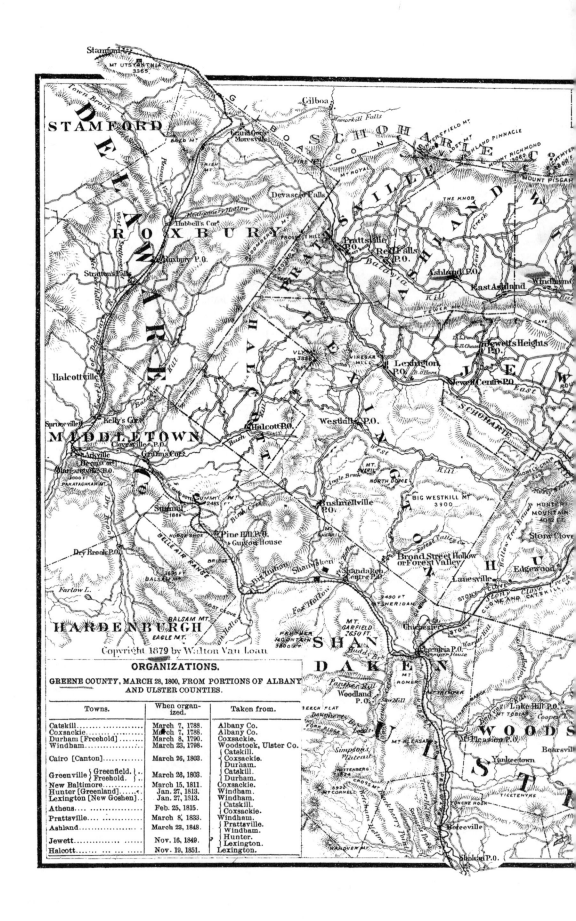

Copyright 1879 by Walton Van Loan

ORGANIZATIONS.

GREENE COUNTY, MARCH 28, 1800, FROM PORTIONS OF ALBANY
AND ULSTER COUNTIES.

Towns.	When organ- ized.	Taken from.
Catskill.............	March 7, 1788.	Albany Co.
Coxsackie...........	March 7, 1788.	Albany Co.
Durham [Freehold]........	March 8, 1790.	Coxsackie.
Windham............	March 23, 1798.	Woodstock, Ulster Co.
Cairo [Canton].............	March 26, 1803.	Catskill. Coxsackie. Durham.
Greenville { Greenfield. } .. { Freehold. } ..	March 26, 1803.	Catskill. Durham.
New Baltimore.............	March 15, 1811.	Coxsackie.
Hunter [Greenland]........	Jan. 27, 1813.	Windham.
Lexington [New Goshen]..	Jan. 27, 1813.	Windham.
Athens.....	Feb. 25, 1815.	Catskill. Coxsackie.
Prattsville.....	March 8, 1833.	Windham.
Ashland.................	March 23, 1848.	Prattsville. Windham.
Jewett..............	Nov. 16, 1849.	Hunter. Lexington.
Halcott...............	Nov. 19, 1851.	Lexington.

MAP OF
GREENE CO. N.Y.
AND PORTIONS OF
ULSTER AND DELAWARE
COS. N.Y.

Scale 3 Miles to the inch

Engraved by J.B. Beers & Co. 36 Vesey St. New York

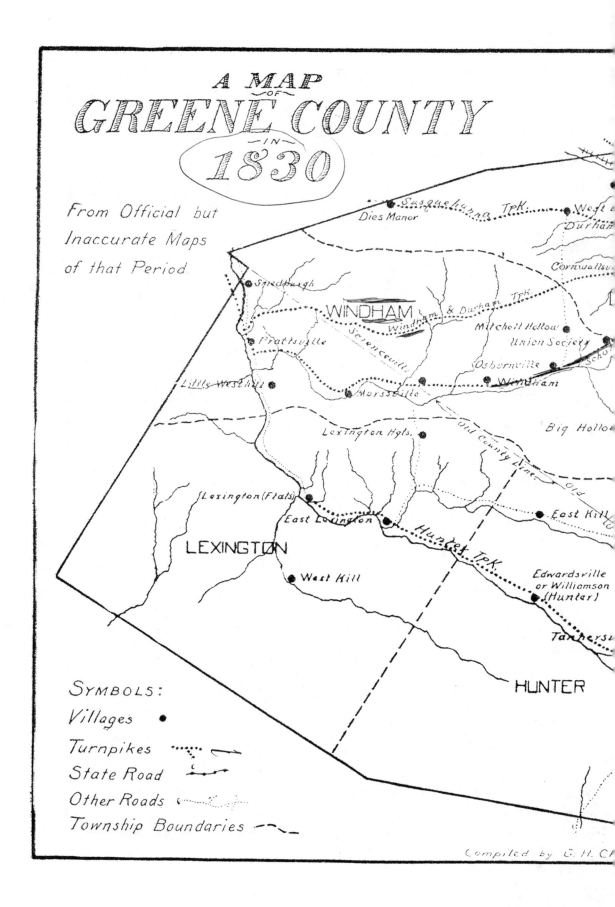

A MAP
OF
GREENE COUNTY
—IN—
1830

From Official but
Inaccurate Maps
of that Period.

SYMBOLS:
Villages
Turnpikes
State Road
Other Roads
Township Boundaries

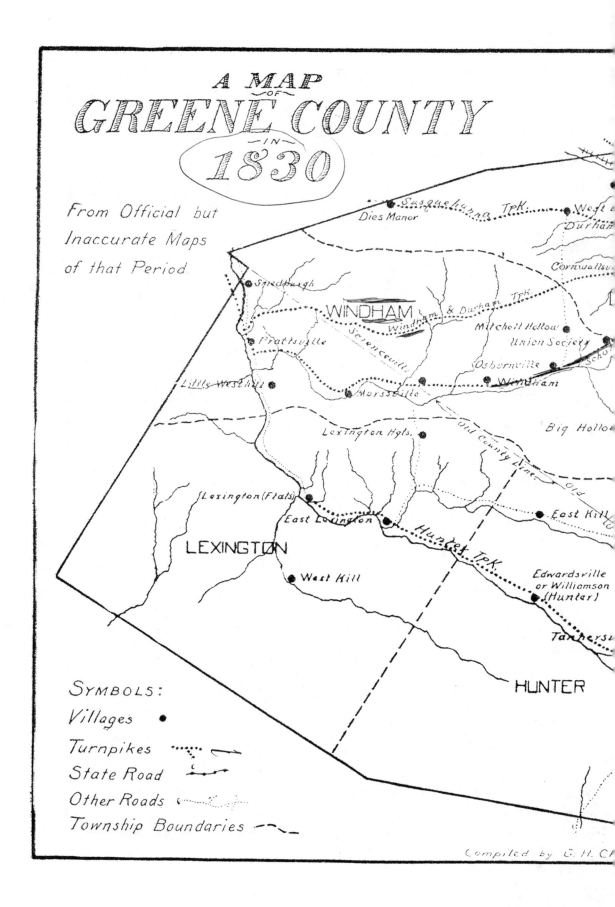

Compiled by C. H. C...

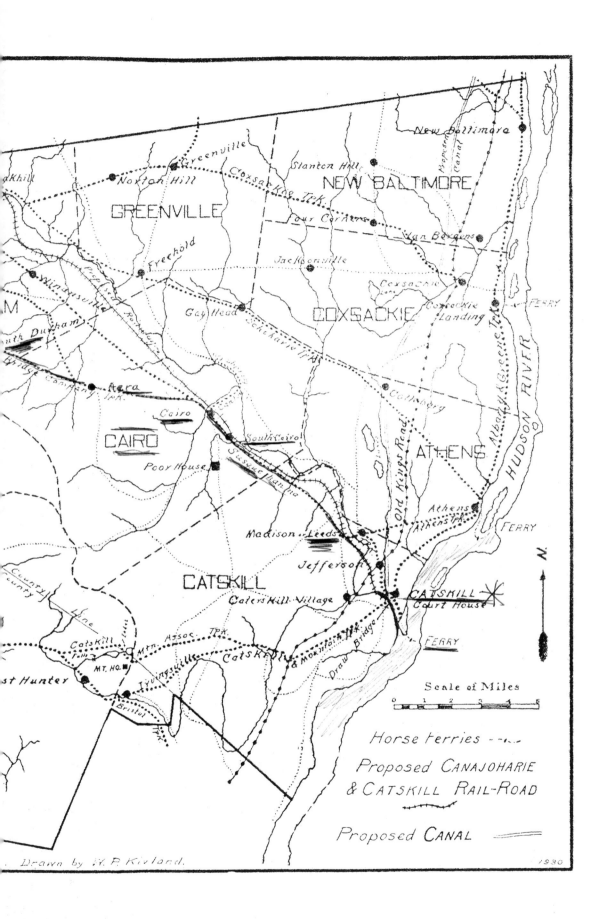

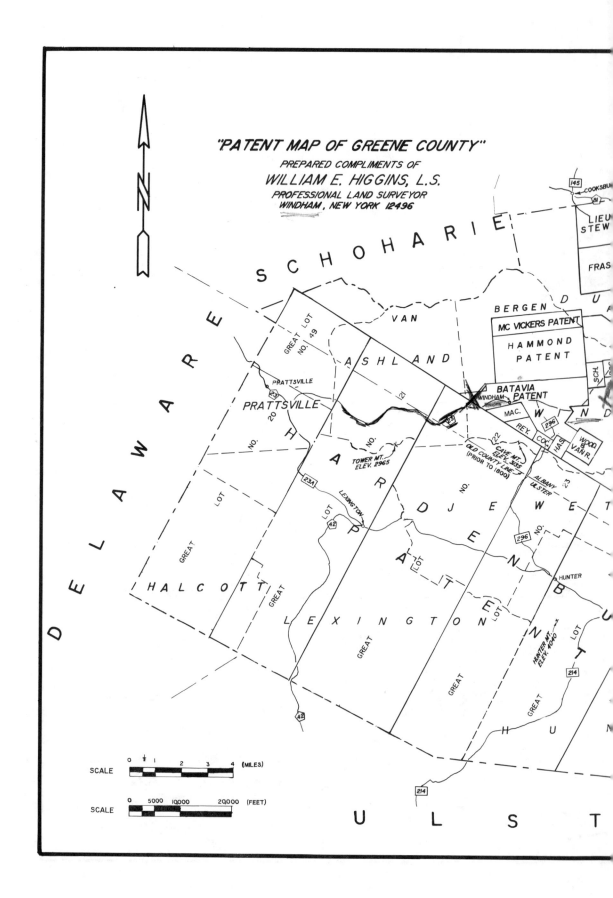

"PATENT MAP OF GREENE COUNTY"
PREPARED COMPLIMENTS OF
WILLIAM E. HIGGINS, L.S.
PROFESSIONAL LAND SURVEYOR
WINDHAM, NEW YORK 12496

SCALE

SCALE

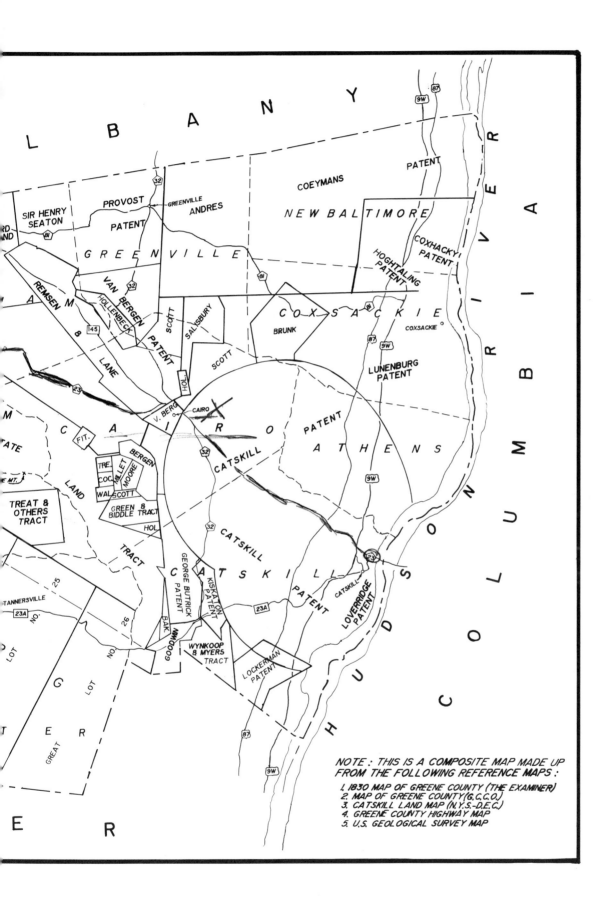

NOTE: THIS IS A COMPOSITE MAP MADE UP
FROM THE FOLLOWING REFERENCE MAPS:
1. 1830 MAP OF GREENE COUNTY (THE EXAMINER)
2. MAP OF GREENE COUNTY (G.C.C.O.)
3. CATSKILL LAND MAP (N.Y.S.-D.E.C.)
4. GREENE COUNTY HIGHWAY MAP
5. U.S. GEOLOGICAL SURVEY MAP

TABLE OF CONTENTS

CHAPTER 1

LAND

*A*n account of a county's history must record and interpret the events which have been the common experience of the county's residents. It is greater than the sum of the parts—the individual histories of its towns and villages—for it encompasses the shared experiences as well as those which are distinctive to individual communities. Greene County has an identity of its own which has evolved in its nearly two centuries of existence. Though its borders cut across the natural landscape except along the river, the experience of people in the adjacent counties has been different, for their political, social and economic lives are lived in another complex of environment, institutions, and central cities. What Greene residents share has created a distinct—and unique—"sense of place," as some interpreters of social history have termed it.

The most basic aspect of this sense of place is the physical environment. Greene County is located in a peculiar juxtaposition of river valley, escarpment, and rugged mountaintop that has made it a place of travel and shipment, of natural beauty, of physical isolation, and of challenging, difficult agriculture. Without these dominant influences, the same people operating in the same broad economy would have formed a very different community.

Today, the relative nearness of New York City is the chief determinant of Greene County's future. The city has always been near and yet far. We enter Greene County a little more than one hundred miles above the city line on the New York State Thruway; it is "centrally distant" 130 miles. While travel time was vastly greater in the past, the city has always been relatively close. Greene's long river frontage provided it with easy access to the port city and to the state capital.

Not a large county by New York State standards, Greene is roughly 20 miles from north to south and 32 miles from east to west, and encompasses 686 square miles.[1] But its rough and varied topography makes it seem much larger.

Mountains are Greene's most visible characteristic. Its hills and valleys are the result of erosion which followed the upheaval of an ancient ocean floor, especially by glacial action. A spur of the Appalachian chain runs northwesterly from a point on the county's south border about seven miles from the river, dividing Catskill, Cairo and Durham and other northeastern towns from those of the "Mountaintop." The north side of this chain is rocky and bare, while on the south side are vast deposits of glacial drift.

Two other chains of hills run parallel to the river; their names remind us of the Dutch settlement of the country. The Kalkberg, or "lime hill," is two to three miles west of the Hudson. The Hooge Bergen, or "High Hills," 500-700 feet high, are four to five miles from the river.

Amongst these hills and mountains are four distinct watersheds which delineate natural divisions of the county. The Catskill Valley runs northwesterly from the Village of Catskill, drained by Catskill Creek. Two miles above its mouth it is joined by the Kaaterskill Creek from the south. Further upstream the Potick Creek and the Basic Creek flow into it from the north.

The Schoharie Kill flows northwesterly on the Mountaintop, and is augmented by its tributaries, the West Kill, the East Kill, and the Batavia Kill. The isolated town of Halcott is drained by the Bush Kill, which flows into the Delaware. Parts of Lexington and Hunter are drained by tributaries of the Esopus, which empties into the Hudson near Saugerties. ❧

CHAPTER 2
PEOPLE

*G*reene County has been inhabited by humans for over ten thousand years. Its high mountains, however, many of which are today forest preserve land, have never been hospitable. The migrant native people occupied only small amounts of land, almost always along the rivers and creeks.

The earliest known inhabitants of Greene County were a people termed the Paleo-Indians, living between 9500 and 8000 B.C. The Paleo-Indians travelled in small groups, hunting big game. They left signs of their presence at two Greene County locations: on West Athens Hill and on Kings Road in the Town of Catskill. Their characteristic spear point, the Clovis Point, may have been mined at Flint Mine Hill in Coxsackie. This important archaeological site includes some 200 pits as well as sorting and chipping stations, workshops, and refuse dumps, used through much if not all of pre-European history.[2]

Following major climatic changes and the disappearance of the big game herd, the Paleo-Indians were superseded by people of the Archaic culture: migratory hunters, fishers, and gatherers, who camped near waterways.

A number of rich archaeological sites reflect the presence of Archaic people. The East Ridge site, a half mile east of Flint Mine Hill, was a camp and tool-making area about 5000 years ago. Lotus Point on the Embought, a campsite about 2500 B.C., reveals freshwater mussel shells, mammal bones, and stone projectile points. The Peloubet site on Four Mile Point revealed pestles and mullers, two kinds of hand-held grinding stones. The Fred Young site, in New Baltimore on Coxsackie Creek, contained points, knives, scrapers and bone dating from 1900 to 1350 B.C. The Vedder site in the Town of Durham is also believed to be Archaic.

During the brief Transitional Stage, from 1300 to 1000 B.C., ancient peoples commenced making stone pottery from steatite. A greatly increased variety of implements and containers emerged during the Woodland culture. The Woodland period, which continued until the European invasion, was characterized by agriculture, clay pottery, new types of projectile points and, eventually, by semi-permanent villages. Remains of this culture have been found in many locations in Greene County, particularly along the Hudson's shore. Among them are the Tufano site on Four Mile Point, holding fish bones, sturgeon plates, mammal bones, pottery and flint from about 700 A.D., and the Black Rock site, south of Athens village, where shells, sturgeon, and triangular projectile points from about 850 A.D. were unearthed.[3]

Archaeologist Arthur C. Parker identified ten pre-historic village sites in Greene County in addition to a number of camp and burial sites. Nearly all the villages were along the Catskill, Kaaterskill, or Hudson. According to Parker, "with the possible exception of a few rock shelters and hunting camps, so far as is now known there are no traces of aboriginal occupation in the mountains west of the river."[4] His map identifies only a single rock shelter in Windham.

By the late sixteenth and early seventeenth centuries, the territory now encompassed by Greene County was home to two tribes of native people. The Munsee, also known as the Lenni Lenape, controlled the land south of Catskill Creek and ranged westward to the headwaters of the Delaware and the Susquehanna: they did not wander beyond the ridge of the Catskills into Mohawk territory in the Schoharie Valley. North of Catskill Creek—and on the east side of the Hudson—lived the Mahicans.

These two tribes established villages in river or creek valleys where the soil was rich and the game plentiful, relocating every 8-12 years. They subsisted primarily on corn and other crops from small garden plots tended by the women, supplementing their diet with nuts and berries, and with fish and game. T.J.Brasser provides a concise description of Mahican life:

> Usually the Mahican Indians selected hilltops near the rivers for their palisaded villages, consisting of about 3 to 16 bark-covered longhouses each. The average longhouse was provided with 3 fireplaces, implying room for at least three nuclear families. . . . The available data suggest an average of about 200 individuals in each village. Every 8 to 12 years the village had to be moved due to the exhaustion of the nearby garden plots, a shortage of firewood, and the increasing filthiness in and around the village.
>
> Around these villages the people burned the woods and layed out their gardens among the charred tree stumps. The gardens were usually quite small, but by means of intercropping they appear to have produced relatively large quantities of food, primarily maize, beans, squash, and probably sunflowers.[5]

In spring, the men fished for herring and shad, followed by freshwater mussels in summer. The women gardened and gathered groundnuts and berries. After harvest, collective hunting drives were organized and, in November, families scattered through the hunting territories until midwinter, when they returned to their villages. They rarely visited the mountaintops where game was poor and where, they believed, evil spirits dwelled.[6]

These traditional ways were little altered over many years. But in the seventeenth century, adventurers and traders from the European continent sailed up the Hudson River, and forced change on the people on its shores. ❧

Etow Oh Koam
Oil painting by John Verelst, 1710
Collection of National Archives of Canada, Ottawa.

Etow Oh Koam, or Nicholas, was a Mahican who went to London with three Mohawks in 1710. He holds a ball-headed club and wears a scarlet cloak given to him in London. The turtle at his feet indicates his clan. Near his left foot is a metal trade tomahawk. This image is one of very few early portraits of Native Americans.

CHAPTER 3
CONQUEST

*T*hough explorers had come from Europe to the northeast coast of America in the sixteenth century, it was Hudson's exploration of the river for Amsterdam's Dutch West India Company that resulted in the first European foothold in the valley.

The journal of Robert Juet, ship's mate on Hudson's vessel, *De Halve Maen*, provides the earliest written record of Greene County life. On September 15, 1609 the ship sailed north along the Greene County shore, anchoring that night just above the site of Athens where the crew was visited by Catskill Indians whom Juet called "very loving people." The following day native people brought corn, tobacco and squashes for trading. That evening the ship sailed six miles north and anchored, proceeding onward the next morning.

On their southbound voyage, on September 24, they ran aground, very likely between Hudson and Athens, and gathered chestnuts on shore. On the 25th, near the site of Athens, Juet recorded they "went on Land to walke on the West side of the River, and found good grounde for Corne, and other Garden herbs, with great store of goodly Oakes, and Wal-nut trees, and Chest-nut trees, Ewe trees, and trees of sweet wood in great abundance, and great store of Slate for houses, and other good stones."[7] Unfortunately, the ship's crew viewed the natives with suspicion and killed a number of them on their way downriver, beginning with one who "stole" a few articles from the cabin. Thus began the clash of cultures in the Hudson Valley.

There was conflict, it is true, before the coming of the Europeans. The Iroquois Confederacy—of which the nearby Mohawk were a part—was far stronger than the association based on shared language or culture among the tribes of the Algonkian group, which included the Munsee and Mahican. In general, the Algonkians were losers when confronted with Iroquois might. Between 1624 and 1628 a protracted conflict between Mohawks and Mahicans resulted in the Mahicans giving up their foothold on the west side of the Hudson; subsequently they used it only for hunting. A village located on the flats a half mile below Freehold was swept away by a Mohawk invasion, probably about 1626, though stragglers later returned.[8]

Added to this equation was the impact of the Dutch settlement, which slowly began in the Albany and Manhattan areas in the 1620s and 1630s. The

Unknown Native American
Detail from "The Van Bergen Farm"
Oil on boards by John Heaten, c. 1733
Collection of New York State
Historical Association, Cooperstown.

In the so-called "Van Bergen
Overmantle", this tiny figure, probably
a Mahican, appears, bearing witness to
the continuing presence of the
indigenous peoples during the period
of settlement.

Munsees were decimated by wars with the settlers and by smallpox, so that by 1670 their survivors mostly migrated westward. Meanwhile, part of the Mahican tribe moved or returned to the Catskill Valley about 1650, remaining there for half a century, during which they and the Munsees were active as fur traders in the southern Alleganies and the Ohio Valley, competing with the Iroquois and the Cherokees. Philip Bronk testified in 1786 that he heard his father say "there used to be 60 fighting Indians, besides women and children, at Old Catskill [Leeds]." Most Mahicans, on the east shore, were pushed away from the river when the Dutch appropriated their choicest agricultural land, forcing them into the Berkshires by 1680. About 1700 the Catskill Mahicans moved higher up into the Catskills, eventually merging with the Munsee on the upper Susquehanna.[9]

There were still stragglers living, probably seasonally, throughout the county. Their tribal identity is seldom given in these chance records—indeed, the settlers probably understood or cared little about those traditionally important distinctions which were becoming blurred by mergers.

The pressure of the fur trade with the Europeans increased the native preoccupation with hunting and inter-tribe conflicts at the expense of agriculture and handicrafts. Securing trade goods, guns, and liquor, the natives became culturally mixed; in Greene County they lived in log cabins, used muskets, iron kettles, hoes and adzes, and wore cloth garments. Still, basketmaking remained a native craft; in 1774 Temperance (Loveridge) Van Orden's estate inventory listed "Indian baskets."[10]

As settlers moved into new districts of Greene County they often found a few Native Americans. Even at the old village site just west of the confluence of the Catskill and the Kaaterskill, natives named Rube, Wancham and Jan de Bakker were living in the 1740s. Mohawks camped before and during the Revolution at the *wildenhausje* (Indian cabin) a quarter mile south of Peter Dederick's house on the Kaaterskill west of the Embought, and during the same war "Peter the Indian" served in Capt. Samuel Van Vechten's Company. Beers also reports "an indistinct tradition . . . in the days of our grandfathers" of a band that came from beyond the Mohawk each summer to camp in a chestnut grove on William Salisbury's farm at Potick. When Stephen Lampman settled in Greenville in 1759-60 he found three families living there to shoot deer at a salt spring.[11]

In later records most references to native people are to individual families, solitary individuals, or medicine shows. At the time Ashland was newly settled, a migratory family of six or more people spent the winter in a log house eight feet square covered with bark and brush a mile from the Batavia Kill near the West Settlement road. They traded in brooms and baskets. Another basketmaking family was that of Nelse and Till, who came to Coxsackie each year until 1852, making willow baskets at their camp along the stream just north of Union Street. Ben, an Oneida, visited Catskill until about 1825; "his last appearance was of a summer evening, with a Bible in his hand." The Johnson family of Durham, early in the nineteenth century, called themselves

Portuguese but were half Indian. Even in Halcott there was a tradition about the "last Indian," called Froman; in that late-settled town, he must have lived as late as the 1810s or 1820s.[12]

While such anecdotes are void of the racial hostility bred by misunderstanding and warfare, we hear also the story of Capt. Hinman, a French and Indian War veteran. He attended an "Indian show" at Oak Hill and became very excited: he "had to be restrained."[13] This probably took place around the turn of the nineteenth century. By the end of the century the tourists at Hunter were treated to an "Indian encampment" on Main Street where, as in many American resort towns, Iroquois from Canada or northern New York made and sold baskets and beadwork, and "put on medicine shows."[14]

While evidence is anecdotal and too scattered to establish a real pattern, it suggests that Indian occupation ended by about 1700, with some small bands and families holding on at least seasonally until the Revolution. In the nineteenth century, Native Americans in Greene County were stragglers. Today, like the majority of Greene County residents, the Indians amongst us have relocated from other counties and states for reasons of employment. ❧

CHAPTER 4
SETTLEMENT

$\mathcal{T}$hough the Patroonship of Rensselaerswyck and the present City of Albany were just to the north, Greene County was not settled quickly or heavily. Land ownership, which was mostly vested in land grants to individuals, simply did not encourage the growth of villages or farming districts in the early years.

In his journal for April 27, 1640, the explorer David Pieterszen de Vries wrote:

> Arrived about evening, as it blew hard, before the Kats-kil. Found the river up to this point stony and mountainous, unfit for habitations. But there was some lowland along the Kats-kil, and here the savages sowed maize.[15]

The first European settlers of the present Greene County faced that discouraging wilderness when, in the following decade, they established their first farms near the creek. They were probably motivated by a desire for improved access to the beaver trade. The events of the 1640s which first settled Old Catskill were traced by Jonathan W. Hasbrouck:

> The nearest settlement antedating that of the town of Kingston, of which we have an authentic record, was Katskill. During the year 1643, Adriaen van der Donck, sheriff of the patroon of Rensselaerswyck, ambitious of becoming a landed aristocrat, undertook to buy the Indian title to this section, and engaged settlers for his estate. Killiaen Van Rensselaer was highly incensed at this independent procedure of his liegeman, and took possession of it himself, claiming no one had a right to buy within eight miles of his estate without his consent. August 22d, 1646, Cornelis Van Slyck obtained a patent for it. Van Schlechtenhorst, director for the former, waged a war of words about it, and settled a plantation there. Either through these would-be lords, or a desire to be independent, some few families had, in the meantime, fixed their homes on the banks of the Catskill Creek, and thus began the nearest settlement to Esopus. Herman Vedder, Jan Dircksen of Bremen, Jan Jansen of the same place, and Peter Teunnisen were among them.[16]

In 1650 one of these men, Jan van Bremen, leased land at Catskill and agreed to build a house, barn and barrack, with Van Rensselaer paying the workmen; Hans Vos, a German, was sent to help. Van Rensselaer's land purchase was ultimately declared void by the colony but settlers remained. Van Bremen then obtained a durable patent at Catskill in 1653, the first of 71 grants of land within the borders of Greene County. In April 1657 Hans Vos was tried at Fort Orange for selling liquor to the Indians at Catskill, and later that year John Anderson ("Jan Andriessen van Dublin") was living west of the creek.[17]

Until the fall of the Dutch colony in 1664, the Catskill settlement—the only European foothold in Greene County—must have consisted of a handful of farms along the creek between the Hudson and Leeds, raising provisions for their own use and shipping wheat and furs to the port.

It was the English colonial government, established in August 1664, that provided the land patents which drew settlers to Greene County. The bloodless "conquest," born of the trade rivalry between the two nations, made no attempt to extinguish the Dutch cultural identity in the Hudson Valley.

In the early years of settlement four large land patents made by the English government and a few rather small ones made land available. The four major ones were Loonenburgh, Coeymans, Catskill and Hardenbergh. While an in-depth exploration of all Greene County patents is not possible on this scale, these four deserve discussion.

The first patent after the English takeover was purchased from the Indians in 1665 by three Dutchmen, and patented in 1667. It encompassed the eastern half of Athens and the southeast quadrant of Coxsackie. Later named Loonenburg, it was not fully divided until 1750. Like the other river valley patents it was settled by "Dutch"—a term which included Germans, Scandinavians, Huguenots, and English, as well as occasional Poles and others, all sharing the Dutch language and culture.[18]

Coeymans Patent, including much of New Baltimore and part of Coxsackie but largely in present Albany County, was confirmed by the Governor to Barent Peters in 1673. Evidence of earlier occupation is found in the boundary description, running up Coxsackie Creek "as far as the place where Jacob Flodders did use to roll down his timber" and it was given under the condition that Peters build a sawmill.[19]

Catskill Patent followed. This circular tract of fertile land included the five great plains at present-day Leeds with all the land four miles around, totalling 35,000 acres. Purchased from the Indians in 1678 by Salisbury and Van Bergen, it was patented two years later.[20]

The last and largest of the four main patents was the Hardenbergh Patent, two million acres, of which 140,000 were in Greene County, granted to Johannes Hardenbergh of Kingston and six others in 1708. The Greene County portion of this vast tract was almost entirely on the Mountaintop, and the first attempts to divide it among the owners and their heirs did not begin until 1739. Unlike the three earlier patents, its Greene County lands were virtually vacant until after the Revolution.[21]

A number of other parcels were patented in Greene County prior to the 1760s; as was true of the large patents, they were all to individuals or small companies. There were no manor grants, with their feudal privileges; nor were there any town charters, as was common in New England. At first the patentees "purchased" title from the Indians, and the patents confirmed their ownership; after Indian titles had been obtained by the colony through treaties, the government made grants directly.

Peter Bronck of Albany received a rather modest patent in what is now Coxsackie in 1662, and the following year built a stone house at West Coxsackie, the oldest building still standing in Greene County.

Settlement of Bronck's Patent and the other river valley patents proceeded slowly but steadily throughout the colonial period. In 1714 a census of Albany County found only 242 residents in "Coxhackie and ye northern part of ye Mannor of Livingston."[22] Three churches were established on the three river valley patents and provided a focus for population. Zion Lutheran Church was the first, in Loonenburgh [Athens], 1708. In 1732 Dutch Reformed congregations were organized at Old Catskill [Leeds] and at [West] Coxsackie, sharing the services of a dominie (pastor). Near each of these churches there was a modest concentration of population and services, very likely including a shopkeeper, a blacksmith and a tavern. At least at Loonenburgh a school was taught early in the century.

The site of Catskill village was probably occupied during the last years of Dutch rule but, despite docking facilities and perhaps some boat-building, it did not grow until just after the Revolutionary War. In 1738 John Lindesay of Cherry Valley received a patent for the village site; three years later he sold it to five men, who partitioned the tract from the present Main Street to the Creek. Although they agreed upon the location of Main Street it was not laid out until 1773. This new settlement was called "Het Strand" (The Landing), to distinguish it from Old Catskill [Leeds]. The name was in use until 1800.[23]

Catskill had a number of mills at an early date. Between 1681 and 1686 Dirck Van Vechten built a sawmill and a gristmill 100 yards up the Hans Vosen Kill. Robert Livingston found it in poor condition in 1712 when he described "a little mill at Catskill [which] grinds so course it cannot be bolted."[24] Probably in the second quarter of the eighteenth century the Salisburys and Van Bergens built a gristmill just east of the falls on the Kaaterskill, and there was probably an early mill at Old Catskill [Leeds].

Enslaved Africans were brought to Greene County by the Dutch farmers. Little is known about their lives, apart from what can be extrapolated back from the census records in 1790, which show many farmers owning slaves, including three households in Catskill and Coxsackie with ten or more. By contrast, Freehold, in the newly settled Catskill Valley, had very few slaves. In 1714, 22 percent of the small population of present Greene and Columbia Counties were slaves. This dropped to 8.5 percent in lowland Greene County in 1790, where the only free Black head-of-household was Charles Cudjo of Catskill, whose household consisted of three Black persons and a white woman.[25]

The records of the Lutheran church at Loonenburgh provide a surprising window on the life of one slave. Peter Christian, slave of Jan van Loon, Sr., was baptized by Reverend Justus Falckner on January 28, 1712. He was about 30 years old, born in Madagascar. In 1714 Peter Christian married a white woman, Anna Barbara Asmer; two years later he married Elizabeth Brandemoes and they had seven children who were born free. By 1738 he served as baptismal sponsor for Hendryk, illegitimate son of his daughter Catharina, and he was living in "Freehold," an area not clearly defined but probably west of the Hoogebergen.[26]

Another important group of later immigrants were the Palatines from Germany. During the War of Spanish Succession (1702-14) the Palatinate was repeatedly devastated. A severe winter in 1708-09 and religious persecution of Protestants provided a strong motive for emigration. In 1710 the English government, anxious to stimulate economic development of the underpopulated Hudson Valley, arranged to bring a number of them to the colony where they were settled at East Camp [Germantown, Columbia County] and West Camp, Ulster County, to produce naval stores. The experiment was a dismal failure and collapsed almost immediately. Many, though not all, left for the Schoharie Valley.[27]

Others moved northward. Beginning in 1726 many Palatine children from Kiskatom were baptized by the Lutheran minister from Loonenburg [Athens]. Similarly, Lot No. 2 of the Loveridge Patent, in the Great Embought district, was settled in 1728 by five young German families named Brandow, Overbaugh and Diedrick. The Germans favored the uplands for their farms while the Dutch usually chose the river bottoms.[28]

Much later a few Germans and Dutch pushed up the Schoharie Valley into the present town of Prattsville, establishing the first European presence on the Mountaintop.[29]

Settlement of Greene County was limited until well past the middle of the eighteenth century. A foothold was made in Greenville in the spring and summer of 1750, when Godfrey Brandow of Saugerties cleared land in the southeast part of that town; he apparently had no near neighbors for a decade until, in the winter of 1759-60, Stephen Lampman of Coeymans settled just north of him. Jacob Bogardus of Coxsackie joined them in the spring of 1772.[30]

After the French and Indian War ceased in 1763, settlement accelerated due to reduced danger and to new grants of land. The war had brought many British soldiers to the Albany area from 1754 to 1763. George III then made colonial land available to "reduced officers" and men, and from 1767 to 1772 many grants were made in the present towns of Catskill, Cairo, Durham and

Bronck House
Woodcut by A. Little, 1884
From Beers' *History of Greene County, N.Y.*

The house of Pieter Bronck, built c.1663 of stone, is the earliest surviving dwelling in the upper Hudson Valley. In 1738 his grandson, Leendert, built the brick house which forms the right side of the present structure. Along with its barns and outbuildings, it is maintained as a museum by the Greene County Historical Society.

Gristmill on the Normanskill
Detail from "Abraham Wendell"
Oil portrait by John Heaten, Albany
County, c.1730-45
Collection of Albany Institute of
History and Art. Gift of Governor and
Mrs. Averill Harriman and three
anonymous donors.

While this mill was outside present
Greene County, this is the earliest
good view of a gristmill in the region.
Such mills were commonplace on the
Catskill, Kaaterskill, and the smaller
creeks which empty into the Hudson.

Windham.[31] Greene's Patent, for example, was made to 14 soldiers. While
relatively few of the former soldiers actually settled on their land—many in
fact held it for speculation—at least two settlements began during the postwar
years, at Woodstock in the present Town of Cairo, and at Oak Hill in the
present Town of Durham.

Just after the French and Indian War James Barker, an English lawyer, is
said to have brought 23 "former tenants" with their families to Woodstock in
the Town of Cairo. Often called "The Patroon," he was nothing of the kind; in
fact, the story about his former tenants has never been documented. But it is
certain that James Barker and his wife Elizabeth came from Blythe,
Nottingham, where they had been married in 1757, and they settled at
Woodstock about 1765, when he acquired 3,423 acres in two transfers. They
were certainly there in the summer of 1767, when they buried a child there.[17]
Beers suggests there were other settlements in Cairo before the Revolution,
"squatters" who built log houses; Indians are known to have attacked such a
farm in 1780.[32]

DeWittsburgh [Oak Hill] was settled on land owned by the heirs of
Richard Maitland, a British army officer. Lucas de Witt, John Plank and
Hendrick Plank were already farming there in 1774, when they leased the land
from the Maitland executors. De Witt had a portable grist mill—probably a
quern—which he hid in a hollow log during the Revolution. After Indian raids
nearby, the settlement was temporarily abandoned; the families returned
about 1782.[33]

Thus, the limit of settlement in the early 1770s was the river valley in
Catskill, Athens, Coxsackie and New Baltimore towns, three farms in
Greenville, the Barker colony at Woodstock in Cairo with a few homesteads
elsewhere in that town, the new settlement at DeWittsburgh [Oak Hill], and a
few pioneers in Prattsville in the Schoharie Valley. The Blue Hills or Catskills
("blauwe bergen" they are called in a 1742 Lutheran marriage record) were a
howling wilderness.

With the possible exception of some fishermen and a few who provided
services or engaged in trade, colonial residents of Greene County worked
farmland, even if they knew another craft. We have no documentation for the
particulars of Greene County farming, though the testimony of Greene County
Loyalists at the end of the Revolution, if available, might provide specifics of
acreage, crops and livestock for a small sample.

By the time of the Revolution, methods of transportation had changed
little for generations. There was a rough road along the west side of the river,
the King's Road, used by those travelling on horseback from New York to
Albany, but most people making the trip preferred the comfort of the other
great "road," the Hudson River, as did Richard Smith of New Jersey in 1769:

*These Albany sloops contain very convenient Cabins. We eat
from a regular Table accommodated with Plates, Knives and Forks
and enjoyed our Tea in the Afternoon.*

Smith also gives us our earliest view of Catskill Landing, such as it was:

*Two Sloops belong to Kaatskill, a little beyond the Mouth
whereof lies the large Island of Vastric [Rogers]. There is a House on*

the North Side of the Creek and another with several Saw Mills on the South Side but no Town as we expected. Sloops go no further than Dyer House about Half a Mile up the Creek. The Lands on both Sides of Kaatskill [Creek] belong to Vanberger, Van Vecthe, Salisbury, Dubois & a Man in York. Their Lands, as our Skipper says, extend up the Creek 12 Miles to Barker the English Gentleman his Settlement. The Creek runs through the Kaatskill Mountains said hereabouts to be at the Distance of 12 or 14 Miles from the North River but there are Falls above which obstruct the Navigation.[34]

The business accounts of Teunis Van Vechten, storekeeper and saw and grist mill owner, list a number of residents of Catskill and adjacent territory between 1753 and 1782, providing us with information on the trades of the inhabitants. Old Catskill [Leeds] had a merchant, Abraham Ten Brock, and John Macrobers, schoolmaster, while Egbert Bogardus was a skipper at Catskill Landing and Walter Norris of Cauterskill followed the same trade. Johannes Van Gorden of Catskill called himself a fisherman. At Loonenburgh [Athens], too, there were merchants, Stephen Haight and Koenrat Vlack, in the early 1770s. Henry Knoll, a doctor, lived at Coxsackie in 1769. Most intriguing of all is Alexander McDugal, a "padler" [peddler]. Instead of a place of residence, Van Vechten wrote that McDugal lived "Everywhere Padling."[35]

Most tradesmen and women combined their work with management of a small farm. Thus Van Vechten recorded carpenters, coopers, wheelwrights and stavemakers. Textileworkers included a tailor, a weaver, flax dresser, flax cleaner, and spinster. Curriers and shoemakers worked in leather, and a "masonner" and a millwright worked with stone. Finally, and no less important to the community life, there were millers and innkeepers.

After a century and a quarter, the Hudson shore and the lower Catskill Valley were developing into a sparsely settled agricultural district of New York colony. The events of 1775 to 1781, although mostly at a distance, slowed or stopped its growth. 🍎

Farmstead at Leeds
Detail from "The Van Bergen Farm"
Oil on boards by John Heaten, c.1733
Collection of New York State
Historical Association, Cooperstown

Perhaps the most important landscape which survives from colonial New York, the "Van Bergen Overmantle" shows Marten van Bergen's house, Dutch barn, two hay barracks and a blacksmith shop, built about 1729; the house was demolished in 1862.

13

CHAPTER 5
REVOLUTION

*M*any books have been written about the causes of the American Revolution and its progress. Greene County was seriously affected by the War in many ways. Yet its leading men were not, for the most part, involved in Albany and New York politics; the great armies did not fight, nor even march, across it; and the threat of attack by hostile Indians, though it caused the removal of settlers from the frontier, became a reality only a few times. Greene County's participation in the war was in a supporting role: through participation in the committee system which provided a form of government, by providing supplies, and by sending its men to fight.

The committee system was organized around the existing local government. For Greene County this was limited to the "district" structure of Coxsackie and Great Imbocht. Both belonged to Albany County, which had been organized in 1683 and ran as far south as Sawyer's Creek. In 1718 the "precincts of Catskill and Coxhacky" had been allowed to elect a supervisor; they were also served by a justice of the peace and a constable. An act of 1772 organized districts with some of the powers of a town: keeping highways in order, raising public money, caring for the poor, etc. Greene County's former precincts then became districts. They were authorized to elect a supervisor, two assessors, a collector, two overseers of the poor, two constables, two fence viewers and a clerk on the first Tuesday of the month of May.[36]

After the Battle at Lexington in April 1775, committees formed throughout the colonies to oppose British policies. Both Coxsackie and Great Imbocht districts organized local committees in April or May 1775 and were thus answerable to the Albany County Committee of Safety, Protection and Correspondence, which convened a general meeting on May 10, 1775 to choose a delegate to a Provincial Congress. The Provincial Congress had sent a "general association" document to the county committees and they, in turn, sent it to the districts in May.[37]

On May 17, 1775, 225 citizens of Coxsackie signed the document, which resolved they would "never . . . become slaves" but made clear their hope for a "reconciliation between Great Britain and America on constitutional principles (which we most ardently desire) . . . "

After this stirring start—and long before the colonists voted for independence—the committee system got down to business. From 1776 to 1778 the Albany Committee assumed control of the county government. On the local level it worked to discover those who conspired against the developing independence movement. On September 14, 1776 its minutes record:

> Resolved that full Power be and is hereby given to the presiding Chairman to order and direct the Company of Rangers under the Command of Capt. Baldwin to march to such place of the District of Coxsackie . . . to apprehend and secure such Persons in and about that District as are turbulent and Dangerous to safety of the good People of that District and have concealed themselves in the Woods and are sculking about to the great Terror of the Inhabitants.[38]

This patrol apparently got out of control, because Coenraadt Hooghtieling complained on the 27th of the same month that they took two gammons, two sides of pork and forty-odd fowl, and made his wife cook it all, paying only in part.

Soon the committee began procuring provisions and supplies for the Continental troops. In February 1777 they sought blankets and in April the army needed flour and wheat. Money, food, clothing, arms and ammunition were solicited from the civilian population throughout the war. For example, in August 1780 Leonard Bronk of Coxsackie received a requisition for ten tons of flour and 20,000 weight of beef or its equivalent needed by the army.[39]

By 1778 the new state government was in place and the committees were no longer needed in their quasi-governmental capacity. The committee's role of investigating Tories was taken over by the Albany County Commission for Detecting and Defeating Conspiracies.

Meanwhile, farmers-turned-soldiers filled the ranks of the Albany County Militia. The Eleventh Regiment was raised from Coxsackie and Great Imbocht, and at least 303 men served in it during the war. The militia served in place of Continental Troops when they were occupied elsewhere on the continent. They were used against Burgoyne during the Saratoga campaign; they protected the districts when Indians and Tories retaliated in the Catskill Valley for the Sullivan-Clinton campaign against the British-sympathizing Senecas and Cayugas, and they generally helped repel the raids on the Mohawk Valley.[40]

The war came closer to home when nearby communities were attacked. Kingston was burned by the British on October 16, 1777 and residents of Great Imbocht "drove their swine and oxen into the woods upon the Kalkberg, and packed their more valuable furniture for speedy removal." Soon afterward, when John Overbaugh "heard the beating of drums at sunrise on the hostile ships at East Camp, and from the top of the Kykuit saw the smoke rising from the burning houses of Livingston Manor . . . ," the Tories of Great Imbocht District were exultant, and "even began to discuss what division of the lands of their Whig neighbors they should make among themselves."

Finally, in the last full year of the war, there were raids on several isolated farmsteads in Greene County. At David Abeel's near the Bak-Oven a party of Indians accompanied by one or two Tories plundered the house and took captive David and his son Anthony. The slaves had been forewarned and removed the priming of the muskets. One slave, Lon, "heaped on his master all manner of abuse, complaining chiefly that he had not been allowed enough to eat, and, at last, snatched his master's hat from his head, giving him his own in exchange, and saying in Dutch: 'I am master now, wear that.'" The Abeels along with Lon and another servant, Jannetje Van Valkenburgh, were marched to the Schoharie Kill and through the Delaware Valley to Fort Niagara. Thence they were taken to Montreal and imprisoned; David was released in 1781 and Anthony escaped the following year.[42] A second and more brutal attack took place in the same year at Round Top. A party of Indians seeking revenge from Bastiaan Strope attacked his parents' isolated farmhouse, killed his parents, and took captive his brother-in-law's brother, Frederick Schermerhorn, who happened to be visiting. He too was marched to Fort Niagara and forced to enlist in the British forces, serving four years before he was able to return to his family.[43]

The final impact of the Revolution on the farmers of Greene was the confiscation of the property of those "indicted or convicted of adherence to the enemy," authorized by a 1779 act of the new state government. Coxsackie and Great Imbocht were heavily Dutch and German, and had relatively few whose wealth or status depended upon the English regime; thus, a list by John T. Reilly of confiscated estates includes only twelve Coxsackie names and three from Great Imbocht, though there were certainly many more sympathizers.[44] This property was sold by the new state; such sales often went to speculators, though ultimately they were purchased by small farmers and returned to freehold status. ❦

CHAPTER 6
NATIONHOOD

*T*he surrender of the British army in 1781 and the treaty which followed two years later ushered in changes of tremendous importance. For the first time the former British colonies had full opportunity to develop their economic potential, free of tariffs and other restrictions. This, in turn, led to expansion westward and to technological innovation which further stimulated the economy.

But the former colonies were not starting from a position of strength. The underdeveloped economy of the colonies was largely shattered by the war, which had interfered with trade and destroyed infrastructure. In many districts farmland, too, had been devastated and families uprooted. Still, the optimism born of victory and the successful government structures developed out of the committee system gave the new nation a running start.

When compared with neighboring communities at Albany and Kingston, there was not much in Greene County in 1783. The well-established farms near the river had probably not been disrupted as much as those in other parts of the colonies, for there had been no major campaigns here. Beyond the Hooge Bergen there were only the scattered pioneer farms and a few clusters along the Catskill. The riverfront trades amounted to little more than fishing and some boat-building, and had no doubt continued except when the men were off with the militia. Here and there, a few men ran sawmills and small tanneries using hemlock bark from the forest and local hides for leather making.

Greene County was to benefit from a number of fortunate circumstances over the half-century which followed the Revolution. Once land was in production, it produced surplus grain, cheese and butter, salted and fresh meat, all of which was easily transported to the landings on the river and thence to New York—and, to a lesser extent, to Hudson and Albany. Its forests produced lumber for the building of the coastal cities; a still greater amount of wood was burned to make potash and pearlash, which had far higher value per pound than did lumber. After a slow beginning, the leather industry exploded after the War of 1812, using local bark and firewood along with imported hides.

The great highway of the Hudson allowed easy and cheap shipment of these products to an almost inexhaustible market in New York City. Catskill Landing's first two sloops, in 1787, "were employed in carrying lumber to New York," shipping 15,000 board feet along with 2,980 pounds of potash. After 1807 the steamboat, which was first successfully used on the Hudson, revolutionized river transport.

"Sketch of the Town of Kaats-kill"
Woodcut after a drawing by A.P. Fecit, 1797
Frontispiece of *The New York Magazine,* September 1797

The illustration is depicted as it originally appeared and is printed in reverse.

Even so, it was east-west transportation that made Greene County boom in the first three decades of the nineteenth century. As the Revolution ended, New England's coastal regions were already overpopulated. Individuals and even whole communities from Connecticut soon began moving into the northern tier of towns, the upper Catskill Valley and the Mountaintop. They were also pushing into the Susquehanna region and, in a very few years, beyond it into central New York. Greene County was in a direct line from Connecticut to this vast territory—and from its new farms eastward to the Hudson's shipping. By the last decade of the old century turnpikes were being built to carry this two-way traffic. These individuals on the move further stimulated the local Greene County production of butter, cheese, meat, flour, timber and leather; but they captured the transport of so vast an area to the west that four new river towns grew into prosperous, bustling ports by 1810.

Finally, the conditions in the young republic which encouraged manufacturing had a modest effect in Greene County, and a few small iron forges and foundries, paper mills, and textile mills were established by entrepreneurs or stock companies. Each of these trends was evolutionary, over decades, and each influenced the others and was influenced by them. ❦

CHAPTER 7
MARKETS

*A*round the turn of the nineteenth century, Augustine Prevost of Greenville wrote his wife Ann a report of the late July wheat harvest on his farm:

Yesterday my Dear Ann we finished Cradling our wheat, if we can but get it in safe, we shall be fortunate for it is the finest grain I ever saw. Both fields were cut in one day—poor Lucretia had her hands full, upon an average she cooks for 21 every day exclusive of her washing, milking, etc.[45]

Though it is hard to imagine in light of today's conditions, the Hudson Valley was then a prime wheat-growing region. Greene County's valley towns had success with wheat for a number of decades. Unfortunately, good agricultural statistics begin in 1845, after the wheat crop had been reduced dramatically. There is plenty of evidence, however, of its importance—and the importance of many other farm products—during the early national period.

Horatio Spafford prepared an impressive gazetteer of New York State in 1813, with entries for each of the towns. It's interesting to compare Cairo and Windham, for example. Cairo was sending its "surplus products," including grain, to Catskill and Athens, while Windham had "much good pasture lands that yield dairy of superior excellence."[46]

Corn, however, was the best cereal crop; acquired from the Indians, it was well-adapted to the American land. Farmers raised oats for their horses; with relatively few Scottish immigrants in Greene County, it was not widely raised for human food. Barley was a minor yet significant crop, which was used for beermaking. In 1820, two-thirds of the barley raised in the United States was grown in New York and marketed at Albany and Catskill.[47] Buckwheat was also raised by Greene County farmers, and used to feed poultry and swine and for pancake meal. Rye was grown for whiskey and bread.

Gristmills were necessary for processing nearly all the grain crop, except the portion destined for distilleries. Both anecdotal and statistical evidence demonstrates the extent of gristmills in the early nineteenth century.

The few mills of the colonial period multiplied rapidly during the period of expansion. Yet new settlers often had long distances to travel with their unground grain. John Munson of West Settlement, Ashland, "used to go with grain, on horseback, to Hardenbergh's mill, two miles west of Prattsville,"[48] and the first settlers of DeWittsburgh [Oak Hill] used DeWitt's quern or rode to Old Catskill [Leeds] with their crop.

At the early date of 1794 there was a mill operating in newly settled Hunter, as advertised for sale in the *Rising Sun*:

> *To be sold, a valuable Grist-mill and Saw-mill, on a double stream, with 100 acres of good land, subject to a yearly rent of one shilling per acre for ever, situate near the head of the main branch of Schohary-Kill, and on the main road from Esopus through Schohary-Kill, and about 24 miles from Esopus.*[49]

One of the largest mills during the height of Greene County's grain crops was described by Reverend Clark Brown in 1803:

> *Four miles from the mouth of Catskill creek, in the village of Madison [Leeds], stands a flouring mill, lately erected belonging to Ira Day and Company, a few rods west of the Susquehannah turnpike. It was set in motion in February, 1803. It is the most curious and complicated piece of machinery, which perhaps is of the kind in the United States. It daily manufactures between five and six hundred bushels of wheat into flour. It has two water wheels, each of which carries two stones for the grinding of the wheat, &c. The whole of the wheat, as it is purchased is poured into a hopper containing fifteen bushels, in which it is weighed, the hopper being erected for the purpose upon a scale fashion. Hence it descends into different bins, according to its quality for goodness, conducted by different spouts. From these bins the wheat is taken by elevators, and is conducted through screws, fanning mills, smut machines, into the hoppers over the stones for grinding. After having descended into a long trough, it is conducted up into the bolts, and thence to a large cooling room, and there cooled by stirring; after which it is carried into a room for packing. All these various operations, with a packing screw, are performed by water, effected in consequence of different gear by the two large water wheels only. These wheels are turned with rapidity, with not more than half the quantity of water, which is necessary for one of our common grist mills. The flour made in this mill is principally sold in New York.*[50]

Clearly, this mill was unusually large and technologically innovative, but it demonstrates that wheat culture in the Catskill Valley was both successful and economically important at the time. Spafford reported this mill in operation, but it apparently failed in 1818[51] and by 1820, operating only three run of stones and employing two men, it was dwarfed by Jacob Haight's mill at Catskill.

Haight had four run of stones and employed 15 men and ground 40,000 bushels of grain yearly, in contrast with the 15,000 reported at Madison [Leeds]. Products included wheat and rye flour, middlings, cornell and shorts.[52]

Another atypical operation was a tide mill on Dooper Island, reported in Beers without further detail.[53] This type was common along the seacoast but little known along the Hudson, despite the river's tidal nature.

Our first statistics for gristmills are in Spafford; he reported 46 mills in the county in 1813. By 1820 they had increased to 49, with as many as nine in Coxsackie and eight in Durham. On the Mountaintop, however, Windham, which then included Ashland and Prattsville, had only three and Hunter a single grist mill.

These mills produced flour for home use and for the New York market, and they ground animal feed. Some of the flour was processed further in Greene County; in the first decades of the nineteenth century a Mr. Titcomb operated a cracker manufactory at Coxsackie's Upper Landing, probably for maritime use.[54]

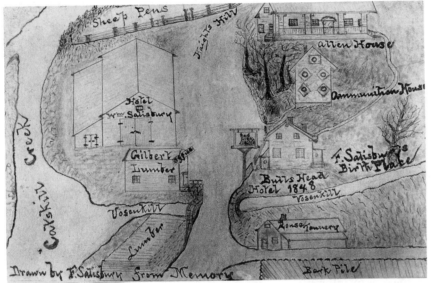

The foot of Jefferson Hill near Catskill as it was c.1848
Drawing by Franklin Salisbury, c.1900
Collection of the Greene County Historical Society

This interesting drawing reveals the importance of the back country to Catskill in the 19th century. Lumber piles, apparently milled elsewhere, are shown next to Gilbert Lumber; a tannery with its adjacent bark pile probably made use of hides from slaughters in the village. Sheep driven for slaughter or shipment to New York were confined in the pens at the upper left. The Bulls Head Hotel and its large barn probably catered to the needs of the farmers and drovers from the upper Catskill Valley, the Mountaintop, and beyond.

After 1825, with the opening of the Erie Canal, Greene County mills faced competition from those in western New York. With the decline of the wheat crop and the marketing of western flour, mills were increasingly used for grinding feed. By 1845 the number of gristmills had dropped substantially to 33, but they remained an important local facility. There were still 33 in 1865, but only three made flour. The first mill using steam power rather than a waterwheel was then in operation. The Powell Gristmill near Grapeville, as an example, first replaced its waterwheel with a turbine about 1884, changing to steam about the turn of the century.[55]

Not all grain remained in solid form, however. The most profitable grain product was whiskey.[56] In the days before the ascendancy of the temperance movement about 1830, there were a number of distilleries in Greene County. Four are recorded in 1810 and 1820, and three of these can be identified with some certainty. Russell Leffingwell's distillery near the shipyard at Athens operated from 1802 to 1814. Daniel Gunn began operations in Windham about 1808 to 1810, and in 1820 his two copper stills produced 7,500 gallons of whiskey and gin sent principally to New York City. And Ard Reynolds called for 6,000 bushels of corn and rye at his distillery at Madison [Leeds].[57] In 1825 there were no fewer than ten distilleries in the county but, by 1835, due both to temperance and the rise of western grain production, there were only three. Aaron Butler at East Greenville later operated a cider press and distillery, closing in 1859, and the Rundles made brandy, but the business was insignificant after the 1830s. There was a brewery at Prattsville in 1856, and another at Catskill about the same time.[58]

Another crop of major importance was hay. By the late eighteenth century uplands were commonly seeded with timothy and red clover to be cut for winter use. Early in the new century hay became a profitable market crop, thanks to increasingly efficient river transport, the growing urban market and the development of the screw-type hay press. Judge Anthony Van Bergen at Coxsackie upper village is said to have had the first of these; another historian reported that Silas Deane of Coxsackie manufactured them. Yet another commented that Garret W. Sager, who left Athens for Illinois in 1853-54, had become prosperous through shipping hay to New York using the hay-press.[59] Though hay was a bulky crop, the press compacted it into bales for practical shipment.

Several lesser crops were locally significant and provided contributions to the local economy.

A great maple sugar boom began about 1783 and was at its height in 1791. Maple sugar was favored partly because it was made by free persons, rather than by slaves as was cane sugar, and it was a relatively pure product since it was made outside of insect time.[60]

In the mid-1790s some families near Haines Falls manufactured sugar from the "large maples" which Samuel Mitchill observed within half a mile of the divide.[61] Gordon's 1836 gazetteer reported "large quantities" of sugar made on the Mountaintop. Barlow's store at Jewett Heights took in "maple sugar cakes" in 1837; syrup, which required containers, was less in demand until the twentieth century. Unfortunately, actual statistics are not available until 1855.[62] Honey was produced in smaller quantities yet, although late in the early national period, a single Coxsackie beekeeper achieved national recognition. In 1828, Moses Quinby reported:

> With money earned from working in a Coxsackie township sawmill at the age of eighteen years, I earned my first money to purchase my first hive of bees. I commenced without any knowledge of the business to assist me save a few directions about hiving, smoking them with sulphur, etc.[63]

Quinby devoted a major part of his time to the honey business after 1832; once his shipment of honey was so large it caused the market price of honey to fall. He later developed a sectional wooden beehive and published *The Mysteries of Beekeeping Explained*. In 1853 he went to St. Johnsville, N.Y. to be in a better bee-keeping area.

Cattle and sheep were raised by many Greene County farms and driven to the landings where slaughterhouses butchered and packed them. Swine were raised as well but, apparently, were more for home consumption. Chickens, it goes without saying, provided meat and eggs but are seldom mentioned in historical sources; their monetary value was slight. There's little record of large-scale horse trading; Philetus Reynolds of Windham dealt in horses "which he bought, fitted for market, and then took in droves to market" at Bangall, Dutchess County. He "removed from the county" in 1816.[64]

The early national period did not witness as many technological advances in farming as did the Civil War era. A few innovations, however, were of profound importance. By 1825 the cast-iron plough, which was soon to replace the wooden plough, was in limited use in the Hudson Valley.[65] To what extent and how quickly Greene County farmers adopted the new tool cannot be determined. The same is true of the revolving hay-rake, introduced shortly before 1820 to replace the hand-held rake. Since it first came into use where hay was a cash crop, it may have been quickly taken up in the river towns. Threshing machines, for beating the grain from the straw, were adopted in the 1830s and 1840s to replace the ancient flail.[66] Though Cyrus McCormick's patent for his reaper dates from 1834, it remained in an experimental stage until the years 1848 to 1852.

By mid-nineteenth century wheat culture in Greene County was largely superseded by the developing dairy industry. During the second half of the century, the pastures of Greene County farms provided food for thousands of cows, and their products—especially butter—provided a chief source of income for farm families. 🐚

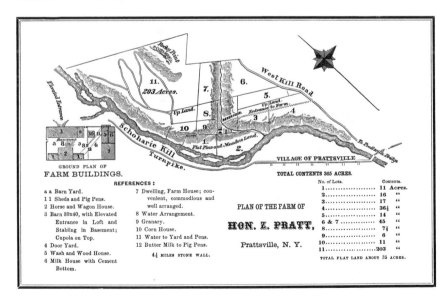

"Plan of the Farm of Hon. Z. Pratt, Prattsville, N.Y."
Engraving, 1861
From *Proceedings of the New York State Agricultural Society*

This is the only detailed farm layout we have found from 19th century Greene County. Zadock Pratt was wealthy and was interested in scientific agriculture, so his farm was not typical.

CHAPTER 8
BOATS

*T*he marketing of the agricultural produce of Greene County for nearly a century, from 1783 to 1882, was almost entirely dependent upon river transportation and the network of local and long-distance roads. The roads running parallel to the river, however, though first used early in the eighteenth century, were of little importance through the period. It was the east-west roads, together with the river, that made Greene County a crossroads of great importance in the regional economy.

Rochefaucault recorded his observations of Catskill's fast-growing shipping industry about 1796:

> *Seven vessels, mostly sloops, belong to this little town, and are constantly passing and repassing between Kaatskill and New York. A single brig, of a hundred and fifty tons burden, is employed during the winter in the West India trade, and even goes to Europe; it is owned by Mr. Jenkins, of Hudson.*[67]

From the time Catskill Landing began to develop it was a home port for river sloops, the graceful sailing vessels of the Hudson. The *Catskill Packet*, a newspaper begun in 1792, even carried the vignette of a sloop as its symbol. A Catskill native recorded his recollections of an early sloop voyage:

> *. . . about the year 1818, I made my first trip to New York, on board the good sloop Delaware . . . At that time but few persons travelled by steamboat, and almost every incident of that voyage is as distinct to my recollection as though it occurred but yesterday. The dropping of the anchor when the tide was unfavorable; the rowing ashore to procure milk, butter and eggs at the farm houses on the banks; the assisting our headway, in the absence of wind, by getting up a "white ash breeze"[by rowing]; the excellent fare; the jolly stories of the passengers, and my emotions when, after a three days passage, we came in sight of the great city . . . will probably never pass from my memory.*[68]

Though the use of sloops continued through the nineteenth century, an event of the year 1807 immediately altered transportation patterns on the Hudson. Robert Fulton's first commercially viable steamboat was tried on the river on August 17-19, and began regular operation on September 4. *The North River Steamboat*, as it was then called—evidence suggests it was never known as the *Clermont*—was a sidewheeler, built at New York, and powered with an engine imported from England; it was fitted with sails in case the engine failed. In the following year the steamboat stopped at Catskill on Wednesdays going south and on Sundays going north, charging $5 for the 24-hour trip to New York City, with berths and meals available.[69]

Many years later Thurlow Weed, a Catskill native who became one of the century's most influential American journalists, wrote in his autobiography:

> *I remember to have gone with other boys to the Point, where we packed our clothes in our hats, and our hats upon boards, which we pushed before us, thus swimming out to the island, where we dressed, and passed two days in succession waiting for the steamboat, which finally came, vomiting smoke and fire, and looking more like a visitor from the infernal regions than the beautiful steamers that now glide through the waters.*

Others agreed with his impression. One farmer said he "had seen the devil going up the river in a sawmill."[70]

At first Fulton and his financial backer, Robert Livingston, had a 20-year monopoly and the price for passage remained relatively high. After the Supreme Court case of Gibbons vs. Ogden broke the monopoly in 1824, the fares dropped in competition and became affordable.

There were three steamboats on the river in 1814, 16 in 1826, and nearly 100 in 1840. In 1828 the first steam vessel began plying the route from Catskill to New York on a semi-weekly schedule; it was called *The Richmond*. Soon there were many others.[71]

Though railroad competition began in the 1840s, the steamboats continued to thrive. That decade saw the peak number of vessels on the river, and in 1848 the *New World* reached the vast size of 352'8". Anthracite coal replaced firewood for fuel about 1840; the travel time to Albany decreased, from 32 hours in the beginning to 18 hours by 1817, and a mere seven hours in 1864.[72] The reduced time inspired the development of "day" and "night" lines which made the New York-to-Albany trip in the normal nine or ten hours achieved by mid-century.

The heyday of Hudson River steamboats was ushered in by the efforts of Van Santvoord and Davidson, who organized the Hudson River Day Line in 1861 as a New York to Albany service with stops at Catskill due to strong business ties with the Beach family, owners of the Catskill Mountain House. A large proportion of the travellers to the Greene County Catskills arrived at Catskill Landing by the Day Line. Two other companies operated at night: the Peoples' Line and the Catskill Evening Line, which stopped first at Coxsackie and Hudson.[73] Another short-lived company was the New York, Catskill and Athens Steamboat Company, which built the *City of Catskill* in 1880; unfortunately it burned two years later. One Catskill native remembers the boats of his boyhood:

Hudson River sloop
Detail from "Pau de Wandelaer"
Oil on canvas, attributed to Pieter Vanderlyn, c.1730
Collection of the Albany Institute of History and Art. Gift of Catherine Gansevoort Lansing

This image of a sloop, the essential vessel on the Hudson River throughout the eighteenth century and well into the nineteenth, appears in a fine portrait of a young man of Albany.

Ah the Day Line! The giants, the Hendrick Hudson and the Washington Irving, were floating palaces with every imaginable extra, lounge chairs indoors and deck chairs outside, space for picnics, a luxurious dining room with huge windows, an orchestra, and a continuous panoply of views on either side of the river.[74]

At first steamboats were of little value to farmers because their freight rates were much higher than those of sloops and barges. Beginning in the 1840s they offered a faster alternative at affordable rates.

Steamboats also were more dangerous than sailing vessels. Accidents caused by racing occasionally claimed lives on the river, as did boiler fires. In 1845 the *Swallow* hit a rocky island off Athens and sank; about 25 lives were lost. It was thought the accident was caused by a reckless race with another boat which had taken the main channel on the east side of the Middle Ground.

The success of steamboats stimulated some major improvements on the river, including the construction of three lighthouses along the Greene County shore. The Catskill Landing wharf at the end of Bomptjes Hook was extended in 1804 by a 100-foot dock and in 1820 fill was extended to a small island to create the Steamboat Landing, which still bears the name, though now surrounded by more fill.[75]

"Long Dock, or Catskill Landing on the Hudson River"
Pen and ink on paper by Thomas Cole, 1847
Collection of Albany Institute of History and Art. Purchased from Mrs. Florence Cole Vincent

Congress appropriated funds in 1828 for a light beacon and light keeper's cottage off the north end of Wells [Rattlesnake] Island. It was built in the two years following. In 1831 the present Four Mile Light was erected. Rebuilt in 1868, it was operated by a keeper until 1940 when it and the Rattlesnake Island light went automatic. The Hudson-Athens Lighthouse, now preserved, was put in operation just south of the Middle Ground in 1874; its last live-in keeper, Emil Brunner, moved to "land" some years prior to his 1949 retirement.[76]

While the Hudson has always been a natural water "highway", it was also an east-west barrier. Private entrepreneurs assisted by state-designated monopolies, and later the villages of Athens and Hudson, provided ferry service. While there were probably ferryboats throughout the eighteenth century, the first recorded operation was that of the Athens-Hudson ferry about 1778. About 1816 it became a "horse ferry": a horse walking a treadmill provided the motive power. A scow with oar or sail was kept on hand for small trips or emergencies.

By 1826 commutation tickets were sold, suggesting that some Athens residents were working in the growing city of Hudson; the ferry realized $35.50 in income that year from them. In 1858 the *John T. Waterman*, a steam ferry, was built at Athens and the horse ferry was retired.

Until the railroad was built on the east shore, the Athens-Hudson ferry was no doubt the most important of the three in Greene County, for Hudson was a substantial city for its time. It had one disadvantage. Directly between the two towns was the "Middle Ground," a shallow area. In 1814 the legislature passed an act giving Athens and Hudson the right to establish a lottery for the purpose of raising $10,000 to remove it. As Gallt said half a century ago, despite the best intentions, "the Middle Ground is still there."[77]

The ferry from Catskill to Oak Hill, a landing on the east shore of the Hudson, was leased as early as 1788. The horse ferry, patented by Troy men in 1819, was in use at Catskill in the following year. The Catskill *Messenger* of October 8, 1831 advertised "a new TEAM BOAT . . . of sufficient capacity to carry at one trip with ease, 8 two horse wagons, 50 oxen or six hundred sheep." This crossing switched to a steam ferry operated by the Beach family in 1853, which made the all-important railroad connection on the east side.

The Coxsackie-Newton Hook crossing began as a monopoly given to Ephraim Bogardus by the legislature in 1800. It, too, switched to a horse boat in 1820, built in Samuel Goodrich's Coxsackie shipyard.[78]

Only with improved roads to the west could the Hudson carry its full load of people and produce. By various means Greene County citizens set out to expand this critical network. ❦

CHAPTER 9
TURNPIKES

*T*he three ferries were critical links in the westward movement across Greene County. Early in the nineteenth century this included immigrants from Connecticut heading for the Susquehanna region; backwoodsmen from the upper Delaware and upper Susquehanna returning from rafting trips to Philadelphia and Baltimore; and teamsters hauling goods to northern Pennsylvania and southern New York State.[79] Once beyond the Hudson, the travellers moved by oxteam, on horseback, even on foot—and, in the winter, in the luxury of sleighs on smooth snow-covered roads. The roads were originally the paths used by the Indians, following the watercourses and passing through the natural cloves.

In 1769 Richard Smith noted that the Duchess of Gordon and Col. Staats Long Morris had just left from Dies' at Catskill to travel to Cherry Valley. They were going via Freehold with two wagons.[80] In May of 1793 a mail route was established from Hudson through Catskill "to the Painted Post in Tioga, there to meet the post from Reading, Pa."[81] The conditions experienced by these overland travelers can only have been wretched.

By the 1790s the stream of immigration westward was a flood. Captain Peter Van Orden, Sr., who built a two-room log hotel with a ladder loft at East Windham in 1788, recalled later that he entertained "many families of emigrants at his house; so many at times that he could not cross the floor without walking over their prostrate forms."[82] With the great increase in traffic, improved roads were needed. The legislature sanctioned the formation of private corporations to build better roads. Many investors and even small business owners in the line of travel invested in stock to encourage the projects; since they expected increased trade from the new settlements, they hoped to realize substantial returns from their investments. While the roads were indeed important, they were mostly unprofitable, as an examination of the record shows.

According to research by Raymond Beecher, the stock transactions show that the backing for these turnpikes came from residents at their eastern terminii. The roadbed of the Coxsackie Turnpike, as an example, was to be 33' wide, of stone, gravel or other hard substance, crowned; as a rule the charters required the roads to be 18 or more feet wide, surfaced with stone, ground, or other hard surface crowned and compacted. Each turnpike had toll gates, usually ten miles apart; on the Coxsackie Turnpike there were three, five miles apart. Tolls were established and posted, as were fines for avoiding payment: $25 in one instance for avoiding it by force, or $5 otherwise. No tolls were levied on persons travelling to mill, church or funeral or on farm business.[83]

Windham teamster
Photograph by E. Van Dyke, Catskill
Collection of the Greene County Historical Society

In the 19th century, teamsters hauled produce to market and returned with manufactured goods. This Windham man delivered produce in Catskill.

The first, and by far the most important, turnpike through Greene County was the Susquehanna Turnpike. According to a 1796 geography book, "A road also has been lately cut from Kaat's-kill, on the Hudson, westwardly . . . "[84] By an act of 1797 the legislature authorized the use of lottery income "to improve the great road from Catskill landing to Catherine's town" in Tioga.[85] A corporation was chartered in 1800 to build the improved road, which actually began in Salisbury, Connecticut, and ran through Catskill to the Susquehanna. As the *Western Constellation* reported in late 1800:

> *[It] exceeds anything of the nature heretofore known, and is at once an evidence of the wealth and public spirit of the inhabitants living on the Road, and also of the immense travel through Catskill to and from the Western Counties of this State.*
>
> * * *
>
> *The shares in the above Road have hitherto been chiefly taken up by gentlemen residing in Catskill, and its vicinity . . .*[86]

The turnpike's first section was in use by August 1801. In Greene County it ran from the Landing through Jefferson, Madison [Leeds], Cairo, East Durham and Durham, and thence due west. Soon the westbound emigrants and the eastbound products of forest and farm were moving along the road in a continuous stream. It contributed to the shift of population from New England to New York and the West; from 1800 to 1820 Connecticut increased only 10 percent while New York's population doubled. It made possible the shipment of vast quantities of produce to the river; as many as 256 wagonloads of hay and butter passed a single point in one day. John Burroughs the naturalist recalled that in his boyhood his family delivered two loads, each with 20 or more firkins of butter, at Catskill Landing each November. Colonel George Robertson opened a hotel on the Schoharie Kill Bridge Company Turnpike 3-1/2 miles east of Windham village in 1828; one night he had 600 head of cattle with 13 drovers staying at his place.[87]

The Susquehanna Turnpike's success encouraged the building of others, with financial backing from the other river towns which desired a share of the shipping, or even from mountain towns seeking to break their isolation. The Windham and Durham Turnpike was conceived in 1800, and the Windham Turnpike in 1808; both were tributary to the Susquehanna. From Athens the Schoharie Turnpike ran to Freehold, Oak Hill and beyond, begun in 1802. Coxsackie was linked with the Susquehanna Turnpike via Greenville by the Coxsackie Turnpike, begun in 1805. The following year a charter authorized the New Baltimore and Rensselaerville Turnpike. The company advertised for laborers in June 1807:

> Wanted at New Baltimore, 20 miles above Catskill, by the subscriber, 10 or 15 sworn TURNPIKERS to work on the Baltimore and Rensselaer [sic] Turnpike, to whom good wages will be given. No Dutchman need apply unless he is pretty well Yankeyfied; and no Irishman unless he can demolish a quart of Rum per day.
> Daniel Ives[88]

In 1809 Athens sought to divert Susquehanna Turnpike business from Catskill Landing by building its short Athens Turnpike to Madison [Leeds].

"Kauterskill Clove, Near the Old Tannery"
Photograph by J. Loeffler,
Tompkinsville, S.I., c.1890 Collection of Mountain Top Historical Society

The early turnpikes were a vast improvement over ordinary roads. This view shows the Hunter Turnpike as it began its ascent through the open pastures above Palenville.

Turnpike hotel at Prattsville
Photograph, c.1865-70
Collection of Zadock Pratt Museum

Before boarding houses were widespread, turnpike hotels were built on the east-west roads to accommodate travelers. This unidentified hotel was probably at the north end of Prattsville near the bridge.

The Hunter Turnpike Company was in operation by 1814 but did not build its road, an improvement of a 1793 road to Schohariekill [Prattsville] through the clove via Haines Falls and Hunter, until 1824 when the increased traffic from the tannery at Hunter made it profitable. It connected with the Bristol Turnpike from Palenville to Malden (1825) and the Catskill and Mountain Turnpike from Palenville to Catskill (1827).[89]

The earliest turnpike running parallel to the river was authorized in 1806: the Albany and Greene, which ran from Coeymans to Catskill along the river road. A turnpike from Greenfield [Greenville] north to Rensselaerville was begun in 1806, while the Prattsville Turnpike from Shandaken to Prattsville was a late comer, in 1843. By that time turnpikes were no longer profitable and it was abandoned to become a town road 14 years later.[90] While not a turnpike, a "bark road" through Stony Clove was built privately by young Colonel Edwards, the tanner, and many years later a Hunter native recalled, "I have seen ten to twenty of his teams come home at night in Winter with full loads of hemlock bark, two cords each, drawn through the notch."[91]

Many other turnpikes were chartered but never built. A good example is the Cairo and East Kill Turnpike, chartered 1812 and 1831 to run "over the mountains" into the East Kill Valley through Dutcher Notch.

Similar charters were issued for two bridge companies which built important links in the system. The Catskill Bridge Company incorporated in 1801 and opened its toll bridge in September 1802 on what is now Bridge Street. In the same year the Schoharie Kill Bridge Company was chartered, erecting a bridge at Prattsville and later a toll road through Windham to Cairo.[92]

Though most of the turnpikes reverted to town roads after a few years, the more heavily travelled sections were still privately maintained for many years. As late as 1894 deLisser wrote "A 'toll gate!' how romantic! how delightful!" when he encountered one on his travels, but soon changed his mind, calling them "remnants of barbarism."[93] The last section of the Coxsackie-Greenville Turnpike was finally sold in 1910 and the Climax tollgate closed; only the Mountain House Turnpike remained a toll road.[94]

"The Old East Windham Toll Gate"
Postcard, c.1905
Collection of Larry Tompkins

Turnpikes erected toll gates every five to ten miles. By the time this postcard view was taken the turnpikes were public roads and the toll gate was an archaic building and a real curiosity. Left to right: Laura Humphrey, unknown, Marcus Sherman, Robert Sherman, Madge Austin, Clifford Sherman.

There was some provision for travel by stage to accommodate those without horses or vehicles. Even along the river, the winter closing of navigation created a seasonal need for stage travel. An act of 1803 granted seven men the right to operate a stage line from Albany to the New Jersey boundary on the west side of the river; these vehicles passed through the county twice a week in each direction. The men advertised that:

> *the public may rest assured that the utmost attention will be paid by the proprietors to render this line respectable. For that purpose they have furnished themselves with sober and careful drivers, gentle and substantial horses, and strong, convenient carriages.*[95]

A similar monopoly on the line from Catskill to Unadilla, via Cairo and Windham, was granted in 1805. Once the terms of monopoly expired other lines entered the competition. A line through Cairo and Durham later competed with the original route, and Zadock Pratt is said to have operated very fine stages.[96]

In the winter of 1821-22, two lines competed for the Albany to New Jersey business. When the upper Hudson froze, there was strong economic incentive for stage travel from Catskill northward; a December 1833 poster advertised a daily line of coaches between Catskill and Albany "during the suspension of steam-boat navigation." Shorter lines away from the river and in areas never reached by rail remained important into the twentieth century; the pioneer short line was the one run by Erastus Beach twice a day in summer to the hotel at Pine Orchard [the Catskill Mountain House] starting in 1824.[97]

In mid-century an enthusiasm gripped New York State for "plank roads," which were essentially wooden plank turnpikes. Intended as feeder roads, usually to rail lines, they were unprofitable to their investors; the excitement

Working the roads, Huntersfield
Photograph, 1898
Collection of Zadock Pratt Museum

Each landowner was responsible for providing a number of days of labor each year to maintain the town roads. These men, farmers in an isolated district northeast of Prattsville, were (left to right): Wesley Cammer, John Plankenhorn, Lafayette Reed, Raymond Doyle.

over them was based on mistaken estimates about the durability of the timber. There seem to have been only two in Greene County. A short, three-mile plank road from New Baltimore to Aquetuck was placed under contract June 17, 1850; it required 420,000 feet of plank and stringer! Organized in 1852, the Coxsackie and Oak Hill Plank Road Company built a highway via Earlton, Greenville and Norton Hill, but its western section was abandoned only four years later. The rest was given up between 1881 and 1884.[98]

There was little lasting improvement of village streets during the nineteenth century. When Catskill incorporated in 1806 it quickly built sidewalks for Main Street and, in 1811, Main Street was graveled. About 1825 a committee explored a plan to "McAdamize" Catskill's Main Street but reported in favor of scraping off the mud in the spring and doctoring up the street in the old way.[99] Typically, plank sidewalks were built for pedestrians with some stone crossings through the mud of the street; these conditions were accepted until after 1910 in most places. The hard surface road encouraged—and was itself a product of—the popularization of the automobile, which gained momentum in the 1910s. ❧

CHAPTER 10
RIVER TOWNS

*T*he process of settlement in Greene County following the Revolutionary War depended upon a number of interrelated, contrasting forces. The mountaintop and Catskill Valley towns filled in as surplus population moved westward, as markets opened for forest and farm products, as transportation to these markets improved, and as improvements in technology allowed the processing of additional raw materials. The river villages grew as a secondary result of the growth of the back country from Greenville and Cairo to Ithaca, and were encouraged by improvements in transportation, particularly the steamboat.

The present village of Catskill was a product of the boom years of the young republic. During those years a vast trade from the West passed through Catskill and enriched it, creating a substantial village with the amenities of a small city. But in 1783 it was nothing more than a landing along the creek with a few tradesmen.

In 1787 this village had five dwellings and one store; two sloops sailed from the landing. In that year 257 bushels of wheat, 15,000 feet of lumber and 2,980 pounds of potash were shipped. Its growth over the following 15 years was explosive. It had ten dwellings, a newspaper and a physician's office in 1792, acquired a drug store in 1795 and, by the turn of the century, had increased to 180 dwellings, with 12 vessels sailing to New York, two to Boston and one to southern states, "which are constantly employed in transporting the produce of the country to New York and other seaports." These ships carried, in 1800, 46,164 bushels of wheat.[100]

William Van Orden, master of the sloop *Catherine*, sailing from Catskill to New York, advertised in January 1797 that he had rum imported from Jamaica and salt from Turks Island and that he took "all kinds of country produce" in exchange for these imported goods at his store.[101] Rochefaucault visited the young village in 1796 and emphasized the importance of one of the country products:

> *pot and pearl ash, which are a considerable article in the trade of new country under clearance, are brought to Katskill from the distance of above a hundred and fifty miles. The pot-ash is sold at present for a hundred and seventy-five dollars the ton. The usual price is a hundred.*[102]

Potash, which was relatively valuable by weight, is the salts of potassium and was used for soapmaking, bleaching, and fertilizer. It was produced by boiling down lye made from wood ash; these ashes were the residue of clearing the forest. Pearlash—potassium carbonate—is refined potash.[103]

When the Susquehanna Turnpike was commenced in 1800, it directed more trade than ever toward the landing. By 1803 the young river town had a population of 2,000, 31 stores, 12 wharves and 12 warehouses; local landowners laid out the level summit into building lots. Three years later, in 1806, the Village of Catskill was incorporated by act of legislature.[104]

The village was a creation of New Englanders, yet the Dutch were a part of the cultural mixture. Pinckney recalled that "perfect cordiality was never fully established between the first generation of the Dutchmen, and those whom they looked upon as 'Yankee interlopers.' In fact, when I was a boy the low dutch was the prevalent language in the town."[105] English was soon to supersede it; the Dutch Reformed Church in the village called Reverend Henry Ostrander to "preach in the English language at the Landing at Catskill" in 1810.[106]

Butchering and shipping of meat became a major part of the business of Catskill in winter. Even before the turnpike trade began, Rochefaucault noted, "here is a regular market, where beef is sold at eight pence a pound."[107] The slaughterhouse was originally "near the middle of the main street" and opened about 1802; it was soon relocated at The Point, near the present Steamboat Landing. We know the extent of business in 1820 from census returns. The single large firm was that of N. Wilson and Company, employing 32 men and slaughtering in one year 2,750 cattle and 250 hogs. The company, in which "Uncle Sam" Wilson had an interest, produced beef, pork, tallow, hides, and smoked beef. Another one-man firm produced 500 barrels of beef, sold at its own shop; its proprietor, James Lounsberry, reported that business "exceeds my ability to supply."[108]

"Mrs. McCormick's General Store"
Catskill, 1844, oil
by A.D.O. Browere
Collection of the New York State
Historical Association, Cooperstown

35

The men who worked in the slaughterhouses were remembered vividly. Jonas W. Gleason, one of the "boss butchers...was quite a character in his way. He had lungs like a smith's bellows." Another source reports that "when pay day came he would climb up a ladder and announce to the men that they had spilled more blood than Napoleon ever did."[109]

The cattle, sheep and, presumably, hogs were driven to the slaughterhouse by way of Jefferson; Jessie Van Vechten Vedder recalled:

> Often the hills were covered with cattle which were taken to the slaughter-house at The Point, where there were four beds, as they were called, and four beeves were killed at a time, one man knocking them in the head, others following to finish the job. The meat was shipped to market by sloops. Cold storage cars by which meat was shipped from the west put an end to this industry in Catskill.[110]

In 1820 census schedules also reveal two industries closely linked to the slaughterhouse. Four shops employing 16 men produced 16,000 barrels for flour and 8,000 for beef or pork. J. Gregory's shop used 10,000 cattle horns to produce combs for sale at Hudson and other places on the river. The shop employed 4-1/2 men and one boy, and used three machines to prepare the stock and one to saw the teeth. F.N. Wilson was still slaughtering 4,000 cattle and packing 8,000 barrels of beef annually in the 1840s.[111]

Andrew Backus wrote home to his father in Massachusetts on July 16, 1815 describing the growing village:

> There is a good deal of business done here. There is considerable building going on this season. There is building in one block one dwelling house and four stores all of brick three story high. The Catskill Mountains are plain in site. From here they are a bought ten miles distant from this place. The soil here is quite clayey so that the streets are very muddy if there is much rain, but they dry very quick again in fair weather and are hard. There is two meeting houses here, one for Presbyterians, one Episcopalian. There is a court house, jail, academy and bank. There is a good many stores here for a place this size. There is mechanicks shops here of a most all kinds. A great many wagons come in here every day from the westward that bring in lumber of a most all kinds, flour, corn, rie, &c.. The inhabitance here are part Dutch but more than half of the people of this village come from Connecticut. Mr. Whittimore that I am at work for moved from Stonington two years ago.[112]

Other than the village at the Landing, there was no concentration of population in the present town except at Old Catskill. It was soon renamed Madison, and then Leeds. There the stone bridge which still stands in a rebuilt form was completed on July 26, 1792 and declared to be "inferior to none in the state."[113] Home to several mills and small factories, Leeds was "left in the dust" by its riverfront successor, though briefly after the Civil War it became a bustling mill town, the only one in the county.

Reed Street, Coxsackie
Photograph by C.C. Wells, c.1875
Collection of the Greene County
Historical Society

Along with Old Catskill, Coxsackie was a "central place" before the Revolution, though it was then little more than a church, probably with the usual businesses nearby—a tavern, a mill, a blacksmith shop—some distance back from the river. A certain amount of fishing, transporting and boat-building took place along the shore, and the small number of buildings at Coxsackie spread from there to the church, much in the same way the village is dispersed today. A few houses stood at the Upper Landing, and the early ferry landed there.[114]

The row of substantial three-story brick stores on the right, with living quarters above, demonstrate the prosperity that boat-building, river trade, and retail business all brought to Coxsackie, as well as Athens and Catskill.

Then, in 1792, Eliakim Reed purchased Water Lot No. 48 from Peter Van Bergen. He built a small wharf, known as Reeds Landing, and a warehouse. In 1804 he sold 25 acres to three partners who laid out a street and lots six years later. Meanwhile, in 1794, Israel Gibbs bought the site of the Lower Landing and established a wharf; later lots were sold at Gibbs Landing as well.[115]

The landings drew trade in back-country produce from the start; a survey of the town made in 1797 listed the exports from Coxsackie:

> . . . *Lumber of all kinds Staves of different kinds about two million feet of pine bords about one & an half Million about 500 Barrels Pott Ashes & Latterly Considerable Beef Pork & Wheat . . .* [116]

The merchants at the landings set about to increase this trade by the building of the Coxsackie Turnpike beginning in 1805. While the landings were growing, the hill country of Coxsackie was being cleared for the first time, for pre-Revolutionary settlement had been concentrated on the valley land, which was the most fertile. In the hilly land on the East Branch of Potick Creek, Greene County's only communitarian experiment took place, short-lived though it was.

In 1824 Robert Owen lectured on communism and attracted the interest of a number of people who formed experimental communities. One, at Haverstraw in Rockland County, quickly broke up but its participants removed to 315 acres on the Potick in 1826. There they joined with several local residents to form the Forestville Commonwealth, operating a mill, tannery, wheelwright shop and shoemaking shop. They had little capital, much debt, and were trying to do too much. As one of them later explained:

> There were few good men to steer things right. We wanted men and women who would be willing to live in simple habitations and on plain and simple diet and be contented with plain and simple clothing, and who would work together for each other's good. With such, we might have succeeded, but such attempts cannot succeed without such men.

They sold their land in October 1827; some went together to Stark County, Ohio.[117]

Athens came into existence from the joining of the pre-Revolutionary hamlet of Loonenburgh with the post-war "plat town" of Esperanza, conceived as a competitor for Hudson. In common with most other Hudson River towns, Hudson City was a product of the rapid expansion of trade which followed the end of the Revolutionary War. In 1794 a company of speculators formed to build a rival town directly across from Hudson, in the northern part of Catskill Town on the Loonenburgh Patent. They imagined a connecting point to the western country, in the way Catskill was becoming, and they dreamed of a Grand Canal to the west terminating at their new town. At the time it was at the head of navigation for ocean-going vessels on the Hudson, and it was directly east of the "Military Lands," the central New York region awarded to Revolutionary War soldiers as bounty for their service. Clearly the speculators recognized a strategic location.

Three-quarters of the shares in this new town of Esperanza were held by members of the Livingston family. Names of the founders were given to the east-west streets while curious names were bestowed on those running north-south. Most of the names were cereals (wheat, rye, barley, corn, oats, rice and their products bread and meal) but others were principles (liberty and equality) and beverages (cider and beer)! An engraved map of the proposed city was made, showing 25x100-foot lots. Also designated on the map were the court house, the market and the city tavern, none of which came to be, but a number of houses were built and the town flourished.[118]

Rochefaucault visited Esperanza a few years after its founding and reported fifty houses, some shops, and a brig which traded with New York. He predicted:

> *This infant town will, beyond all doubt, experience a considerable increase: it enjoys, in common with all the other towns built on the western bank of that beautiful river, the advantage of an extensive back country, which, in proportion as it becomes cultivated, will furnish immense quantities of produce, that cannot find any more convenient or certain vent than the North-River.*

At that time, however, the Duke noted that the back country was still mostly "desert wildernesses," and that Esperanza's merchants would have to conquer the habit of the farmers of carrying their produce to the older landings, such as Catskill.[119]

In 1800 Isaac Northrup acquired the Loonenburg "Lower Purchase," the future site of downtown Athens. In the following year he had it surveyed into lots and began attracting investors and settlers. Its development was rapid and, thanks to Northrup's success in attracting the right businessmen, it outstripped Esperanza. In 1805 the Village of Athens incorporated, taking in both Esperanza and Loonenburg.[120]

Quakers were among the early settlers of Athens. Timothy Bunker, for example, arrived from Nantucket in 1800. In 1811 a Preparative Meeting, the local organization of Quakers, was formed at Athens. They built a meeting house in 1813-1814.[121]

Spafford's 1813 *Gazetteer* repeated Rochefaucault's prediction of a "very great city" and noted that Athens had eight vessels on the Hudson and a rope-walk.[122]

The glory of New Baltimore was in its shipbuilding; it shared, too, in the shipping of farm products from the back country, though never on the scale of the three larger villages.

Cornelius and Storm Vanderzee purchased the land on which New Baltimore landing stands in 1773; in 1786 they ordered a map drawn "for the Regulation of a Town." John Williams was in business as a merchant by 1791, the same year that Paul Sherman arrived from Tiverton, Rhode Island and began acquiring property. Sherman built a number of houses and shops, renting them to boat builders and others. Within five years the two Vanderzees and Sherman jointly owned a storehouse and dock. Sherman also had a schooner and carried on trade with the West Indies.[123]

Growth was sufficiently promising to encourage subdivision of additional land in 1809. John D. Spoor surveyed 112 lots on Main, Green, Washington and Liberty Streets for the partners; on his map Spoor wrote that New Baltimore was "a fair prospect for the Mercantile & seafaring adventurer."

New Baltimore's back country was settled principally during the 1780s and 1790s. A group of Quakers from Dutchess County took land in the ninth allotment of Coeyman's Patent and held their first meeting on March 25, 1781.

Five years later their meeting was constituted and, by 1788, they had a meeting house at Stanton Hill, which was replaced with one 50 by 35 feet, two stories high, in 1797-98. A little to the west, Quakers at Staco began meeting in 1807.

In 1829 there were 342 Friends in New Baltimore, but the division that was then taking place in the sect began its decline. Elias Hicks, a Quaker preacher, appealed to the rural, traditional and generally less affluent Quakers with a more mystical approach to their faith. Most meetings split into Hicksite and Orthodox, as did Stanton Hill.[124]

Many of New Baltimore's other settlers were from Westchester County and settled their land during the 1790s.[125] A small, short-lived colony of three French families who fled their homeland during the Revolution there arrived late in 1794. Honoré Chaurand named his farm "Friendship's Asylum" but, like many of his exiled contemporaries, gravitated toward seaboard cities; the New Baltimore families went to New York City sometime after late 1797.[126]

Sherman warehouses, New Baltimore
Watercolor by Ann Frances Sherman, c.1820
Edward Ely Sherman Memorial Collection of the Greene County Historical Society

Even New Baltimore, though much smaller than the other three river ports, saw a thriving business, as seen in this early watercolor by a 13-year-old daughter of one of its merchants.

Through the nineteenth century, despite vast changes in transportation and shipping, New Baltimore remained a depot for river shipment, especially the products of farms in extreme southern Albany County and northern Greene County. Gallt noted early in this century:

> *Formerly a large amount of shipping was done from New Baltimore village and it was not an unusual sight to see lines of teams and loads of straw reaching from the landing to the top of the hill and for half a mile. With the burning of the big store house of Andrew Vanderpoel this business was lost.*[127]

Coxsackie, Athens and Catskill continued to handle river shipment of produce, but after 1880 the railroad cut into the business substantially. ❧

CHAPTER 11
VALLEY TOWNS

*T*hough Cairo, Durham and Greenville, the towns of the Catskill Valley and its tributaries, each drew some settlers before the Revolutionary War, the process of clearing land for farms in the valley essentially commenced just after the Revolution, as it did on the Mountaintop.

The proprietor of much of Greenville was Augustine Prevost. He and his father received land in 1764 for military service during the French and Indian War: at Greenville, near Lake Otsego, in western Pennsylvania and the Mississippi Valley. Most of the land was lost to him because of his Loyalist sympathies, but he received clear title to his Greenville tract in 1786 and, in 1793, contracted for the building of his house, "Hush Hush." When he came to Greenville he found people squatting on his land; they were hostile not only because he was the legal owner but also because of his Toryism.[128]

In 1781 three men from Woodbury, Connecticut—Benjamin Spees, Edward Lake and Eleazer Knowles—had come to Greenville to scout for land. They returned home and, in the following winter, left Connecticut for good, moving their families to the wilderness. The story is told that one Connecticut woman lost 14 silk dresses in the Hudson crossing: "A judgment on her, she thought it, for presuming to carry such superfluous finery into the wilderness." It was on February 23, 1782 that "the ax was heard" beginning the clearing of land for the Woodbury company.[129]

Other settlers followed, both on Prevost's land and elsewhere in the present Town of Greenville. A large proportion of its settlers were from Connecticut, Massachusetts and Dutchess County.

Rochefaucault, en route to Prevost's, observed the conditions a few years later:

> *Few houses have above twenty acres of ground cleared around them; and many have much less. They are all log-houses: the majority of the new settlers (and they are the better class) have immigrated from Connecticut.*

Prevost, he said, had "a neat little house" on his 9,000 acres, and had built a cornmill, sawmill, and "one for grinding tanner's bark. These he keeps in his own hands . . . "[130] Later, about 1814, Prevost built a carding mill and fulling mill.[131] At these endeavors Prevost was an exception. Most Greenville residents were small farmers, and no major industry has ever located in the town.

In Durham, settlement resumed in 1782 with the return of the Plank and deWitt families, who had abandoned their settlement at DeWittsburgh [Oak Hill] during the Revolution. Saybrook Hill was settled in the summer of 1783 by Connecticut emigrants, some from Saybrook, and Durham hamlet was settled probably in 1784 by families from Wallingford, Haddam, Guilford and Branford. The major thrust was the arrival, probably in the spring of 1784, of the Meetinghouse Hill settlement, consisting of families from Durham, Cheshire, and other points in Connecticut. The first year there were seven families; five more came the second year, and four in the third. To them were added a few Dutch families. The uplands of West Durham were settled from Connecticut between 1790 and 1797, but "some of them did not remain long."[132]

"Truman Ingalls' Family Reunion, at Lorenzo Hunt's Residence, Norton Hill, July 4th, 1884." Collection of Merritt and Ruth Elliot

Along the Catskill Creek and its tributary, the Potick, the relatively good land and easy grades made farming profitable well into the 20th century. As the large families dispersed, they returned to the "home place" for reunions, as seen in this formal group portrait.

In common with most Greene County towns, the construction of gristmills followed quickly after settlement, to permit the grinding and shipping of flour. Before the Revolution, deWitt's portable mill was alone in Durham, and the nearest water mills were at Old Catskill [Leeds] or near Catskill Landing. After the war Stephen Platt built one at Freehold. By 1790, however, Benjamin Bidwell on Durham Creek and Roswell Post on Post's Creek each built mills, followed in 1795 by Lucas deWitt on Catskill Creek. Later there were many others, as may be seen by census statistics, available from 1820 on.[133]

Durham farmers got high marks early in the new century when Timothy Dwight visited and described the Durham valley: "thoroughly cleared, well-cultivated, and divided by good enclosures into beautiful farms. Indeed everything here wears the appearance of prosperity . . . "[134]

CHAPTER 12
MOUNTAIN TOWNS

*G*reene County's Mountaintop, though it slopes into the Schoharie and Esopus Valleys, is so sharply defined from the Hudson and Catskill Valleys that its settlement was delayed until after the Revolutionary War, except for a small outpost at the western edge of the county in the Schoharie Valley.

This first settlement on the Mountaintop was near the confluence of the Schoharie and Batavia Kills. Simon Laraway, a farmer at "Petaveia," did business with Teunis Van Vechten of Catskill starting in 1757. Other Laraway family members—Isaac, Abraham, Jan and Jonas—were also customers from Batavia before the Revolutionary War. Other early settlers there included members of the Becker, Somer, Carlogh, Shoemaker, Taylor, Van Loan and Van Alstyne families, as well as Bastiaan Strope, who removed to Round Top during the war where his farm was attacked by hostile Indians. The settlers at Batavia [Prattsville] were also attacked by a force of British and Indian troops.[135]

Traditionally, the first settlers of the eastern Mountaintop are thought to have been Samuel, Elisha and John Haines and Gershom Griffin from Putnam County. They were Cowboys, essentially Tory guerrillas, and they fled into the mountains by way of Kingston and Mink Hollow. According to Beers they were discovered living in the present Town of Hunter by some Dutch farmers who were bear hunting there in 1786.[136] Aside from the general reliability of early oral tradition, there is no documentation for this. Jennie Haines Dunn, an extraordinary local historian, charted the movement into the Mountaintop, noting that only four families were living in the northern part of Great Lot 25 (Hunter) at the time of the 1790 census: those of William Hains, Samuel Merrit, Abraham Bloomer and John Porter.[137] By 1787, however, James Desbrosses of Kingston, who owned that lot, began leasing land. Two Kingston men, Peter Van Gaasbeek and Jacob Tremper, built a sawmill and later a gristmill on Roaring Brook near Elka Park, helping to open the region for settlement.[138]

Meanwhile the first settlers of Windham had arrived in 1785. Chancellor Livingston owned Hardenbergh Patent land there and experimented with the

Old World custom of pasturing herds in the high country during the summer. His herdsman was George Stimson; he and his family are said to have had no neighbors nearer than Cairo or Prattsville, 16 and 10 miles respectively. Livingston's agent, Stephen Simmons, was also sent to the Batavia Kill valley about that time.[139]

Perhaps an earlier settlement took place at the mouth of the East Kill, now Jewett Center. William Gass is believed to have arrived there in 1783, the first settler in the present Town of Jewett.[140]

Log Cabin at West Settlement
Photograph by M.L. Pangman, 1906
Collection of the Greene County
Historical Society

Log cabins were normally replaced within a few years by framed and clapboarded dwelling houses, but as late as 1855 3% of Greene County houses were of log. By the time this photograph was taken, they were considered very quaint. This one was built by Harlem Tompkins when he came from Darien, Conn. late in the 18th century.

The trickle of the 1780s turned into a flood in the 1790s. New England, settled for over a century and a half, was short of farmland. Its families commonly numbered six or eight and, after the pent-up period of the Revolution, New Englanders began a great movement to the West. As Windham's first historian put it:

> *This unsettled period, when gladness and apprehension seem alternately to have possessed the patriotic mind of the country, when the poverty of the people forced them to struggle to love, and the political troubles invited them to dispute, was the period when emigration flowed in amongst these mountain wilds and forests. It may have been only the peculiar way of Connecticut Yankees: the hive not only swarmed early, but took a stormy day for it.*[141]

A few settlers had other reasons to settle on the Mountaintop. Deacon Lemuel Hitchcock moved his family from Durham to the upper Batavia Valley in order to bring up his children in the isolation of the wilderness, away from the influence of neighbors who were "Sabbath breakers with loose habits and principles."[142]

Jennie Dunn noted that the tanbark business, later so important to the Mountaintop, had no influence on the settlers of the 1790s. They were drawn instead by the availability of waterpower and timber, furs and lumber as sources of income, and the negligible rent charged by most Hardenbergh patentees. In fact, the Putnam County settlers had been tenants of the Philipse family and probably moved to Hunter precisely because they were leased lands: they had not been able to buy farms in Putnam when the new state sold the Philipse estates in 1785.[143] Hardenbergh Lot 25 was sold to John Hunter of New Rochelle about 1790 and surveyed into lots. According to Edwin C. Holton, the annual rates were a "reasonable" shilling an acre. Rents seemed to have been quite low, but one source in 1824 believed differently and, writing about Windham, noted: "If the ground rent is as high as in Lexington, stated by a resident correspondent, they can hardly be full blooded Yankees who pay it."[144]

The leasehold system on the Hardenbergh Patent both advanced and retarded this early settlement, as Dunn noted. It gave the impoverished postwar immigrants a chance to rebuild, but it discouraged permanent settlement by serious farmers.

While most farms were sold outright over the years, there were still two active leases in 1884, and Jason Clum held a perpetual lease on his farm near Tannersville as late as 1910.[145]

As was true in some of the valley towns like Durham, settlers immigrated in groups from New England and the Hudson Valley, or sent word back to draw their former neighbors to the new settlements. Barbertown [North Lexington] was settled by five families, four of them from Canaan, Columbia County. Wallingford, Connecticut families settled Jewett Heights in 1789 and Goshen, Connecticut families settled nearby Goshen Street between 1795 and 1800.

Other individual settlers came from various towns in Connecticut and Massachusetts. Dutch and German settlers came from several directions: Schoharie County farmers settled East Jewett in 1806, while a number of Hudson Valley families cleared farms in Lexington, including at least two Van Valkenburghs, one from Columbia County and one from Rensselaer County. In 1896 the *Examiner* noted that there were 26 families with that name in Lexington, and even today it's common on the Mountaintop.[146]

Oliver Homestead, near Hensonville
Photograph, late 19th century
Collection of Haines Falls Free Library

A typical Mountaintop farmhouse showing Connecticut influences.

The Town of Halcott, then part of Lexington, was settled later and separately. At first, it drew squatters, mostly from Connecticut, who cleared a few acres but soon moved on; Helmus Chrysler, who came in 1809, is the earliest known. He abandoned his "chopping" in 1813 and two Van Valkenburg brothers with their mother took over his place, becoming the first permanent settlers. Within four years eight or more farmers joined them, most getting their start on the abandoned "choppings." Always an isolated town, it was better connected with Lexington and Prattsville in its early years, for three rough, unimproved roads—the only kind anyone was accustomed to—crossed the ridges. Today, these roads are only trails and little used.[147]

With the exception of Halcott, the Mountaintop towns were settled before the days of turnpikes and the process of moving was an arduous one, recorded for us by "old settlers" who arrived as children. Several described hauling their household goods into the mountains on carts or sleds pulled by oxen.[148] Zephaniah Chase from Martha's Vineyard, a former whaler crew member, was bound for Binghamton in 1788. At Windham he found the road to the west was impassable, and a man offered him land at Jewett Center, so he settled there.[149]

Along with the difficult conditions, there were the rewards of community. Curtis Prout, who came from Middletown, Connecticut in 1799, recalled his arrival at Windham: ". . . a cheering spectacle met his gaze. The old meeting house was being raised, and then he halted and met his brother, brother-in-law and others who had come out the previous year."[150] And Samuel Ives, who came from Wallingford, Connecuticut in 1789, remembered the fine welcome his family received:

> Soon after going there . . . the family were startled at night by the sound of a violin, and listened to know whence it came. It moved towards the cabin, and never stopped its melody—the musicians marching right over brush fence and logs till they stood in the cabin of Mr. Ives—three old Wallingford neighbors, settlers upon the ridge, Eb. Johnson, Thorpe, and Sam Peck—marching to musical strains into the cabin and into the arms of their old Connecticut friends, and so giving them a brave welcome to the new country.[151]

Shelter was the most immediate concern of the new settlers. When Henry Goslee came to Jewett in 1788 from Hebron, Conn., he "felled a large maple tree, set up forks by the side of it, laid poles on the forks, and spread bark and boughs on the poles, for their house."[152] Such lean-tos were not used long, but the log cabins which succeeded them were not much better. One major disadvantage of the log house was that it could be enlarged only by lengthening. Yet as late as 1855 there were 145 log houses in Greene County, mostly in Halcott, Hunter, Lexington and Prattsville, somewhat less than 3 percent of all dwellings.[153]

As soon as sawmills were built, the Mountaintop farmers built frame houses covered with clapboard, many of them one-and-a-half story dwellings after New England models. George Stimson, Windham's first settler, initially built a brush shanty. When he replaced it with a frame house, it was an unfinished shell for at least 15 years before it was at last lathed and plastered "and made comfortable."[154]

The next order of business was provision for the winter. The virgin forest allowed an easy wheat crop, despite the poor soil. The custom, as reported by the Bump family who settled in Mitchell Hollow about 1810, was to chop and clear land in the winter, and sow it the first year in wheat, the next in rye. The family of Jabez Barlow in Ashland lived on pounded rye and other grain during their first year.[155]

Perkins Farm, Tannersville
Oil on canvas, c.1850
Collection of Mountain Top Historical Society

The Mountaintop farm struggled with thin soil, rocks, and a short growing season. This painting shows such a farm before the boom in summer tourists after the Civil War, when boarders were found to be a more profitable crop than cows or potatoes. The Perkins Farm became "Roggin's Mountain Home" soon after the war.

Since the clearing of land was arduous, some immigrants apparently allowed several seasons to get settled. Peter Van Orden of East Windham reported:

> *I have heard of some men who came on in the spring and worked all summer to make some improvement, to bring on their families the next spring, and then return and winter east. Some who done so did return and settle, and some never return.*[156]

Henry Goslee of Jewett was among those who returned to New England for the first winter.[157] But, in the long term, the Mountaintop was not meant for farming. Much of the lumber, staves, and potash reported in shipments from the river towns early in the nineteenth century were products of the wild Mountaintop forest. After the passage of about one generation, the leather industry discovered the riches of hemlock bark in the Catskills and the economy was literally revolutionized. 🍎

CHAPTER 13
GOVERNMENT

*A*s settlement resumed throughout the territory which would become Greene County, the final exercises of the Revolutionary War took place. Until Cornwallis' surrender, Americans could not return to normal lives. Even then, the formal peace was nearly two years in the future, and several more years passed before their shattered economy was restored sufficiently to permit growth and expansion.

The town governments evolved from the districts and from the committee system. The present county consisted of Coxsackie and Great Imbocht Districts. In 1786 the residents petitioned to be included in the new county petitioned for by residents east of the river; but Columbia County was formed without them. When Albany County was divided into towns in 1788, the districts became the towns of Coxsackie and Catskill. The line between Ulster and Albany Counties was moved somewhat north, and encompassed much of the Mountaintop in the town of Woodstock.

In 1790 the western part of Coxsackie was made the town of Freehold. Two years later the *Catskill Packet* reported that the freeholders and inhabitants of Catskill, Freehold, part of Coxsackie and New Stamford would meet at Martin G. Schuneman's to "consult" about applying to the legislature to be a separate county.[158] The wheels moved slowly. In the meantime, in 1798, Windham was divided from Woodstock, and Catskill joined it as a town of Ulster County. Petitions flew back and forth, both pro and con, and on March 25, 1800 Green County, as it was spelled for a few years, came into existence. Its four original towns were Catskill, Coxsackie, Freehold and Windham.[159] It was named for General Nathanael Greene, a hero of the Revolution.

The boundaries of Greene County have remained fixed since that time except for minor alterations. However, there were several attempts at major changes. In 1811 the legislature was petitioned to enlarge Greene County by annexing Rensselaerville and Coeymans; the courthouse was to be moved to Coxsackie. In 1824 a Mountaintop county was proposed from parts of Greene, Albany, Delaware and Schoharie; Lexington residents met and decided they were unwilling to cede any land for that purpose.[160]

The court system was the chief function of county government in early years. Greene County had a Court of Common Pleas, later called County Court, held three times yearly; Leonard Bronk of Coxsackie was its first judge.

There was also a Court of General Sessions, held the third Tuesday of September; Circuit Court; Court of Oyer and Terminer; and Surrogate's Court. In the following year a District Attorney's office for Columbia, Greene and Rensselaer was established by the legislature; in 1818 each county became an individual district.[161]

One of the first actions by Common Pleas was a survey of "a plat of ground for the liberties of the Gaol [Jail] of the County of Greene." The courts were held in the Academy at Catskill until a court house was authorized by an 1811 act of the Legislature. Completed in 1813, it was brick, considered fireproof, and provided an auditorium for lectures, fairs and travelling shows. Unfortunately it was not really fireproof and, in 1819, the second court house was built on its site; it was in use until 1910.[162]

The growth of population resulted in rapid division of the towns for about 15 years, with occasional changes until mid-century. A major reorganization took place in 1803: Canton (renamed Cairo, 1808) was formed from parts of three towns; Greenfield (renamed Freehold, 1808 and Greenville, 1809) from parts of two towns; and Windham acquired additional land south and west of the summits. In 1805 Freehold was renamed Durham. New Baltimore broke off from Coxsackie in 1811 and Athens was formed from Coxsackie and Catskill in 1815. Windham was divided in 1813, creating Greenland (Hunter after 1814) and New Goshen (Lexington after 1813). Prattsville was formed from Windham in 1833, and in 1848, those two towns gave the land for Ashland. In 1849, Hunter and Lexington ceded land to create Jewett, and two years later the county assumed its present composition when Halcott was set off from Lexington.[163]

The few urban and semi-urban concentrations of population in Greene County were incorporated as villages under state law. Athens and Catskill, as creations of early economic growth, led the way in 1805 and 1806 respectively; Coxsackie, though also a substantial community, did not form its own village government until 1867. Hunter and Tannersville incorporated as villages in 1894 and 1895 during the railroad-driven boardinghouse boom. Prattsville had incorporated in 1883, but was dissolved in 1900. ❦

CHAPTER 14
BOATYARDS

*A*ll four river towns were centers of boat- and ship-building during the late eighteenth and early nineteenth century. Catskill, the metropolis of the county, took a back seat after the first quarter of the century. At Athens and New Baltimore, the business continued well into the twentieth century.

The building of small river craft probably pre-dates the Revolution; the Teunis Van Vechten account book lists a ship carpenter at Catskill in 1784. In 1786 Dr. John Ely of Greenville leased land at Coxsackie "on which to build vessels."[164] By the 1790s the business was established, probably at all four landings. Rochefaucault noted:

> *At Katskill are built the sloops employed in the trade between that place and New-York. At present their price is from forty-three to forty-five dollars per ton, ready for sea: they are generally of from seventy to ninety tons' burden.*[165]

The first documented ship from a Greene County yard was the *Venus*, a brig built in 1797 at the New Baltimore shipyard for four New Haven, Connecticut merchants. She was a single deck, two-master of 146 tons, square sterned and measuring 72'3" by 22'10".[166]

In 1813 both Coxsackie and Athens claimed eight vessels sailing the Hudson. Of Athens it was said, "considerable shipping is built here," and there were shipyards at Catskill as well.[167]

New Baltimore's first great yard, that of Paul Sherman, started building in 1815. In 1830 it suspended building, but five men began a dry dock. John G. Raymond opened another "side way" in 1835. The 1842 gazetteer lists "two dry docks and shipyards." The first yard closed, but the second carried on—they built two barges in the year 1854—passing into the hands of J.R. and H.S. Baldwin in 1856. Four years later they utilized steam power and employed 16 men. During their two decades of ownership the yard built over one hundred barges, propellers, steamboats and schooners. William H. Baldwin purchased the yard in 1881 and continued the business until 1919; but, as late as 1930, his successors, Baldwin and Stott, were the only important employers in New Baltimore.[168]

Catskill shipbuilding went through a long eclipse after its early years. In 1824 two shipyards and a ropewalk were listed, but the "extensive shipyards of

Mr. [Hiland] Hill contracted to a shed where, almost to his death, he continued to build small craft" including sailboats and rowboats.[169]

Coxsackie had a shipyard and two drydocks in 1842 and, in 1850, William Mayo employed 15 men, but by 1860 shipbuilding was "declining." In 1867 Mayo sold to John Myer, who sold his yard to the Knickerbocker Ice Company six years later; but he continued to build cedar rowboats until after the turn of the century.[170]

Athens sustained the greatest level of shipbuilding and actually boomed after the Civil War. In 1842 it counted three drydocks and shipyards. It was, however, the establishment of the Athens Shipyard and Drydock by William Coffin in the following year that set the stage for Athens' glory days as a shipbuilding center. They began producing large sidewheelers, like the *Buffalo* of 1846. In 1850 Athens claimed two good-sized shipyards, one employing 15 men and the other 12. N.E. and F.R. Edmonds were in business a little north of Second Street in 1867, as was W.H. Morton at the foot of Fourth Street. Five years later the Edmonds sold to Mathias Van Loan and Peter Magee, and it was under their ownership that the yard produced about 200 steam vessels. Late in March 1882 their yard was the scene of the launching of the *Kaaterskill*, the splendid new sidewheeler of the New York, Catskill and Athens Steamboat Company.[171]

For many years there was little or no building at Catskill but, in 1860, Francis J. Dunham began a boat business there at which he bought, sold and rented small craft. In 1884 Henry A. Dunham purchased it and George Benter joined the business, buying out the Cummings and Myers boathouse on the west side of the creek in 1886 and, in 1888, Dunham's share. Benter's brothers, Charles and Worth, took over, and for many decades engaged in building, storing, repairing, buying, selling and renting.[172]

Two views of the boatyard,
Lower River Street, Coxsackie
Photographs probably by C.C. Wells,
c.1875
Collection of the Greene County
Historical Society

The relative significance of boat building to Greene County's economy is not evident from the number of men employed, but census statistics demonstrate the amount of wealth produced, which was comparable to that of the woolen mills. In 1855 there were three shipbuilders (out of 86 in the state) in Greene County, one in each landing town except Catskill, and they employed forty men. Their product, however, was valued at $56,000.[173]

The number of firms and the number of employees were similar five years later, but the product had exploded to $310,000, which was double that of the next largest industry, woolen goods. In 1870, 59 men in five yards produced $725,000 in boats, and only woolen goods exceeded the value of product. The 1880 census revealed four firms employing 109 men.[174]

By the turn of the century shipbuilding was on its way out. At Athens, Magee died in 1899 and his yard was sold to William D. Ford, standing idle from 1903 to 1908. During that period Wentworth Allen at the "Upper Shipyard" produced small crafts and tugs, but died in the latter year. It was a Kingston man, Richard Lenahan, and his son Michael, who modernized the old Magee yard soon afterward, building the powerful Athens Dry Dock. Its shops were equipped with electric and pneumatic tools, and it produced modern diesel tugs, ice and brick barges, deck scows and canal boats. Michael Lenahan retired in 1938, effectively ending riverboat building in Greene County.[175] ❧

Athens shipyard crew
Photograph, late 19th century
Collection of Athens Museum,
courtesy of Lynn Brunner

CHAPTER 15
MILLS

$\mathcal{U}$ntil methods of shipping improved significantly, manufacturing enterprises were small, mostly water-powered, and produced goods which had a high value compared to weight and cost of shipping. These small mills gave farmers cash income from hauling, woodcutting, charcoal burning and the like. Perhaps Greene County's successful role as a marketer for Western agricultural and forestry production reduced the need for manufacturing risks by its capitalists.

At the start of the nineteenth century Greene County residents in various towns established small mills producing paper, textiles and iron. They never became numerous, but were sufficiently successful to survive for generations, usually under a succession of owners.

Papermaker Nathan Benjamin established the Hope Mill on Catskill Creek near Jefferson about 1800, and rebuilt it after a fire in December 1806. In 1813 he sold out to Abner and Russell Austin. In 1820 Abner employed eight men, four women and eight boys and girls. Abner died in 1848 but his two sons continued the operation until the 1880s. It always made rag paper, especially bonnet board, under trade names "Hope Mills" and "Kalkberg." It also produced some straw paper.[176]

Another long-lived paper mill was Croswell's, New Baltimore, established by Nathaniel Bruce before 1826. Here a paper-making machine, an improvement which revolutionized the industry in the century's second quarter, was introduced in 1829. It, too, was still operating in 1884 when it was called "temporarily idle."[177]

Textile production was being mechanized by the turn of the nineteenth century, but progressed slowly. Water-powered mills in various locations provided machine carding (combing) of wool, mostly on order; fulling (processing) of woolen cloth; and, rarely, actual production of cloth. In 1813 Spafford reported 12 fulling mills "or clotheries" in the county, and 11 carding machines, but only one cotton factory, which produced an insignificant 868 yards.[178] Beginning in 1816, however, there was one moderate-sized cloth factory, Horace Austin's Furnace Manufacturing Company in Cairo. It employed six men, three women, and six boys and girls in 1820, producing

"Catskill Mill"
Engraving by George W. Merchant,
before 1822
Collection of the Greene County
Historical Society

This engraving was probably part of a
wrapper for paper produced at the
mill. It bore the words "Geo. Moore &
Co. / Hot Pressed / Superfine Vellum /
Manufacturers of Writing, Bonnet,
Printing, and Clothiers Press papers."

broadcloths and sattinets. Its raw material requirement was 5,000 pounds of
wool and 450 pounds of cotton. The list of machinery suggests a fairly up-to-
date operation: a fulling mill, a napping machine, a picker, two carding
machines, two 30-spindle bills, three 60-spindle jennies, three broad looms,
six narrow looms, a mill for warping, a pair of hand shears, two shearing
machines and a press.[179] It operated until it was transformed to paper
production in 1871.

Still, most textile production remained in the home until the output of
cheap textiles from the mills of New England eliminated both domestic
production and small factories. In 1813 Spafford reported 314 looms in the
county producing 22,189 yards of woolen cloth, 27,300 of linen, and 4,965 of
mixed and cotton cloth. As he said of Greenville, "their clothing is the product
of the household wheel and loom."[180]

The carding and fulling mills supported this domestic production. In 1825
the county had 27 fulling mills and 24 carding mills, well-distributed with
only Hunter lacking at least one. Domestic production began dropping by the
second quarter of the century. In 1825, 242,000 yards were produced, but by
1835 the total had decreased to 105,000 and in 1845 to 64,000. After the Civil
War only 16,000 yards were produced.

In 1845 large factories in Cairo and Prattsville produced woolens, as did
smaller ones in Catskill, Greenville and New Baltimore. As late as 1865, there
were six woolen mills. Still, there has only been one major textile factory in
the county, the one at Leeds, and it was short-lived.[181]

Hat manufacturing was a significant force in the county before the Civil War. Charles Rodgers from Wallingford, Connecticut, "at one time employed many workmen" at Catskill, but it was at Ashland that the trade was most prosperous. It was begun there by Leonard Kingsley, under the direction of Mr. Wadsworth. Zadock Pratt and his partner Smith opened a large hat shop at the north end of Prattsville hamlet in 1851. The 1855 census did not enumerate it, but found 89 employees in Ashland's three shops, producing $56,000 in goods, with another $12,000 produced at Windham's single shop by 21 operatives.

In 1860, Greene County's three hat factories produced $25,000 worth of goods and employed 31 men and 12 women. G. Rundell was Ashland's only hat shop proprietor in 1867, and after that the trade seems to have died out. Pratt and Smith's shop carried on under various owners until 1880 when it, too, closed.[182]

Iron processing and associated tool making were also important early industries. "The Forge" in Cairo, from which Purling received its original placename, was founded in 1788 by Enoch Hyde and Benjamin Hale from Litchfield, Connecticut. Iron was brought from the Ancram mines by vessels and mule carts to be processed into wrought-iron bars for local blacksmiths. A related shop was Beelzebub Barton's bell foundry near South Cairo; after casting, bells were finished at the forge.[183]

A longer-lived iron industry was the Catskill Foundry, established in 1808 by Josiah Dutcher, who produced ploughs. It passed through many hands, growing substantially later in the century. Samuel Fowks was manufacturing iron ploughs at Leeds by 1813 on a model invented by Jethro Wood; this business was carried through three generations, but closed due to competition.[184]

The triphammer of Pliny Barton, operating from 1809 until about 1832 in Cairo, produced 100 dozen scythes and 10 dozen axes in 1820, sold in "this

"Hope Mill"
Letterhead engraving by William H. Spencer, Athens, 1827
Collection of the Greene County Historical Society

Hope Mill, on the Catskill Creek near Jefferson, produced paper from about 1800 until the 1880s.

and neighboring counties." He employed only two boys, so his shop was only slightly advanced from that of a blacksmith. And the factory of Marvin and Company made chisels, augers and other tools beginning about 1818 on Catskill Creek above the falls.[185]

While locally important, both for income and to supply a primary market, these early manufacturing enterprises were never large employers compared to the production and trans-shipment of farm and forest products. And they certainly were dwarfed by the tanning industry, which expanded rapidly after 1815. ❦

CHAPTER 16
TANNERIES

*T*he manufacture of leather by tanning was a dirty, arduous trade. A contemporary scholar has described the process as it was followed at the turn of the nineteenth century:

> *To prepare a hide, the tanner practiced four regular operations: first, the preliminary washing, which took about 30 hours to clean the skins; second, the longer processing to loosen the hair, soaking and scraping the skin, lasting a year; third, the tanning by immersing the dehaired hides in a bath of oak [or hemlock] bark; and, finally, the drying and finishing of them to perfect the quality and appearance of leather.[186]*

If early county histories are correct, Nicholas Parray had the first tannery in Coxsackie about 1750, and other, small tanneries followed. They catered to local demand.

With the push into the Mountaintop after 1783, its riches of hemlock bark became a major factor in the expansion of the tanning industry. Using old surveyors' records, foresters have attempted to recreate the early Catskill forest. On Great Lot 22 North, now part of Jewett, nearly 42 percent of the trees were hemlock, and the average for the northern Catskills was over 27 percent.[187] The bark was peeled off felled hemlocks in May or June when the cambium was soft, but was hauled in the winter. After grinding (in a "bark mill") it was mixed with water to produce the tannin.

Although wood-using industries were to supplement or replace tanning, during the boom most of the lumber was wasted; about 95 percent of the trees were left to rot after the bark was removed. Other bad effects included the "denuding" of the hills with attendant erosion of the already light soils, and the loss of trout in Catskill streams, attributed to the tanneries by the early historian Prout.[188]

While statistics for the tanneries were not consistently gathered by the census, we have some data beginning in 1810, when there were 25 in Greene County, mostly small, processing 12,949 hides. Even in 1820, the 12 for which census forms survive were mostly two- and three-man operations. Ten years

Hunter and its tannery in 1820
Oil on canvas, mid 19th century
Collection of John Ham

Col. William Edwards established his
highly profitable "New York Tannery"
on the Schohariekill in 1817.

later the county produced more leather than all the other counties in the state combined.[189] In 1835 and 1845 Greene County reported 32 tanneries, which were widely distributed throughout the towns.

Two great tanneries established the reputation of Greene County for producing sole leather: those of Colonel William Edwards at Hunter, and of Zadock Pratt at Prattsville. Edwards was a tanner from New Jersey and Massachusetts who had passed through bankruptcy shortly before he made a prospecting tour to the Mountaintop in 1816-17. He saw the vast stands of hemlock, ready water power, the nearby Hudson which offered transportation to New York City. He believed his new method of suspending the hides in the tanning liquor would cut tanning time.

He decided to use an 1811 law which permitted the creation of limited-liability stock companies, even though it had specifically excluded tanneries. He secured passage of a bill which permitted such companies to operate tanneries in Greene and Delaware Counties. And he quickly secured a group of six wealthy investors, five from New York and one from Havana. As his son wrote thirty years later:

> In May or June, 1817, the New York Tannery Company was formed under the manufacturing law as amended, with a capital of $60,000. . . . We had decided on the plan for the tannery, by which all operations were to be carried on within one building; set men at work to clear the ground and prepare the foundation. . . . We marked out the main street (of Hunter Village), and began to build on it as soon as the land was cleared sufficiently. First, a barn, 30x40; then a boarding house, 24x40, one and a half story; next, a substantial store and office, 20x40; and finally the tannery, 200x36, to begin with. . . . Great care was taken to construct the tannery in such a manner as to bring all my father's improvements into the most convenient situation for economical use. . . . the tannery was extended till at length the main building was 500 feet long, and a second building near and parallel with it at its upper end 200 by 30 feet.[190]

Edwards planned to tan 5,000 hides per annum, but soon expanded. He employed six men and nine apprentices in 1820. Two years later he bought out the investors. His grandson remembered Edwardsville [Hunter]:

> It was a busy striving town. The bark and wood gave employment to scores of men, summer and winter, cutting the hemlock trees and peeling the bark, chopping firewood and hauling both bark and wood in. All the hides and supplies for the village were hauled from the river and the leather taken to the river. This gave employment to several teams which were on the road from year's end to year's end.[191]

By the mid 1820s, the proliferation of tanners had driven prices down, but members of the colonel's family continued operation. With the growing scarcity of hemlock bark, "some tanning continued under two or three different forms till about 1855, when the business ended."[192] The village of Hunter lived on, adapting to changed circumstances, subsisting on forest industries and on tourism.

Zadock Pratt was in business far longer than Edwards, and he was so colorful a man that he attracted lots of attention. After his apprenticeship, he became a skillful saddler and later opened a tannery in partnership with his brother a half mile south of Jewett. After about 13 years of operation, he closed it just before the depression in tanning after 1815.

In 1824 he removed to Schohariekill [Prattsville], with $14,000 made in furs and ash oars, with the intention of building a tannery. But, he said, he had "come to live *with* and not *on* his neighbors," and he also created a thriving and beautiful village.

His new tannery, reputed to be the largest in the world, was 550 x 31 feet, with 300 vats, conductors under the vats, 12 leaches, six heaters, three hide mills, and pumps. An inveterate statistician, Pratt kept records to establish the impact of the tannery. He estimated he employed 58 men within the walls, but a total of 200 benefitted directly or indirectly. He had utilized the bark from 6,666 acres of land, equivalent to ten square miles. In 1844 he received 36,839 hides worth $100,972, and shipped 73,590 sides of leather, netting $164,517. After expenses of about $37,000 per year Pratt was left with a handsome profit.

His records, too, establish the sources of the Catskill hides. They came from "San Juan" [probably Puerto Rico], Venezuela, Uruguay, Argentina, Honduras and Mexico, as well as from California and Buffalo. The tanneries like Pratt's were in the Catskills because of hemlock bark and firewood, not a proximity to raw hides.[193]

Throughout his life Pratt demonstrated a penchant for self-promotion in an innocent spirit; Alf Evers called him "beguilingly simple and even childlike," and these qualities have made of the long-dead tanner a Catskill folk hero. He took great pride in his physical strength and agility; he kept minute records of his factory production and other accomplishments; he published autobiographical pamphlets and books. Late in life he commissioned an itinerant stonecarver to record his life's work on the outcrop known as "Pratt's Rocks," just south of the hamlet, including a bas-relief of the tannery, a hemlock tree, and family members.

Pratt was known for odd practical jokes and eccentricities. One Fourth of July he drove into Catskill in a sleigh, wrapped in a fur coat. He re-enacted the Battle of Lodi at the Windham bridge, complete with fireworks. He enjoyed blasting down barns with the militia and artillery under his command, paying the farmers generously for the privilege.

Widowed a fourth time late in life—his first four wives were two pairs of sisters—he remarried at 78 to a woman half a century his junior. This story and many others are still repeated around Prattsville, and it seems as though nothing was ever said against this dynamic and generous man.

Zadock Pratt
Engraving by T. Doney, 1845
Collection of Zadock Pratt Museum

Pratt operated his tannery from 1824 to 1845, but is best known as a benevolent eccentric who created the village that bears his name.

Even after a century and a half, Prattsville shows the effects of Pratt's benevolence, for it is a community of considerable charm. Pratt devoted much of his wealth to improving Prattsville, building workers' houses and public buildings. He built a model dairy farm, firmly believing that when tanning ended, the dairy business would emerge.[194]

Finally, in the autumn of 1845, the tannery closed. But the hamlet still had a variety of small industries including an India Rubber factory, match factory, and the hat shops. And while the economic shifts cannot have been easy, he was correct that Prattsville would become the center of a good dairy country.

Edwards and Pratt, while the largest, were not the only important tanners in the county. Foster Morss at Red Falls, Jonathan Palen at Palenville, and Philo Bushnell at Bushnellville all operated substantial tanneries. There were also concentrations in Big Hollow and Kaaterskill Clove; but during the height of the boom the tanneries were dispersed wherever hemlocks stood.

One significant impact of the tanneries was the arrival of small numbers of Irish Catholics. The churches at Hunter (founded 1836-37) and Ashland were formed before the vast immigration of 1845-48 because the tanneries there had drawn distinct concentrations of Irish laborers.

"The Prattsville Tannery"
Pen and ink, probably by Zadock Pratt, 1845
Courtesy of Zadock Pratt Museum

Pratt was fascinated by statistics and concerned with the historical record; he probably drew this sketch to record the appearance of his tannery at the time he retired from the business.

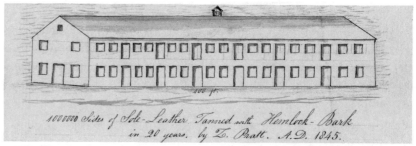

1000000 Sides of Sole-Leather Tanned with Hemlock-Bark in 20 years, by Z. Pratt. A.D. 1845.

The large tanneries began to go out when Pratt did, about 1845. By the mid-1850s the decline was rapid; the 1855 census showed only nine tanneries remaining, one percent of the number in New York State. The virgin hemlocks were mostly gone, the increasing use of steam rendered the location along mountain streams unnecessary, and the use of bark extracts permitted tanning away from the hemlock stands. Some men called tanners after mid-century were really small-scale tanners using local slaughters for boot and shoe production.[195]

George Robertson of Big Hollow [Maplecrest] entered the trade rather late and was one of the last of the Mountaintop tanners. In 1850 his firm of Pratt and Robertson tanned 26,000 sides, but ten years later, he produced only 2,600 sides of California leather. He was still in operation in 1867 but, soon afterward, the bark ran out.[196]

In 1855 Hunter, a town built on tanning, had only two tanneries employing 13. Many of Greene County's tanners went to Sullivan County or to Pennsylvania; there, tanning continued for decades. ❦

CHAPTER 17
CANAL AND RAIL

*D*uring the tannery boom, Greene County suffered a serious blow to its dominance in western produce shipment.

In 1817, New York State began construction of the 363-mile Erie Canal. When it was completed eight years later, it provided a "water level route" for emigrants and manufactured goods going westward, and for eastbound agricultural produce. As stated by the business leaders of Catskill in 1837:

This town was one of great promise before the construction of the Erie Canal, and commanded a large and extended trade with eight or ten Counties in this State, and with a part of Pennsylvania. Since that time it has been Stationary, and its citizens have been compelled to depend upon a limited business.[197]

A document of the following year estimated that two-thirds of Catskill's business had been diverted.[198] This was a hard blow to take, particularly because Catskill's leaders seem to have felt that, 20 years earlier, they had failed to woo the state into digging the canal through the Schoharie and Catskill valleys.

Besides altering shipping forever, the new canal had a revolutionary impact on agriculture in Greene County. With easy transport for the flour from the rich Genesee Valley, wheat farming ceased to be profitable in Greene County. By 1845, the first year for which statistics are available, only five percent of the acreage devoted to small grains was in wheat, and one-third of the gristmills extant 20 years earlier were gone. Oats, rye and buckwheat remained important, however.[199]

A new technology was already poised to threaten the canal's dominance, and Catskill interests attempted to use it to make up for lost opportunities. American railroads began late in the 1820s to forge land links between ports on waterways; many decades passed before it superseded boat travel. But Catskill's main western route was entirely overland, so in 1828 the Catskill and Ithaca Rail Road was incorporated. Curiously, it was authorized to permit individuals to use the rails with "suitable and proper carriages" by paying tolls at tollgates. But this provision, and Catskill's ability to compete with the Grand Canal, were never tested. The Catskill and Ithaca was never built, and the company failed.[200]

A less impractical scheme was launched when, in April 1830, the Catskill and Canajoharie Rail Road incorporated. This shorter route was calculated to turn the new canal to Catskill's advantage by providing a rail connection with the Erie some fifty miles west of Albany, thereby bringing freight to Hudson River landings south of the notorious sandbar near Coxsackie and the early ice closings near the capital.

Ground was broken October 27, 1831 at Catskill but nothing much was done until 1836. There were accusations that the railroad company was a speculative scheme; the contractor on the Mohawk and Hudson Rail Road wrote:

> *I see by the papers that the stock of the Catskill and Canajoharie Rail Road Co is taken up—if this is not a wild speculation I am much mistaken as it is my opinion that the Mohawk river might more easily be turned out of its valley than to divert the western travel from the same valley . . .* [201]

The railroad company finally put the whole line under contract in June 1836. It was a time of wild profit-taking, particularly in real estate, and at a meeting on February 10 of that year a group of Catskill men organized the Catskill Association, "formed for the purpose of Improving the Town of Catskill." They intended to promote the railroad; they hoped for a canal to parallel it to Canajoharie; and they purchased land west of Catskill Creek with the intention of developing it. A circular was printed with a map of the large new neighborhood, showing streets with "high-sounding names."[202] A Catskill businessman wrote his cousin in New Haven, Connecticut, reporting on the big doings:

> *You have probably heard of the "Catskill and Canajoharie Rail Road" which we consider of one the greatest improvements of the progressing age in which we live. According to the speculations of some of the prognosticators it is going to make us a "city" before we are aware of the fact. It connects our place with a small village called Canojoharie on the New York & Erie Canal. It will take the produce from the canal at that place and convey the same to this place, instead of Albany, to be shipped from here to New York. . . . These considerations offer great inducements to those receiving and sending produce from the "West" to the city of New York. Real Estate, in consequence of these contemplated improvements has already [risen] over one hundred per cent and will advance much more. Oh! we are avenues on to the west.*[203]

Then the economy reacted to the 1836 peak in land speculation with the Panic of 1837. The railroad faced slow going; many of the stockholders were unable to come up with the money they had subscribed.[204] The contractors laid stringers of Norway Pine, five by six inches; the rail was an iron strap 5/8" by 2 to 3". Rolling stock was acquired, including a single small engine which apparently was soon sent to Paterson, New Jersey for repair. Ten freight cars pulled by horses operated most of 1839, hauling building materials and hay.

Finally the Catskill *Messenger* announced:

> The Locomotive MOUNTAINEER commenced her regular trips on Monday last, upon the Canajoharie Road, running out as far as Stevens' in Durham.[205]

A vivid description of this train was recorded in 1897 by an eyewitness, John Baldwin:

> When I was a little shaver of about eleven years, my father took me with him one day down below South Cairo, on business. It was rather late in the fall and we drove down near a large mill that stood on the Catskill Creek about three miles west of Leeds.
>
> By and by we came to a place where there was a queer looking machine with what appeared to me a frightful looking chimney and a big stove on wheels, which stood directly across the highway. My father said: "Johnny, that is the new railroad and that is the Indian," as I understood him, but, of course, he must have said "engine."
>
> I was rather skittish yet curious, and our steady old horse was more so than I was, and began to rear so that father had to get out and hold him by the head. Then I had time to look closely at the "Indian." It had a tall, rather tapering smoke stack about seven feet high. There was no cab, I remember, for later on when cabs were adopted, I noticed the difference. There was a tender next to the engine, a short four wheeled affair. There was a single pair of drivers about three feet in diameter, and while the affair would look very small and insignificant to-day, it seemed to me then, as big as a barn would now. The engine and the tender were not more than twelve feet in length, but the brass bell that was on the engine, that they kept ringing, took my eye, and I thought it sounded very pretty. There were three short four-wheeled freight cars that resembled the ore and coal cars of the present day [1897], and in the rear of these were two passenger cars that were simply four-wheeled platform cars with old stage coach bodies thereon and fastened with bolts. In each of the cars were perhaps a half dozen passengers and I, boylike, wondered how they dared to risk their lives in that way. By and by, after the track, which was composed of bar iron about two inches across and half an inch [thick] bolted on string pieces, was repaired, which occupied a few minutes, the bell rang and the engine, slowly at first and then with increasing speed, moved off up the road..
>
> I was told it went to Durham and that the cars did not go any further.[206]

The track was extended to Cooksburg, Albany County, but its entire life as an operating railroad was about two years. In 1841 the company failed to pay the interest charges on $200,000 in state railroad stock, pleading for help to extend its rails another 15 miles to the Schoharie Valley in order to corner the shipment of its rich produce.[207] By some time the following year, "that unsubstantial bubble, the Canajoharie and Catskill Railroad"[208] discontinued operation.

Despite its many disappointments, Catskill was far from dead. In 1836 a gazetteer reported its "exports": 250,000 sides of sole leather, 3 million board feet of lumber, 3,000 bundles of shingles, 15,000 firkins of butter, vast quantities of grain, flour, hay, brick and wood, 600 tierces flaxseed, pot and pearl ash, 3,000 barrels salted herring, 5,000 barrels beef, 500 barrels tallow, 2,500 slaughter hides, 50,000 pounds of wool, and the products of many handicrafts.[209]

Change had been tumultuous from 1825 to 1845, as tanneries boomed and disappeared, the canal was completed and the western lands were opened. The old migration from Connecticut to the Mountaintop and the Susquehanna was over. Now Greene County natives began to join various streams of emigrants, mostly to the midwestern states and to New York City. ❦

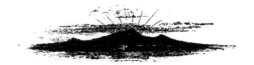

CHAPTER 18
EMIGRATION

*J*ames Pinckney believed that the Erie Canal had started the westward migration:

[it] opened up an Empire of rich, cheap and accessible country, toward which emigration immediately commenced to flow . . . Every town upon the Hudson, as well as the entire East, felt the drain thus created, and measurably ceased to grow.[210]

Yet some emigration took place much earlier. Jennie Haines Dunn found that at least one member of the Peck family had quickly become discouraged on the Mountaintop: "Coldness, sterility of the soil and the inaccessibility of this location induced him to emigrate with his family to the fertile valley of the Chenango River." Alf Evers found that it was not unusual for a mountain farm to pass through three or four tenants in a dozen years.[211]

The Erie Canal seems to have been the chief factor in the emigration of the 1830s. The pioneer families had invested about a generation in their farms; many were tenant farmers. Of some sixty families who settled Hunter in the 1790s and 1800s, Dunn found descendants of only four or five were still in the town in the twentieth century. Most left in groups in the 1830s. A great migration to Michigan from Hunter took place about 1829-30; the Griffins left for Ohio in 1833, and William Miller, a tanner, left in the same year for Bruce County, Michigan.[212] "Westward Ho! is the order of the day," wrote an Ulster County man in 1836.[213]

As tanning declined, ten or fifteen years later, more families followed. Olive Woodworth noted, "As the supply of hemlock on their land became exhausted, families began to move away, those with smaller holdings of course going first."[214] She noted the departure of eight or more families from Jewett in the 1840s and early 1850s. These people were uninterested in developing the Mountaintop's limited farming potential, whether they followed the hemlocks or went to Ohio, Indiana, Illinois or Michigan for prairie lands.

Robert B. Griffin returned from Huron County, Ohio to his childhood home in Hunter in 1866. He was 57 years old:

Nov. 5 Douglass took us to the old place. Made a general inspection of the premises. Took dinner in the old house with Larry Norton, its present occupant. All is changed here. I am a stranger in my childhood home.[215]

Others went even farther. The Gold Rush drew young, single Greene County men in some numbers, for the Catskill *Messenger* reported the departure of at least seven young men of that village and 11 from Prattsville, while "a company" from Coxsackie intended to go in February and another company of 15 from Cairo planned the trip in March.[216] Harriet Crandall of New Baltimore noted in her diary years later: "Met Mrs. Andrew Van Slyke in church home on visit from California. She is very fond of that country."[217]

With constant sloop and steamboat traffic between Catskill, the other three ports, and New York, it is certain that many Greene County young people also sought their fortunes in New York and Brooklyn from the dawn of the new century onward. This emigration continued for a century or more. At the turn of this century, it was a fashion for groups of country-born people to gather in the cities where they made their homes. The Greene County Society seems to have been organized in New York City about 1905, holding annual dinners at grand hotels. Three hundred attended the 1906 banquet at the Hotel Astor. An unsigned note in the Vedder Memorial Library states: "Father, Mother and I attended the meeting [at the Park Avenue Hotel in 1918]. It was the most elaborate dinner I ever ate." Later this tradition was carried on among Greene County "snowbirds" in Florida; they held an annual dinner at Allendale as early as 1924, and still gather in winter at Stuart, Florida.[218]

"Annual Greene County N.Y. Dinner, Allandale, Fla. March 16 1924"
Photograph by Coursen, Daytona, Fla.
Collection of Haines Falls Free Library

The loyalty of Greene County natives to their home is demonstrated by the gatherings held in New York City and in Florida.

Auction at Stannard Homestead,
Wright Street, Town of Durham
Photograph, c.1900
Collection of Durham Center Museum

As farming mechanized and it became
more difficult to make a living on a
small, poor farm, the poorest lands and
most remote locations were
abandoned; this process accelerated
around 1880. In this view we see an
auction, perhaps to break up such a
farm or to settle an estate.

    The census statistics for 1875 are revealing of the relative backwater
Greene County had become after 1825. Perhaps many Greene Countians left,
but rather few people moved in. Among counties Greene had the sixth-highest
percentage of residents born in the county—69 percent—and the third-
highest percentage born in the state—89 percent. Only 8 percent of its
residents were foreign-born, over half of them Irish. While tourism was well
underway by 1875, the forces that encouraged resorters to become residents
were still in the future.[219] ❧

CHAPTER 19
ANTI-RENTERS

*S*ome of the 1830s emigrants were tenants of Livingston and others on the Mountaintop. There were far fewer tenant farmers in Greene County than in neighboring counties, for its many small patentees had generally sold land free and clear. Still, most of the vast Hardenbergh patent was leased land, and tenancy was known to be counterproductive to the development of a town as well as to the building of individual wealth. Beginning in 1839 an angry conflict over tenancy gripped the mountains, in which farmers disguised as Indians rode to each other's support.[220]

The Anti-Rent War, as it is called, began in the Helderbergs in early 1839. Stephen Van Rensselaer, one of the largest landlords in eastern New York, had left an estate burdened with heavy debt. It was nearly equal to the back rents owed by his tenants; a benevolent landlord, he had long ignored the mounting arrears. When his heirs attempted to collect, resentment grew against the defenders of the archaic tenancy system. In that fall's election, the voters—who included most of the tenant farmers—turned out pro-landlord officeholders.

In 1840 Governor Seward demanded changes in the leasehold system, but the legislature dawdled. Too, the tenants were led to believe the Hardenbergh Patent was invalid, and they waited for legal relief. But after a few quiet years the conflict erupted. Early in 1845 an agent attempting to seize logs belonging to the Livingston heirs was tarred and feathered in Woodstock, and Sheriff Steele was shot and killed in Delaware County during a rent dispute.

Reports of costumed "Indian" violence in Greene County began to appear at this time,[221] although most early historians—who must have remembered the conflict themselves from childhood—left it out of their narratives entirely. A few anecdotes have survived.

One landlord owned eight farms in Halcott; when the sheriff came to serve papers a couple of "Halcott Indians" burned the warrants. In Windham, not many years later, Prout wrote:

> *Mrs. Disbrow remembers one day when her father lived near the bridge . . . how they heard a great noise, the blowing of conch shells and tin horns, and shouting till the valley rang again. It was the signal for the advance of an army of Indians, to rescue Uncle Jedediah Hubbard and his family, out of the hands of the cruel land agents, who had come to eject them.*[222]

Martial law was declared in August and many of the conspirators were convicted, but that November's elections sent even more anti-renters to Albany.

In 1846 the voters had their say. The Constitutional Convention abolished perpetual leases and, early in 1847, Governor Young pardoned the men who had been convicted of taking part in the Anti-Rent War. When those headed for home in western villages passed through Prattsville, Zadock Pratt welcomed them with a fine dinner as brass bands played, bonfires blazed and tin horns blew.[223] The "Calico Indians" were to be evermore heroes to the people of the Catskills.

Yet even after the state constitution provided incentive for the landlords to sell, some did not. John Hunter, owner of much of the Town of Hunter, insisted on all back rents before he would issue a deed or a new lease. He wrote his agents, James Powers and John Kiersted:

> *I have not been in any way instrumental in bringing about the state of things which exists. No father was more indulgent than I was or wished less to separate from his children than I did from my tenants—if we are separated, and by force of law, separated, it has been their own act, not mine.*[224]

Whether quickly, by Livingston heirs, or slowly, by Hunter and others, most Hardenbergh farms were sold outright. With the advent of private ownership, "thrift and prosperity" emerged from the neglect of tenancy.[225]

Leather mask used during the
Anti-Rent War
Collection of New York State Office of
Parks, Recreation and Historic
Preservation, Senate House State
Historic Site, Kingston

CHAPTER 20
CIVIL WAR

*G*reene County was not enthusiastic about the Republican administration which, it seemed to many, carried the nation into Civil War in 1861. From Jefferson's presidency through Arthur's, the congressmen from Greene County were all Democrats, including the Mountaintop's own, Zadock Pratt, who served two terms from 1837 to 1839 and 1843 to 1845.

In 1860, Greene County voters favored Douglas over Lincoln—they would again support Lincoln's opponent in 1864— and they voted 4,530 to 548 against Negro suffrage in the same election.[226] The father of Harriet Crandall of New Baltimore was an old-time Democrat with strong Southern sympathies; the daughter wrote on July 30, 1864, "We do not discuss war. Father is with those who blame Lincoln and the North." A few weeks later she wrote, "I went to Albany today to buy books for our district school library and wasn't there a fuss with the trustees because I bought 'Uncle Tom's Cabin' so father paid for it and said I could have it if I wanted it."[227]

So it was reluctantly that Greene County entered the Civil War. But at least 850 young men from Greene County served in the war, and many lost their lives. Two regiments, the 20th New York State Militia and the 120th New York Volunteers, drew most of the local boys.

The 20th New York State Militia was almost entirely from Ulster and Greene Counties; two of its companies were from the Mountaintop alone. Formed in 1857, it was put into service for the conflict, first entering major combat at the Second Battle of Manassas on August 30, 1862. There its commanding officer, Col. George W. Pratt, son of Zadock Pratt, received fatal wounds. The 120th New York Volunteers was recruited from Ulster and Greene in the summer of 1862. Both regiments were at Gettysburg and suffered heavy losses there, about 125 of 300 soldiers in the case of the 20th.[228]

Conscription was necessary by the middle of the war. The draft began May 27, 1863, but very few of those who were drafted actually served, most paying substitutes. Yet many men volunteered "to save the Union," including African-Americans, who served in segregated units; 16 enlisted from Greene County in the U.S. Colored Regiment.[229]

Greene County's only known Medal of Honor winner, William Plimley of Catskill, was recognized for his heroics at Hatcher's Run, Virginia, on April 2,

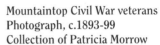

Mountaintop Civil War veterans
Photograph, c.1893-99
Collection of Patricia Morrow

The Grand Army of the Republic
("G.A.R.") organized Union Army
veterans, who continued to meet until
the 1940s. Standing (left to right):
unknown, Mr. Howard, Louis Hadden,
David Vining, Cyrus Tompkins. Seated
in chairs: unknown, unknown,
Addison Hayes, Martin Carr, unknown.
Seated on ground with wide black hat
brim: William Crandell.

1865. There were, of course, many other Greene County men whose devotion
and bravery went unrecognized.

Other than the sad loss of many young men, the war's greatest effects on
Greene County were indirect and economic. Even the men who returned
safely were drained from the labor pool for three years or more, forcing those
at home to explore mechanization on the farm; by 1864 three-quarters of New
York farmers with over 100 acres owned a mower.[230] The long-term impact of
industrialization and the resulting accumulation of wealth contributed to its
future prosperity for, with the return of peacetime in 1865, the Catskills were
poised to become a great resort area, appealing to the burgeoning middle
class. ❦

Officers of the 120th New York State
Volunteers, at Wall Street, Kingston
Photograph, 1865
Collection of Zadock Pratt Museum

The 120th Regiment recruited on the
mountaintop, valley towns and outside
the county.

CHAPTER 21
GENTLEMEN TOURISTS

*T*he extraordinary landscape of the northern Catskills drew the attention of Hudson River travellers from the time of the first explorers. Yet few ventured into the mountains as sightseers until the 1820s.

The Indians themselves had spent little time on the Mountaintop, believing it to be the home of hostile spirits; anyway, it had less of the game and other resources they needed. The Europeans were even less experienced in the ways of the forest. They were frightened both of getting lost in the wilderness and of attacks by wild animals and Indians.[231]

There were a few exceptions. John Bartram of Philadelphia, a pioneer American naturalist, travelled to the Mountaintop in 1741 and 1742 to collect samples of balsam for an English patron. He returned with his young son in 1753; they saw Kaaterskill Falls and camped at North Lake:

> . . . *came to our lodging kindled a fire & I being very weary tumbled down on ye moss that was spread on ye ground for our bed while my guide & son gathered wood to keep a good fire all night & a fine pleasant lodging we had a great rock between us & ye lake which served for a back to kindle ye fire against which reflected heat to ye under side of ye rock that projected over us A bright moonshine night & nothing wanting [to] render all agreable . . .*[232]

There were probably very few other travellers to the Mountaintop until a trickle began at the time of settlement in the 1780s. Spafford's 1813 gazetteer suggests that this was well underway, noting that Windham "attracts the notice of numerous parties in summer. The view from this mountain is inexpressably grand . . ."[233] This brief account was the first widely distributed description of Catskill scenery.

Even so, four conditions were necessary before tourism could really begin: a public that valued the landscape, transportation, accommodations, and public awareness of the Catskills' grandeur.[234] As it happens, new kinds of environmental attitudes from Europe, transported chiefly by literature and paintings, began to influence Americans, particularly after the War of 1812. They were encouraged to take up the arts and, in so doing, turned their attention to the wonders around them.

Palenville, Clove Valley, Catskill
Mountains
Ink on paper by Thomas Cole, c.1835
Collection of the Albany Institute of
History and Art

The Livingstons, who owned much of the Catskills, made their homes on
the east shore of the Hudson facing the Blue Mountains. Their wealth
permitted them to be hospitable; in August 1812, for example, Washington
Irving visited John Robert Livingston at Barrytown. Irving did not then travel
in the Catskills but seven years later he published his story, "Rip Van Winkle,"
set at the foot of the high Catskills although it is based on the German folktale
of Peter Klaus, a goatherd who fell into a long sleep.[235]

Four years later, James Fenimore Cooper published *The Pioneers*, in
which Natty Bumppo described the scene from the Pine Orchard near Haines
Falls: "'What see you when you get there?' asked Edwards. 'Creation!' said
Natty, 'all creation, lad!'"[236] Although the trickle of travelers had already begun,
these two stories published four years apart were so widely read that an
awareness of the Catskills burst upon the public consciousness at exactly the
moment when accommodations were prepared to receive them.

Entrepreneurs, who recognized both the increasing number of city
dwellers who wished to spend money on mountain scenery and the decline in
the local wheat and flour trade occasioned by the opening of western lands,
were the critical players in the birth of Catskill tourism. Elisha Williams, a
Hudson lawyer who served the interests of Hardenbergh Patent landlords,
secured title to the Pine Orchard and Kaaterskill Falls from the state in 1813.
For six years he did nothing; but, in 1819, Hiram Comfort and Joseph Bigelow
built a refreshment stand on Williams' land, soon adding bunks for overnight
stays.[237]

In the same season Erastus Beach, a Catskill liveryman, "finding business
rather dull," took his coach and four horses to Saratoga Springs, where he was
hired for 30 days by a party of four ladies and four gentlemen. After they had
"seen everything," he brought them back to Catskill to see the Pine Orchard.
His tourists spread the word and the trickle increased.

James Powers of Catskill was in control of the Pine Orchard site by 1822, when he built a sixty-foot addition to the 1819 shack. In September he tested the waters. He held a "Rural Ball" at the Pine Orchard, intended to excite interest and secure investors for the next step in the development of a resort.

In March of 1823 the Catskill Mountain Association organized. It proposed to build a hotel at the Pine Orchard and a turnpike from Catskill to the foot of the mountain. A temporary house of hemlock boards was put up late in the summer, consisting only of two dormitories, a kitchen, ballroom and parlor. Late in the year a frame hotel, the "Pine Orchard House," was begun; completed the following year, it was enlarged in 1825. It was to become the first successful mountain tourist hotel in the United States, renamed the "Catskill Mountain House."[238] It was visible from Hudson River steamboats, and it claimed its high elevation gave it a freedom from fever, a real concern of city residents in the summer.

Opening as it did just after the publication of Natty Bumppo's memorable words, the Pine Orchard House drew the attention of the newly emerging "tourist." Late in 1824 William L. Stone noted that not enough "lodging rooms had been provided to accommodate all who needed them"—two thirds of the tourists were being turned away.[239]

Morning
Oil on canvas by Frederic E. Church, 1848
Collection of the Albany Institute of History and Art. Gift of Catherine Gansevoort Lansing

Catskill Mountains
Oil on canvas by Asher B. Durand,
c. 1830
Collection of the Albany Institute of
History and Art. Gift of Miss Jane E.
Rosell

Writers began the movement to the mountains, but it was artists who helped make the Catskills world-famous. Thomas Cole arrived in the area in 1825 on a sketching trip; when he returned to New York City he painted three Catskill landscapes which immediately attracted the attention of his fellow artists and patrons. The Catskills were featured, too, in Wall's *Hudson River Portfolio* completed in the same year. In a guidebook published shortly afterward, James Kirke Paulding wrote:

> *Messrs. Wall and Cole, two fine artists, admirable in their different, we might almost say, opposite styles, have illustrated the scenery of the Kaatskill, by more than one picture of singular excellence. We should like to see such pictures gracing the drawing rooms of the wealthy, instead of the imported trumpery of British naval fights, or coloured engravings, and above all, in the place of that vulgar, tasteless, and inelegant accumulation of gilded finery, which costs more than a dozen fine landscapes. These lovers of cut glass lamps, rose wood sofas, and convex mirrors, have yet to learn that a single bust or picture of a master adorns and enriches the parlour of a gentleman, in the eyes of a well bred person, a thousand times more than the spoils of half a dozen fashionable warehouses.*[240]

Until Thomas Cole helped create the enthusiasm that led to the successes of the Hudson River School, American landscape drawing and painting were limited indeed. They fulfilled utilitarian functions, such as the needs of naturalists, or were supplementary to portraiture, serving as atmosphere and backdrop. Artists were largely discouraged from imitating nature, too, by academic dictates that they should master pictorial conventions.

The growth of the Romantic movement, coinciding with the domestication of most of the Eastern landscape and the rise of American nationalism, captured the hearts and minds of American art patrons, and Thomas Cole showed the way. His pictures of the Catskills embodied the Romantic ideals of the "sublime" and the "picturesque," two concepts which are hard to define. They represent, respectively, the awe-inspiring attributes of landscape and the aspects associated with antiquity, "charm," and variation.

Cole was the first artist to achieve recognition for his Catskills paintings; in fact, he is considered the first artist to embody the romanticization of the American wilderness. He is also the most important artist to have lived and worked in Greene County. Eleven years after his first visit, he married a Catskill woman and made the village his home. Until his 1848 death, he remained in Catskill in sight of the mountains, though his paintings' subjects wandered beyond the landscapes he had pioneered to encompass allegories as well as other genres.

Cole's influence on the Hudson River School and on American Romanticism was magnified, however, by his friendship with other artists whom he introduced to the beauties of his chosen countryside. During Cole's final four years, Frederic Edwin Church was his pupil and a member of his household. Later Church ranged throughout the world, commanding some of the highest prices ever paid to an American artist, but he returned to build his home, "Olana," across the Hudson River from Catskill.

Asher B. Durand was a well-established engraver and portraitist when he met Cole in 1825. Soon he, too, was spending summers and autumns painting directly from nature in Cole's favorite haunts and, by the late 1840s, was at the center of the early art colony at Palenville. Although he never gave up his New York City home and he painted extensively in other regions, including the White and Green Mountains, his Catskill work was early and influential; he engraved and published his view of the "Catskill Mountains" from Jefferson Heights as early as 1830.

Several artists were drawn by Cole's reputation and influence to settle in Catskill. Albertis D. Brouwere (1814-1887) arrived in 1841. Although he made two long visits to the West, prospecting for gold and painting its landscape, he eventually settled permanently in Catskill and continued to paint "the native scene." Sanford R. Gifford (1823-1880) took up landscape painting in 1845 and lived and worked most of his life in Catskill, though he visited the West as well as making the customary long visits to European art capitals. B.B.G. Stone (1829-1906) settled in Catskill by 1858 and thereafter devoted himself to painting, along with journalism and politics. Briefly, too, Charles Herbert Moore (1840-1930) lived in Catskill for some time, painting the Greene County landscape until 1871, when he left for a teaching position at Harvard and the directorship of the Fogg Art Museum there.

Other members of the Hudson River School were occasional visitors to the Catskills and painted some canvases here, including Thomas Doughty (1793-1856); John Frederick Kensett (1819-1872); Jervis McEntee (1828-1891) who painted around Lanesville; Alexander H. Wyant (1836-1892); Jasper F. Cropsey (1823-1900), who painted a superb view of the Mountain House; and Winslow Homer (1836-1910).[241]

Though Cole and Durand were active as early as the 1820s, most of the Catskill Mountains work of this roster of artists was created between 1848 and the early 1870s. Their large output of canvases riveted national attention on the natural beauty of the Mountaintop and of the Catskill Valley. Most sought more bohemian accommodations than the Mountain House, but the landmark remained an artistic subject and an increasingly famed geographical reference point.

During the 1830s the Catskill Mountain House suffered financial trouble; twice it was close to foreclosure. In 1839 Charles L. Beach, son of liveryman Erastus Beach, became the manager. Horace Greeley visited in 1843, noting:

> *Although nearly everything but milk and mountain berries must be hauled up from Catskill and New-York, his table would do honor to a hotel in the City, and the arrangements for the comfort of visitors are well-designed and ample, though the house itself about as inconvenient as possible, its windows port holes, its kitchen at one end while its dining room is at the other . . .* [242]

View of Catskill Creek
Oil on composition board by Thomas Cole, c.1833
Collection of the Albany Institute of History and Art

The Catterskill Fall (From Below)
Engraving by W.H. Bartlett, c.1840
Collection of Deborah Allen

In 1845 the hotel was sold at auction to Beach, and he set about improving it and modernizing. He added landholdings, enlarged the building substantially, and added the trademark Greek Revival portico facing the river. A large proportion of visitors stayed only one or two nights, because that was the time necessary to see the "sights" nearby.

The next quarter century was the Mountain House's most prosperous period. A guidebook, *The Scenery of the Catskill Mountains*, published in many editions beginning in 1846, provided advice on sightseeing in a more popular form than the gentlemen's travel journals which originally had spread the mountains' fame. During the 1850s and 1860s Mountain House overflow spurred the development of the boarding-house business, and the supplies, transportation, and transient business contributed to the prosperity of Catskill, whose economy had metamorphosed from long-distance trade to equally successful local trade since the Erie Canal opening. Beach controlled the great hotel privately until 1871 when, in order to preserve the family interests, he set up a corporation. ❧

CHAPTER 22
BOARDINGHOUSES

*I*n early America most travellers stayed in the tavern, but private houses offered an alternative. William Darby reported in 1819 that it was easy to get lodging "anywhere" in homes.[243]

Despite the Catskill Mountain House's great fame and considerable success, few other hotels were built for half a century. Instead, growth in lodgings through the mid-century was in boardinghouses, primarily in Hunter, Cairo and Catskill towns. As increasing numbers of tourists came to the Catskill Mountain House, the overflow enriched the surrounding farmers.

Beers' important 1884 history, published at the peak of boardinghouse business, carefully enumerated the accommodations in each town. The opening dates provided give us a good idea of the development of the boarding business.

Very few boardinghouses extant in 1884 had entered operation before 1850. Winter Clove, at Round Top, was begun in 1838, and a few other houses in the towns of Cairo and Catskill, which were relatively convenient to the steamboat, started in the 1830s and 1840s, most of them at Leeds, South Cairo, Acra, and Palenville. The Summit House in Durham opened in 1848. The Laurel House at Kaaterskill Falls, close to the Mountain House, dated from 1831. With The Vista, built in Haines Falls in 1849, there were a trio of hotels on the Mountaintop.[244]

The great expansion of the boardinghouse business took place after the Civil War. Fueled by the War, the American economy resumed expansion, and the newly burgeoning middle class sought pleasant ways to spend summer weeks and months. In Catskill, four houses opened during the four years after war's end, and in Lexington, where there seems to have been little or no boarding before the war, several houses opened. In Windham, the Soper Place opened in 1866; in Beers it was called the "third oldest summer boarding house in the valley." Palenville, which attracted artists and others starting in the 1840s, lost its remaining industries in the mid-1870s and thereafter blossomed as a boarding hamlet.[245]

Hunter, which acquired rail service in 1882, prepared for it by building many new boardinghouses in 1881 and 1882. By 1884 "the principal business of its citizens in summer [was] caring for guests; either boarding, staging, acting as employees of numerous houses, or furnishing vegetables, meats, etc." Though they pursued lumbering in winter and maple sugaring in spring, Hunter residents even devoted off-season to the tourist business as they cleaned, renovated, and improved the boardinghouses, employing "many native carpenters."[246]

A sign of its importance is the great growth in Hunter from 1880 to 1900. While the town started growing after the Civil War when the forest products industry became viable, it boomed during the first two decades of railroad service, gaining 48 percent.

It had become impossible to overlook the vast potential of summer boarding to the Greene County economy. "In sections," Beers reported, "almost every farm house has become a boarding house on a small scale," and the 1890 census showed its 900 boardinghouses increased the winter population of 31,000 to about 70,000 in summer.[247] City folks chose their boarding places by recommendation from friends and by reading guidebooks. Walton Van Loan's *Catskill Mountain Guide*, first published in the late 1870s, was the most widely distributed. It was reissued annually at least through 1915. The longest-lived series was *Summer Homes*, issued by the New York, Ontario and Western Railway from 1878 through the early 1930s.[248]

In 1894 deLisser reported a comparable figure of over 800 boardinghouses and said that "Hundreds of thousands of dollars are left in Greene County every year by the summer visitors." After the turn of the century a railroad guide covering the southeastern Mountaintop enumerated 10 at Lanesville, four at Edgewood, 63 at Hunter, 59 at Tannersville and 33 at Haines Falls, in addition to its two grand hotels.[249]

Yet parts of the county benefitted little from the summer boarders. In New Baltimore "the only hotels" in 1884 were two in the hamlet. Although Freehold "has of late become quite a resort for city people," and there was a

High Peak Tower near Haines Falls
Photograph by C.O. Bickelmann,
c.1896
Collection of Mountain Top Historical Society.

Boarders with walking sticks
Photograph by C.O. Bickelmann,
c.1890
Collection of Mountain Top Historical Society

Hiking was one of the most popular amusements among Mountaintop boarders in the late 19th century.

S. White in a maid's uniform Postcard, East Durham, c.1905 Collection of the Greene County Historical Society

The boarding business provided employment for many Greene County residents during its heyday. Here a young woman is seen, in a postcard made purposely to send to her friends, proudly posing in her maid's uniform.

large boardinghouse at Gayhead, deLisser reported that Greenville was "one of the few villages in the county that does not encourage the taking of summer boarders. I do not know as the citizens object to them, but they do not seek them, leaving the entertainment of such as do come to the one hotel in the centre and a few boarding-houses near by."[250] Halcott apparently had no boarding business despite its proximity to the railroad, until 1897, when Mrs. Fannie Cohen bought a farm in Elk Creek and built three houses there, followed by "The Snowdon" at the end of West Settlement in 1904-05.[251]

Summer boarders in the Catskills were remarkably interested in the scenery and in enjoying the out-of-doors, rather than in social activities, as at many other Victorian resorts. Hiking, driving, fishing, hunting and sightseeing were the chief objectives of the tourists throughout the century.

Nature provided most, though not all, of the sights. The Kaaterskill Falls, a magnet even in the eighteenth century, remained a particular favorite of visitors, but the clearing of the Mountaintop affected its flow. Later in the nineteenth century, a dam was built to control the water level; as Longstreth remarked:

> *They meet the situation triumphantly . . . They save up the waterfalls by doing without them at night and at other times when they are not of much use, and are thus able to provide a life-size cataract at certain hours when somebody happens along who can afford one.*

This peculiar arrangement struck people differently. DeLisser said he felt "little interest in seeing the caged waterfall perform," but Bayard Taylor called it "an admirable arrangement."[252]

Domestication of mountaintops was not unknown either. Mount Pisgah, on the border of Durham and Windham, was cleared in 1853. Walter Doolittle

Winter Clove House, Round Top Photograph, c.1875-80 Collection of the Greene County Historical Society

Winter Clove, still an important resort, is said to have begun as a boardinghouse in 1838.

Jewett Bowling Alley/Store
Postcard
Collection of Larry Tompkins

General stores served boarders as well
as residents and many offered
additional attractions.

purchased land there in 1876 and built a carriage road up the mountain in 1880-81; it was used by about 3,500 people in 1883. An observatory and a hotel provided additional amenities. As one Durhamite told Oriana Atkinson years later, "Oh, yes, my dear, if you hadn't been to Pisgah top, you hadn't done ANYthing."[253]

Fishing, too, could be man-made. In 1880 A.W. Marks had 190,000 speckled trout at his Palenville hatchery, ready to be released; and 20 years later George A. Dykeman released 10,000 trout there.[254]

And surprisingly reminiscent of modern Greene County and its famous Catskill Game Farm was the "group of little houses to the rear" of the Platterkill Falls Mountain House, which contained a menagerie, including a black bear, foxes and raccoons.[255]

Souvenir shop and post office,
East Durham
Photograph by Hastings, c.1900
Collection of Durham Center Museum

CHAPTER 23
RAILROADS

*D*uring the years after the failure of the Catskill and Canajoharie Rail Road, most parts of New York State were linked by rail. Greene County was a latecomer; it was the hotel and boardinghouse business that forced the construction of the only line on the Mountaintop.

Even the main line along the Hudson River—on the east shore—was nearly twenty years in coming. Successful railroads were in operation before the Canajoharie and Catskill was commenced, yet the Hudson River Rail Road was not built until 1847-51. A station was established at Oak Hill in the summer of 1851, later called Catskill Station, and connection to the village was made by ferry.[256] Later that year the line was completed from New York to Albany.

Due to improvements in steamboats and the general cost-effectiveness of river transport for freight, there was little incentive to build a second line on the west shore. Instead, two years after the east shore line was completed, a proposal was made to improve the river above Catskill where "that confounded 'overslaugh'," a sandbar, prevented navigation at low tide. A report urged "a ship canal and basin from Albany to New Baltimore," which would "afford an uninterrupted navigation to the city of Albany for such classes of vessels as are required to navigate the ocean, and thus permit the transfer of freight received by the canal to be made at Albany instead of New York."[257] Apparently, nothing was done.

But the west-shore towns, like those on the east shore, desired railroad service, for each winter the river froze over for many weeks. At Albany the river usually froze over in December and opened up sometime in March. Harriet Crandell of New Baltimore wrote with relief on March 25, 1864: "River open so we do not feel so far from everything. I wonder if I shall ever see that West Shore [Rail] Road."[258]

The incentive to build this railroad, when it came, was not freight expense or isolation, but the frustration of a transportation baron thwarted in his expansion. Daniel Drew was heavily invested in the New York Steamboat Company (the "People's Line") and sought a franchise for railroad tracks along Albany's Quay Street to the Steamboat Landing so his boats could easily connect with rails to the west. Thwarted in his plan, he joined with his rival, Vanderbilt, to organize the Saratoga and Hudson River Railroad. Thirteen investors filed incorporation papers April 13, 1864.

The new line was intended to connect with steamboats at a terminal just north of Athens and run to Schenectady, where it would meet rail lines to the west. As its name suggests, it was originally planned to continue to Saratoga Springs. Its 38 miles were built by Irish laborers; the freight yards at Athens had room for storage of hay, grain and other farm products, and oil from western New York.

When Vanderbilt acquired the Lake Shore line with its connection to Chicago, the Athens line became insignificant and was soon dubbed the "White Elephant." Service was discontinued late in 1867, resuming briefly a year later. Then, in the spring of 1870, Vanderbilt's New York Central decided to divert its heavy freight with the exception of livestock to the Athens road. Fred Coons remembered the days of busy freight shipment:

> When I was a boy in Athens, I often walked to the White Elephant Terminal to see the trains and steamboats. There were many tracks with engines switching cars to and from the docks. There was one dock for oil from Central New York wells, another for grain and other produce, and one for livestock. During the summer they were busy into the night; and with hundreds of lights ashore and on the boats, it looked like a little city.[259]

Tonnage was heavy until an 1876 fire, on a steamboat tied at the dock, spread to the big brick terminal and the freight sheds; service continued afterward on a reduced scale.

The relative usefulness of the "White Elephant" was ended by the

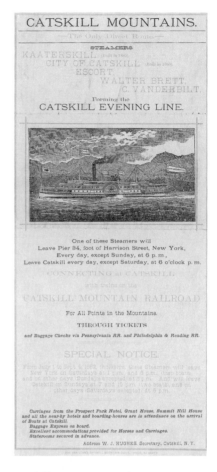

Catskill Evening Line advertisement
Handbill, 1882
Collection of the Greene County
Historical Society

Hudson River Day Line Office, Catskill Point
Photograph, 1914
Collection of Robert Carl

Boarders disembarking the steamer
New York at Catskill
Photograph, c.1900
Collection of the Greene County
Historical Society

construction of the long-awaited West Shore line. The New York, West Shore and Buffalo, which was building a double-track line of heavy steel rails ballasted with stone, leased the White Elephant in November 1881. On July 9, 1883 the West Shore began operations, providing both freight and passenger service to the river towns. The White Elephant track from Athens to West Coxsackie was soon regarded as superfluous, and in the fall of 1888 the tracks were taken up.[260]

The construction of the West Shore line seems to have been the first introduction of Italians to Greene County. Not mentioned in the 1875 census, they came as laborers on the railroad and either stayed or returned later. The Brick Row near the old White Elephant Terminal above Athens became home for many Italian families; in a 1917 photograph of the Upper Village School, 32 percent of the students are identified with Italian-American surnames. Roman Catholic churches, established to serve the Irish immigrants in the river towns beginning in 1847, expanded to embrace the new residents. A new mission was begun at Smith's Landing [Cementon] in 1897.[261]

Due to the lack of inland railroads, stagecoach travel remained the norm on the Mountaintop and in the Catskill Valley through the 1870s. Charles L. Beach and his nephew Charles A. Beach formed a company in 1869 to take over the Beach stage company from Charles L.'s brother Addison. The firm was well-equipped, but the business made money only in the first three years, after which it was marginally profitable at best. The company's loss for the decade, as of February 1880, was $176 on receipts of $108,000. Yet Van Loan's *Catskill Mountain Guide* for 1880 encouraged the traveler:

> *Ho! For the Mountains! The stage-coaches of the past have been*
> *superseded by light platform wagons and the time from the Landing*
> *to the Hotel is now about one hour less than in former years; the*

stage fare reduced to $2.00 including hand luggage—trunks extra according to size.[262]

And about the same time *Lippincott's Magazine* saw the old method of transportation as an asset:

> *Let not the Catskills be made more accessible; they are accessible enough. We want no more railroads, no improved means of transportation to transform pleasure-paths and byways into highways. The old lumbering stagecoach was the vehicle best suited to mountain roads.*[263]

Despite the brave advertising, the Beach family knew they were in danger of being left behind. By August of 1879 Beach and some Catskill investors began planning the construction of a railroad.

Stage service for the Mountaintop already connected with the Rondout and Oswego Railroad (later the Ulster and Delaware), which had reached Phoenicia in 1869 and soon afterward provided service to Prattsville and Windham from a station at Moresville [Grand Gorge]. When the Kaaterskill Hotel was proposed by a rival of Charles Beach, S.D. Coykendall of the Ulster and Delaware planned a narrow-gauge line from Phoenicia to the new house. The 14-mile Stony Clove and Catskill Mountain Railroad was organized in January 1881, and the Kaaterskill Railroad from Kaaterskill Junction to South Lake was completed in 1883. It transported freight as well as passengers; freight cars were lifted onto narrow-gauge trucks without unloading.[264] The tiny railroad line passed through a clove of extraordinary ruggedness; years later Longstreth read a guidebook description of the "crags" in Stony Clove and wrote:

Construction workers on the "Otis"
Photograph, 1892
Collection of the Greene County
Historical Society

Otis Elevating Railway
Photograph by J. Loeffler,
Tompkinsville, S.I., 1892
Collection of the Greene County
Historical Society

Well, there you get one notion: crags and crags and crags, until the neck is cricked and the head dizzy and with the vertiguous display. One might almost suppose that the traveling public would hesitate to intrust itself to a passage imperilled by such overwhelming crags.[265]

Meanwhile Charles Beach, who owned the Mountain House and held controlling interests in steamboats and stagecoaches, took steps to meet the challenge of his competitor. His Catskill Mountain Railroad, also a narrow gauge, followed the bed of the old Canajoharie as far as South Cairo, then struck southward to Palenville. It operated only in the summer. Narrow-gauge cut costs by nearly half: it followed contours more closely and its equipment was smaller and more economical to operate.[266]

A railroad was proposed from South Cairo to East Durham, but never built. A Durham man reported in 1884 that the town had potential as a fruit-growing region but "the great hindrance to the enlarged development of this industry is the entire lack of railroad communication." Instead, a short spur, the Cairo Rail Road, was built in 1885.[267]

The competition on the Mountaintop continued. The Catskill Mountain Railroad, begun during a recession, suffered and was forced into court by its investors in 1885. In November of that year the directors organized to build the Otis Elevating Railway from Palenville to Pine Orchard; and by mid-January "crews of southern Negroes were soon blasting and cutting their way upwards on the steep slopes."[268] The engineering feat was completed in 1892.

The railway made the ascent from the valley to mountaintop using two railroad cars attached to opposite ends of a long cable; adding to the dramatic effect was the high wooden trestle constructed to carry its tracks at a more gradual ascent than the mountainside.

Beach then built the Catskill and Tannersville Railroad to tap the boardinghouse traffic running up the Stony Clove; he arranged cooperation with the Ulster and Delaware and built the line from Otis Summit as far as the Kaaterskill, where it connected with the U&D.

In 1898 the Ulster and Delaware shifted to standard gauge, discontinued its cooperative service, and cut its fares. Beach's short line was marooned, so he extended it in 1899 as far as Tannersville.[269] But the railroad improvements were all in vain. The locomotive had little more than a decade of dominance ahead. ❦

Track workers at Cairo Junction
Photograph, c.1900
Collection of Robert Carl

Catskill Mountain Railway steam engine on Water Street at "second" village station, Catskill
Postcard, c.1900
Collection of the Greene County Historical Society

CHAPTER 24
GRAND HOTELS

*T*he definitions of boardinghouse and hotel were somewhat vague. Some boardinghouses were quite small, taking ten or twelve; others were very large indeed, with accommodations for 90 or even 125. It's hard to say when an overgrown boardinghouse was termed a hotel, though it likely had to do with proprietorship. If the owner lived in, it remained a "house."

Relatively few lodgings in Greene County in the late 1870s and early 1880s could sleep more than 100. The Catskill Mountain House, still first and foremost, had two such neighbors near Haines Falls: the Laurel House and Hilton Hotel, holding 125 and 200. In the Town of Catskill, there were several large hotels at Palenville—Maple Grove House, Drummond's Falls House and the Winchelsea—and three large ones in or near the village—Grant House, Prospect House and Summit Hill House—which offered river access and distant views of the mountains. In Cairo, Durham, Windham and Lexington were other, smaller hotels, as well as the omnipresent boardinghouses.

By 1879 economic prosperity had so expanded the boarding business that new resort hotels appeared a good investment. The Mountain House still held its own, though refusing to change with the times. "How can you complain about your room and board?" Charles Beach would say. "You don't pay a cent for either. I charge only for the mountain air. I throw in your room and board free."[270] It was, of course, a situation that invited a challenge.

George Harding was a determined and resourceful Philadelphian who visited the Mountain House summer after summer. In July 1880 his sick wife and daughter wanted fried chicken. It was not on the menu, and the Mountain House wouldn't budge. He began immediately to plan a rival hotel, higher up the mountain and close to the planned branch of the Ulster and Delaware.

On June 27, 1881 the vast Hotel Kaaterskill opened. It introduced modern plumbing and gaslights and many of the amenities of the highly materialistic, late Victorian era: all of which Beach and his Mountain House, in upholding tradition, had refused. During the flush period other houses, like the Laurel, enlarged. Evidence suggests that the hotels overexpanded the higher-priced room capacity. Business slowed down by about 1883. But it was the decade of

Carpenters building the Sunset Inn, Haines Falls
Photograph, 1902
Collection of Mountain Top Historical Society

Construction of cottages, boarding houses and hotels provided employment for Greene County tradesmen; in this view the only identified worker is Milton Peck, holding a saw with his fingers.

the 1890s that was especially difficult for the big hotels. DeLisser wrote in 1894: "The days of the great hotels may have gone by, but people are coming here just the same, and they will go where they can get the best for their money."[271]

Kaaterskill Hotel
Photograph by A. Doncourt, c.1881
Collection of the Greene County Historical Society

The Catskill Mountain House
Photograph by J. Loeffler,
Tompkinsville, S.I., 1892
Collection of Black Dome Press

Hotel advertisement from
Van Loan's Catskill Mountain Guide
(New York: Aldine Publishing
Company, 1881)
Collection of Greene County Historical
Society

Even the Mountain House in its stodginess was challenged by the changing tastes. In 1899 Beach turned the house over to his sons, and in the summer of 1902 they installed electric lights and flush toilets, provided tennis and golf, created lawns and flower beds, and altered the dining room to include small tables and printed menus.[272] 🍂

CHAPTER 25
JEWISH BOARDERS

*T*he arrival of an entirely new contingent of resorters was a dramatic change late in the century.

During the post-Civil War era, German-speaking vacationers constituted an increasing proportion of the Catskills trade, especially along the Ulster and Delaware. They were Catholic, Protestant, and Jewish and, at first, no attempts were made to limit the patronage of any group. Reflecting the human tendency to associate with people who share history and interests, the three groups tended to patronize separate boardinghouses. But at the Mountain House, for example, Jews had always been among the visitors.

There were, of course, few Jewish residents at the time outside the cities. David Friedman, a German Jew, worked in Edwards' tannery in the 1840s, and Jewish peddlers, forerunners of the successful dry-goods merchants, were in evidence throughout New York State. DeLisser noted in 1894, "All through the county we shall find these thrifty, hard-working sons of Israel on every by-path, along every highway, more often with great packs on their backs, but sometimes . . . with an antiquated team of some description."[273]

An incident of prejudice at Saratoga Springs set in motion the exclusion of Jews from some Catskill resorts and ultimately opened Hunter to their patronage.

In the summer of 1877 Judge Henry Hilton, manager of the Grand Union Hotel and, at best, an unpleasant person, refused lodging to the wealthy Jewish banker Joseph Seligman. A storm of protest broke. Charles Beach revealed his essential conservatism by sending out a dispatch: "There is none of the shoddy aristocracy here. New England furnishes more than her usual proportion of appreciated guests . . .," although he admitted he served a few Germans, "lovers of fine scenery."[274]

Responding to the debate, the Catskill *Examiner* wrote: "In the limits of our village we have a number of these descendants of Solomon and if we have observed rightly a better class of visitors could not be desired."[275] But, for Beach and others, the Jewish visitors comprised a poorer class of travellers; the railroad had made mountain vacations possible for them.

The debate heated up again a decade later. In 1888 it was said that half of the summer travellers on the Ulster and Delaware were Jewish. When one small village in Ulster County, Pine Hill, tried to restrict its hotels and boardinghouses, the *Times* took notice of a rumor of an "anti-Hebrew crusade." While it was indeed only a rumor, there was hostility behind it.[276] In August 1889 ruffians raided Simon Epstein's Jewish boardinghouse at Saxton, Ulster County. They were arrested and sentenced and there was no further violence. But boardinghouse keepers, particularly with the apparent overbuilding and general downturn in business, found they were losing money by excluding Jews. What a sense of fairness could not accomplish, economics eventually did.

Epstein moved to Hunter in 1893 and opened the Grandview House. It was the beginning of a wave; many older hotels there were purchased and entered the new market, which included a niche for the "high-class" Jewish trade of clothiers, furriers and textile men. Harry Fischel, for example, a New York real-estate magnate and distinguished philanthropist, built a summer home at Hunter in 1904.[277]

By early in the new century the neighboring villages of Hunter and Tannersville attracted large numbers of Jewish vacationers from varying backgrounds. The establishment of synagogues between 1899 and 1914 reflects first the summer vacationers and later the presence of year-round businessmen.

Temple Anshi Hashoran, Tannersville
Photograph by John H. Frank, c.1900
Collection of the Greene County
Historical Society

Tannersville's Congregation Anshi Hashoran was incorporated by German-American Jewish vacationers in 1899; a synagogue was built five years later. In the same village, Russian and Polish immigrants including the mercantile family of Honigsbaum organized Congregation Talmud Torah in 1911. The two synagogues merged soon after 1920.[278]

In Hunter, residents like Harry Fischel had found it difficult to secure a place for services, so they built a 250-seat synagogue in the summer of 1905. Another synagogue was begun in 1909 by the more traditional Eastern

European families including the Slutzkys; it was completed in 1914. These two congregations merged in 1939.

The impact of Jewish resorters on the Town of Hunter was considerable. In 1907 Tannersville hosted the tenth annual convention of the American Zionists.[279] By the early 1920s over one hundred Tannersville area boardinghouses served Kosher food, keeping seven Kosher butchers busy.[280]

Some were not happy with the contrasting community in their midst. A guide-book editor made his prejudices clear in 1914 when he noted that Tannersville was ". . . a great resort, in particular, of our Israelitish brethren, who love to gather where they can be together." He lobbed a final insult at Tannersville:

> *If one goes to the mountains simply to join a rollicking, highly varied crowd, which is bent on having a "good time" without much expense or attention to conventionalities, the Tannersville district will suit them . . .* [281]

But before the Depression hit, Hunter lost ground. Sullivan County was far closer by automobile; there are suggestions that bank financing during the slump was easier for Jewish hoteliers in Sullivan than in Greene. Much of the resort trade shifted to the Sullivan County "Catskills."[282] 🍂

CHAPTER 26
COTTAGERS

A very different community of summer residents had its start at almost the same time in the same town. Tannersville came to be the center of the private parks, where wealthy and cultured people built substantial cottages in which to spend much of the summer in private surroundings.

The cottage was made possible by four related forces following the Civil War: urbanization, the growth of a vacation "ideology," the growth of a middle class with disposable wealth, and the expansion of railroads. The railroad reached Tannersville in 1882 and made it possible to travel from New York City in somewhat less time and, more importantly, without transfers from river or rail to the slow-moving, uncomfortable stagecoach. The park cottagers of the Catskills were distinctly upper-middle-class, and sought privacy from crowds and social climbers, relief from the formality of the hotels, fellowship with "their own kind," and an atmosphere that would nurture their children.[283]

Onteora Park was the first of six communities within a few miles of Tannersville, all of which came into existence between 1883 and 1889. Its founder, Candace Wheeler (1827-1923), was an important figure in the decorative arts movement. In 1877 she formed the Society of Decorative Arts of New York, teaching the application of the craftsmanship of William Morris to needlework. From 1879 to 1883 she was part of the so-called Associated Artists, a group of New York interior decorators, and in the latter year founded her own textile firm.

In 1883 she joined her brother and husband to look for summer home property. Coming upon an old field on a farm north of Tannersville, they made their decision. Candace called it "Lotus Land." Their cottage was the first of many:

> *It is built of solid logs, with the bark peeled off, which shine like silver in the sun. Inside . . . the walls are of logs too, covered with skins and rugs and wasps' nests and wildflowers and everything that is mountainous, beautiful and unconventional.*[283]

Very soon the Wheelers decided to expand upon their discovery—to invite friends to join them:

> It entered into our minds to buy the mountain and the farm sloping eastward to which it belonged, and bring some of our friends to build homes and share permanently with us the joys of solitude; not realizing that solitude and society cannot live together. We thought we could take the latter in small doses, forgetting that it was a cumulative medicine.[285]

These friends were not so much wealthy as they were part of the cultural elite of the day. Many were writers and artists, including quite a number of independent women. Mark Twain and his family visited the Wheelers the first summer, returned to the "Bear and Fox Inn" on the grounds the second year, and rented a cottage in 1890 or 1891. John Burroughs was also a frequent guest of the Wheelers, and Dvorak visited between 1892 and 1895. Mary Mapes Dodge, author of *Hans Brinker*, built her own cottage.

In the summer of 1887 the Wheelers decided to buy more land; with the principals of the Ulster and Delaware, Candace's husband and brother organized the Catskill Mountain Camp and Cottage Company. Over the following six years, 20 rustic cottages were built. Beginning in the mid-1890s the cottages became more complex, to include examples of Shingle, Queen Anne and Tudor architecture.

From the beginning this park was a boon to natives, particularly those of East Jewett, just to the north. It provided employment for plumbers, carpenters, gardeners, truck farmers, cooks, laundresses, housekeepers and winter caretakers.[286] It also must have caused quite a bit of amusement. On an occasion celebrating the opening of a new road around Parker Mountain, the cottagers organized a procession:

> It was led by yokes of oxen whose necks were wreathed with ropes of daisies, carrying bunches of wild roses at their horns. Guided by a man in a long smock with girdle and scarf of green, they drew a great wainful of children dressed as wood-land gods, tossing daisies and field flowers as they went along . . . they were followed by a Roman Centurion on horseback, and a Roman Emperor and Empress . . . after this equipage walked a company of girls in straight white gown carrying long wands of meadow lilies . . . when the west side of the mountain was reached a green arch spanned the road and a chorus of voices among the trees hailed the procession.[287]

In 1903 the Onteora Land Company bought out the old owners and renamed it the Onteora Club. It added modern improvements including water, sewer, telephone and a post office, and became more like a group of country estates than a retreat for eccentrics.

Twilight Park came into existence almost simultaneously, in the summer of 1887. Its founder was Charles F. Wingate, who visited Haines Falls for a convention. A member of the Twilight Club in New York, a forum for free expression on current subjects, he had already conceived a park project and enlisted some of his fellow members. On August 26 of that year he signed a contract for 160 acres of sheep pasture overlooking the clove. His vision was not unlike Wheeler's:

> . . . *we do not want too many rich people here to put on style and make us dress. We would frown down anything like fashionable display . . . We would rather have an artist, teacher or writer, a doctor or a clergyman, with a little money to invest safely, than any millionaire, unless he is a clubbable fellow. Nor is the Bohemian element desired.*[288]

By the end of 1887 five foundations were in place, and those cottages were built quickly by Alexander Van Wagner and a crew of men. By the close of 1888, 75 people were in residence. The original concept was to provide meals in a central dining room and, as a result, the first cottages had no kitchens: on June 15, 1889 a resident wrote, "We build without kitchens so far; the eating is done at the Club-house; $7 a week. We leave housekeeping cares behind us. It is a family-vacation." But by August cottages were being built with kitchens and dining rooms.[289]

The early cottagers at Twilight included progressive and reform movement people, and many authors and editors, women among them, not unlike Onteora.

Aerial view of Twilight Park
Photograph by Rusk's Foto Factory,
Haines Falls, c.1890
Collection of the Greene County
Historical Society

The association was incorporated May 31, 1888 and owned the land outright, dividing it into 100-foot-square lots on 99-year leases. The Wingate family held the controlling interest. Later, in 1905, a membership corporation—Twilight Cottagers—organized, and assumed management of the park. The two boards merged in 1933.

Recreational facilities were an early asset of Twilight. The first tennis court was built in 1889, as well as an independent but adjacent golf course. Bowling alleys followed in 1890. A total of three clubhouses for meals, dances, theatricals, cards and lectures were built; one burned in 1926, a second was razed in 1944, and the last in 1977.[290] The swimming pool was a latecomer, in 1921.

The club's season was always May to October; in the mid-twentieth century a resolution was proposed that Twilight develop itself as a ski resort but it lost unanimously. As the park's historian concludes, "But slowly, more winter use of the Park developed, cottagers 'winterized' their houses, and a few selected to retire in permanent homes in the Park or even to commute between Twilight and their city jobs."[291]

Two other, smaller parks came into existence uphill from Twilight almost immediately after the more famous park incorporated. Sunset Park was not a "club" in that its lots were sold outright to the cottagers, mostly between 1888 and 1906, with a few as late as 1924.[292] The Sunset Park Inn was built in 1902, and stood until its 1990 demolition, but Sunset Park as an organization lapsed during the Depression. The Santa Cruz Falls Association organized in 1889 on 600 acres adjacent to Twilight; an inn opened in 1893. Santa Cruz became a stock company in 1910, and merged with Twilight in 1935.[293] Even smaller was Philadelphia Hill, south of Tannersville; its first cottage was built by Dr. August F. Muller in 1884, and was soon followed by St. John's Church, reflecting founder Mrs. Alexander Helmsley's interest in the Cowley Fathers, an Episcopal brotherhood. This quiet community comprises about five cottages and the church, all in use seasonally.[294]

The last of the six parks, and the only one with a distinct ethnic character, was Elka Park. In July 1887 members of New York's elite German social organization, the Liederkranz Club, visited the Hotel Kaaterskill. In the spring of 1889 six members went searching for land and acquired the park tract. From 1890 to 1896, 21 cottages were built. Two of these have been destroyed and one additional cottage has been built since 1896.

The Elka cottagers were wealthy German-born residents of New York and Hoboken, New Jersey; a significant number were industrial chemists, mechanical and civil engineers. They were seeking a less consciously rustic experience than their neighbors. All cottages had indoor plumbing, gaslighting and water tanks, and the park, which held lots for more than eighty cottages, was provided with a high-quality overall design, including good roads, stone walls and stone sluiceways. Most Elka cottagers had their own tennis courts. Since a dining facility was not essential, Elka Park was slow to build a clubhouse; a hotel known as "Schoharie Manor" was adjacent to the

Cottage at Elka Park
Postcard, 1905
Collection of Justine Legg Hommel

park from the early years. The facility now in use for meals and guest lodging is Elka Park's second clubhouse, erected after a 1949 fire.

All the parks came into existence at a particular time in history and no others followed after 1889. A number of factors in the twentieth century resulted in their decline. The institution of the personal income tax in 1913 and the rising popularity of the automobile meant that "it was no longer felt necessary, or even desirable, to own a second home at which to spend vacations."[295] In the case of Elka Park, the impact of the financial crises in 1893 and 1907, the desire of residents to maintain the park's German character, and the decline of German language and customs as a result of World War I were followed by the Depression, during which seven of 20 cottages were either given back or purchased by new owners at tax sales.[296]

Yet the three largest parks remain a part of the Catskills scene after over a century. As Twilight's historian observes, "Twilight hasn't changed a great deal. We still gather around a wood-burning fireplace. We still party on the 'piazza' and elsewhere. We still picnic. . . . We still come back, generation after generation."[297]

CHAPTER 27
SCHOOLS

*T*he growth and progress of Greene County in the nineteenth century was dependent upon its public school system, which provided at least a basic education to all of its children. The colonial foundation for public schools was a cooperative one; neighbors or the members of a church agreed together to support a school. There was no government provision for education.

Evidence suggests that in the settlements surrounding the churches at Coxsackie, Athens and Old Catskill, schoolmasters taught the children of the vicinity before the Revolution. The earliest evidence is of a school at Athens before the 1751 death of Domine Berkenmeyer. Teunis Van Vechten traded with schoolmasters Martin McGee of Great Embought and John Macrober [Macomber?] of Catskill.[298]

After the Revolution, with the influx of settlers from Connecticut, where schools were more common, such neighborhood endeavors were no doubt begun in many parts of the county; we know that Polly Chittenden was teaching a school in Durham in 1787 and 1788.[299]

When a law was finally passed by the State to encourage communities to create schools, it merely permitted residents to "associate together" to hire schoolmasters. The act of 1795 provided 20,000 pounds a year for five years to help pay salaries, and required towns to elect commissioners to supervise such schools. The act expired in 1800 and, although funds were again voted in 1805, the public school system in New York State really did not come into being until 1812.[300]

Scattered evidence suggests Greene's citizens acted on the 1795 offer. In Coxsackie and Freehold towns, a list of teachers and trustees of that year demonstrates that there were at least nine public schools in operation: Coxsackie village, Athens, New Baltimore, Jacksonville [Earlton], east of Jacksonville, Greenville, Cairo, and two other unidentified locations.[301]

Catskill Landing provided for education in another manner. On August 23, 1793 subscriptions were taken for the construction of an academy, which was completed about 1794-95. Such a school was essentially private, intended for any children in the community whose parents could pay tuition, and it provided a more thorough education than most "common schools," usually including classical languages. Its students in 1797-98 numbered 21 boys and 13 girls.

Henry Hill, who came to Catskill with his shipbuilder father at the age of one in 1796, remembered his early schooling:

In 1799 Mrs. Ball had a school for small children in the Brockway House. I was in my fifth year. Some of my playmates went, and as I wished to be with them I was permitted to go. All that I remember of that school is that Mrs. Ball pointed with her scissors to the letters when teaching the alphabet . . . For five or six years I attended school in the large room on the first floor of the old court house . . . .[302]

By 1803 there were two other schools in the village and 12 others in the town, nearly all of which were one-room schools.[303]

After the Revolution schools were apparently taught in English, despite the survival of Dutch speech in the families. About 1800 Fred Overbagh went to a schoolhouse on the Saugerties road south of Catskill Landing; its teacher, Master Macomber, would not allow Dutch spoken during school hours.[304] Even today there are a few people who remember the Dutch language spoken in Greene County as late as the 1920s. Philip DuBois, who grew up in Catskill, remembers the fragments of the language in his family:

My mother was three-quarters of Dutch descent, and proud of it! In her mother's childhood in the 1840s, the children were forbidden to speak Dutch while the parents spoke Dutch when they did not want the children to understand. But the children did understand and even remembered a bit of the language into adulthood. At good night time at The Ridge we were often wished "Schlaven-sie voll!" and Aunt Hattie could recite the nursery rhyme which begins "Trippe! troppe! trontje!"[305]

On the Mountaintop, part of Ulster County until 1800, evidence of early schools is more scarce. The present Town of Hunter established three schools before the 1812 schools act: one in the Olmstead district, one at Haines Falls, and one at Hunter called the "Nigger House." Jennie Haines Dunn found the earliest reference to a school in an 1809 town record. At Windham the first schoolhouse was built of logs. There were probably other schoolhouses on the Mountaintop prior to 1812 but, having little government support, the documentary evidence of them is scanty.[306]

Finally in 1812, "an act for the establishment of common schools" provided all the ammunition necessary for public schools throughout the state. Each town was to elect three commissioners to create the districts; the inhabitants chose the site for the district school, voted taxes for its support, and elected three trustees to manage it. To receive state aid, the school was to be taught by an approved teacher for three months or more. Two years later another act made it mandatory.[307]

Thereafter schools were built wherever settlement was thick enough. Halcott's first log schoolhouse was built in 1816; three districts, each with new frame schoolhouses, were created between 1834 and 1836.[308] The pattern of school building was repeated throughout the county. In 1844 Greene County had 130 schools; six years later the number had increased to 176.

The quality of such schools was not especially high. Teachers were often little more than children, as an 1844 report makes clear: "The time of many teachers who had been permitted to enter the school-room in that capacity, might be profitably employed in improving their education in a common school for some time to come." And their methods were no better: "The minds of their pupils are not trained to habits of thought and reflection. Mere isolated facts are substituted for ideas."[309]

Oversight of the schools above the town level was limited. An act of 1843 created the office of County Superintendent, but it was abolished four years later. An 1844 convention of town superintendents appointed a committee to develop Teachers' Institutes, which provided a limited, one-day exercise in teacher training from 1845 on. After 1858 School Commissioners oversaw the schools throughout each assembly district.[310]

To supplement the common schools, particularly for high school education, Greene County residents founded and supported a number of academies in addition to the one at Catskill. Greenville Academy was incorporated in 1816. Zadock Pratt endowed Prattsville Academy with $5,000 in 1842. These two later became the foundations of the public high schools in those communities.[311]

Jewett Heights Academy
Photograph, 1903
Collection of Larry Tompkins

Students and teacher at an unusually fine rural school building. Front row (left to right): Mildred Bailey, Milton Goslee, three unknown students, Leonard Baldwin. Middle row: Allen Peck, Walter Bailey, Wynford Bailey, Roger Sweet, Neal Longyear, unknown. Back row: Olive Persons Bailey (teacher), Ray Persons, unknown.

In more isolated locations, such schools had short lives. West Durham Seminary was certainly not located in a spot to draw large numbers of local scholars,[312] nor was Ashland Collegiate Institute. Located in a five-story, 200-by-100-foot edifice on West Settlement Road, this college-level institution flourished from 1854 to 1860 and included John Burroughs, the naturalist, among its alumni. Its library amounted to a substantial 1,500 books, and music, painting, trigonometry, surveying and astronomy were among the course offerings. Its 1858 catalogue announced that "a farming class has been organized," an unusually progressive move. But the Institute burned in 1861 and never reopened.[313]

In 1853, the Union Free School Act permitted districts to combine their resources; this made possible public schools with academic departments, or high schools. Catskill formed a union district in 1856 and added academy or high school instruction in 1861. Its large brick school was built in 1869 and consisted of ten departments: six on the primary level, grammar, intermediate and academic, as well as a "colored" department.[314]

Reports for 1882 provide us with a comprehensive survey of public schooling in Greene. Each town had its district schools, ranging in number from four in Halcott to 20 in Catskill, most of them one-teacher operations. However, some were quite large. District One of Catskill employed thirteen, and even in rural Ashland the "village school" drew 89 pupils.

Of 185 teachers in the county in 1884, only 19 had a Normal School education or State Superintendent license. Their average weekly wage was $6.57, and in 46 of the 151 districts, the teachers still "boarded around," receiving room and board in rotation from the parents of their pupils.

Most schoolhouses were frame. There were 143 of wood, with only nine brick schoolhouses (including several multi-story village buildings) and five of stone. The days of the log schoolhouse were long gone in 1882.[315]

By an 1838 state law, the small school district libraries were open to public use. Other early libraries were independent; there were a few surprisingly early attempts to make books available. The Greenville Library Association was formed before 1808, and Spafford reports a Durham public library with 400 volumes in 1813. The fate of the Durham library is unknown, but the Greenville library was absorbed by the academy late in the century; the present institution dates from 1928. In Coxsackie, printer Thomas B. Carroll made room for a subscription library in his place of business during the 1830s, while the present Heermance Library dates from 1909. Strangely, in Catskill, there was "a well-regulated library in the Landing, cointaining six hundred and seventy-two volumes of well-chosen books" in 1803, but the present institution was formed in 1893.[316] Haines Falls established its library in 1900, a few years after Hunter. ❧

CHAPTER 28
IMPROVEMENT

*T*he prevailing mood of the nineteenth century was optimism. Small wonder, for growth—in numbers, education, productivity, and well-being—was evident on every side. And in keeping with their time, Victorian Americans set themselves to work to solve the problems of their society. If the amount of effort expended is any indication, efforts to advance religious faith and to eliminate the causes of intoxication seem to have been their chief concerns. Care of the poor and, after mid-century, public health measures also attracted some attention. Equality for women was seldom broached, and in Greene County woman suffrage was essentially a twentieth-century movement. Slavery was abolished in Greene County by an 1817 state law, which took effect on Independence Day 1827. After that, equality for African-Americans was scarcely a guarantee but, with their numbers small and work opportunities for Blacks plentiful, the issue seldom appears in records.

Church membership in nineteenth-century America was far from universal; statistics of 1884 suggest that about 10,000 of Greene County's 32,000 residents were church members. About 25 percent were Methodist Episcopal, a denomination with 32 churches thoroughly scattered across the countryside. The five Roman Catholic churches—three rather large and two small—were next, with 20 percent of the church members. Dutch Reformed was close behind at 19 percent and Presbyterian a distant fourth at 12 percent, though each had ten congregations. Smaller numbers were claimed by the Baptists at 9 percent and Episcopalian at 7 percent. In addition there were Greene County congregations of Christian Connexion, African Methodist Episcopal, Evangelical Lutheran, and a handful of other churches.[317]

Although percentages of church membership were comparable to the late-twentieth century, there was a marked contrast. Society and the media perceived the role of faith and of the church very positively in the mid-nineteenth century. Religious affiliation was associated with the advance of civilization, the improvement of communities and progress in general. Many newspaper editors—whatever their personal beliefs—seemed to endorse religion.

Their columns often carry congratulatory accounts of revivals. The camp meeting movement, which originated in Kentucky in 1799, had little impact on the Greene County scene—residents may have travelled to Round Lake or elsewhere for camp meetings, and in 1883 they did organize the Catskill Mountain Assembly Grounds Association at Hunter, of which no further evidence has been found—but as early as 1821 there was a great church-based revival at Coxsackie, and 400 members were added to the First Reformed Church there.[318]

The greatest figure in revivalism in Greene County was Maggie Newton Van Cott (1830-1914). She first came to Cornwallville on a visit in 1867 and stayed to conduct revival services, preaching the following winter and spring in Durham and Cairo. In 1869 she became the first woman licensed to preach by the Methodist Episcopal church.

Van Cott used an odd method to reach crowds. In 1882 she bought an old church in Cairo and resumed the manufacture of patent medicines, including "Frog-in-the-Throat," a lozenge with a big green frog on the package. Despite her business interests, her "deep-seated purpose was to win Christian converts," selling medicines and preaching at any opportunity. In 1896 she built a house on Liberty Street, Catskill, where she lived until her death. As late as 1903 and 1904 she held revival services at Ashland and Windham.[319]

Another factor in the spread of Christianity in nineteenth-century America was the Bible Society. The Greene County Bible Society organized in 1815 at Cairo to collect funds to buy and circulate Bibles "wherever they were needed." In the following year it helped organize the American Bible Society. Members often raised as much as $1,000 a year, but it was reported in 1884, "Its mission being measurably filled, the society has for several years been on the decline."[320]

The church provided many women with opportunities for self-fulfillment. An example is the "Female Benevolent Association," which met at the Reformed Church at Leeds; it reorganized in 1853.

In the second quarter of the nineteenth century the role of women was increasingly circumscribed by the doctrine of "Separate Spheres." As the male workplace left the home, the participation of women in generating income was

County Almshouse, Cairo Photograph, c.1900
Collection of the Greene County Historical Society

The care of the poor was shifted from the towns to the county early in the 19th century; in 1883 this substantial almshouse was erected. It serves today as offices for the Cooperative Extension and other agencies.

substantially reduced. This shift may, in fact, have precipitated the beginnings of the women's rights movement. The Leeds association noted the conflicting theories in their constitution, and came down firmly on the side of domesticity:

> *Whereas in these days of excitement and innovation there is so much dispute with regard to the appropriate sphere of women, we . . . take this opportunity to state the ground which we assume on this disputed point: While we distinctly repudiate the doctrine advocated by many, that women should sally forth into the field of action side by side with man, . . . neither do we fall into the opposite extreme and hold that she is required to fold her hands in idleness or spend her days in vain pursuits. We believe that woman has a sphere of action appropriate to her sex—modest but important, unobtrusive but influential. To this field she is appointed by her Maker and Judge.*[321]

Women exerted considerable influence in the communities through the church; but guarantees of rights had to wait until the twentieth century.

Jessie Vedder reported a reform attempt by a Catskill woman, Ruth Pierce Croswell, sister of the famous Sally Pierce, founder of Litchfield Seminary. She established the first female prayer meeting and amidst ridicule and reproach formed a Women's Temperance League against "custom of furnishing intoxicating cordials at afternoon tea, breaking up the custom."[322]

Both women and men were players in that largest of reform movements. We have already noted the expansion of distilleries from four in 1810 and 1820 to 10 in 1825. Yet 10 years later there were only three, and in 1845 only two. Since the farmers continued to produce grain, historian Henry Whittemore concluded that it was "probably owing to the decrease in consumption of the article." As examples, Osborn's large distillery at Windham, begun in 1824, ceased operating about 1832, and the smaller one of William Tuttle and Hiram Clearwater was discontinued by 1830 after only four years.[323]

Certainly heavy drinking was a part of the pioneer experience in Greene County. Hunter's historian commented that " . . . the evil of intemperance was then unnoticed by press and even pulpit. Temperance among the best men consisted in not getting drunk, but a little boozy."[324] At Peter Van Orden's tavern at East Windham, "During a day and evening, on a special occasion, three barrels of cider were drunk in this inn."[325]

But in 1829 the Greene County Temperance Society formed, reflecting the tide of concern over alcohol abuse then sweeping the country. In Catskill, the citizens associated drinking with crime and poverty; the Mountain House, with its busy bar and its sophisticated visitors, seemed a similar, if less disruptive, threat. One-third of Catskill's inhabitants signed the pledge to abstain from spirits.[326]

Not everyone stayed with temperance. At Broadway in Durham, Richard Tryon "had several sons, and one of them joined the temperance society on condition he might drink when he washed sheep; and it was said that he had one old sheep that he washed every day."[327]

But the movement continued strong for two generations, its message often conveyed through lectures, illustrated with horrifying examples of the results of alcoholism. A lecturer from the American Temperance Union delivered about fifty lectures in the county on one tour, and new temperance organizations sprouted. In the flush years following the Civil War, the Sons of Temperance were a fast-growing lodge, numbering 21 "divisions" in the county, the largest at Windham having 144 members. But just 14 years later Beers admitted, "There is no county temperance organization in existence here now, and but little attention is paid to the subject." Interest revived periodically, of course, until Prohibition was enacted in 1919.[328]

Progress in sanitation was rather slow through the nineteenth century, though the purity of mountain air and water were a selling point from the earliest years of the resort business. Many visitors came to Greene County in the summer to escape health hazards in the city; in 1832 and 1854 fatal cholera outbreaks even reached Catskill.[329] There was an increasing awareness of the importance of pure drinking water, though really adequate village systems were not in place until early in the twentieth century. Health ordinances were enacted in 1850 in Catskill; an 1884 revision includes twice-weekly rubbish collection from the street in front of each house.[330] Most Greene County residents, of course, drew water from wells, the quality of which varied widely, and most disposed of their refuse on the farm or in public dumping grounds.

Catskill and Coxsackie initiated water systems very early, in 1803 and 1804. The first Catskill system piped water from Cold Spring to most houses

Haying on the poor farm, Cairo
Photograph, c.1900
Collection of the Greene County
Historical Society

Residents of the county farm were fed from the farm's produce; the able-bodied were expected to work.

Drilling Mulbury's well, Oak Hill
Photograph, late 19th century
Collection of Durham Center Museum

in the village through wooden troughs. It was succeeded by the Aqueduct Association, founded in 1818; this aqueduct was in use as late as 1837. Coxsackie's Union Aqueduct Association, incorporated in 1804, placed log water pipes underground from a stream near Climax; these 10" diameter pipes had a 2-1/2" bore but were never adequate, and Coxsackie also drew from the Hudson and a town pump. (A dam at Climax provided a modern system in 1899.) Even at Hunter, hemlock logs carried water from hillside springs.[331] Modern water systems in the larger villages and water supply in the smaller towns began to be a priority in the 1880s. Catskill began pumping from the Hudson in 1883. Athens began study for an improved system in 1885, though its Hollister Lake gravity system was not put into operation until 1927. Greenville's water company incorporated in 1896 with investors from Stamford and Roxbury. In Prattsville, an electric pump was available to draw water from the kill when dry weather affected wells.[332]

The construction of water systems in the villages facilitated real progress in fire protection. A fire company was authorized for Catskill in 1797, but about 1805 both Catskill and Athens organized fire companies; they purchased "engines" which pumped water from ponds or rivers and forced it through hoses onto the fires. Prattsville formed a fire company in the 1830s, and Windham acquired its first engine in 1854. Coxsackie finally acquired organized fire protection in 1860, and New Baltimore in 1896.

The resort communities, with their large frame boardinghouses which were subject to devastating fires, organized fire companies. Between 1886 and 1904, Cairo, Hunter, Tannersville and Hensonville fire companies formed, bringing the total number to ten at the time of World War I. Most were still dependent upon standing water for their hoses.[333]

The care of the poor was also primitive. From colonial times the poor were a town responsibility, and their care was turned over to the lowest

Fire at Horton's Stable, Catskill
Postcard, 1913
Collection of the Greene County
Historical Society

Bomptjes Hook Hose Company #50
Photograph, after 1912
Collection of Robert Carl
The Bomptjes Hook firehouse,
founded 1912, was located at the
present 80 Main Street and served the
Catskill Point area.

bidder. The humiliation of this system deterred many from applying for help, while many of the bidders were themselves desperate and in need of the extra income. The conditions in Greenville were noted in an 1824 report:

> *This town for a few years past, have sold their paupers at public auction, on the day of the town meeting, and those who purchased give in proportion to the supposed ability of the paupers for labor. There are some, however, who are entirely incapacitated for labor, in consequence of disease; there are others again, capable of occasional labor, probably enough to earn their bread.*[334]

The system was unsatisfactory, and led to the county poorhouse act of 1824. In sixteen counties, Greene among them, the poor became an exclusive county responsibility.[335]

In October 1825 the Board of Supervisors appointed a committee to select a site. An eleven-acre tract in Cairo was chosen for the wooden poorhouse. In 1839 it was moved to another site. Construction of the last poorhouse was begun in the summer of 1883. This two-story brick "alms house" held 90 people, with a frame building adjacent for 35 to 40 more; the 198-acre farm included 100 acres in cultivation to supply the tables.[336]

With the growth of skilled nursing and the advent of "home relief" in the twentieth century, the facility was no longer needed. It closed by resolution of the Board of Supervisors on June 1, 1962. ❦

CHAPTER 29
FAIRS

 *E*ducation and reform met in the agricultural fairs, which were originally organized for the improvement of agriculture and the "amelioration of morals."

The "modern" agricultural fair was created by Elkanah Watson in Pittsfield, Massachusetts, when he exhibited pure-bred sheep on the town common in 1807. In 1819, living in Albany, Watson secured the enactment of a Board of Agriculture to encourage county fairs in New York State, and he sent out a circular to stir up interest.

The newly formed Greene County Agricultural Society held its first annual "cattle show and fair" at Cairo on November 2, 1819. Livestock was exhibited in a field, and domestic manufactures, fruits and vegetables were shown in an unoccupied store. At noon the participants assembled at Osborn's Tavern, received diplomas and a head of wheat tied with green ribbon for their hats, "then sat down to a good farmer's dinner." The 1819 state act included appropriations—Greene received $200 for its fair—but expired after seven years. There is no evidence that the Greene County fair continued even as late as the mid 1820s.[337]

The society was reorganized in 1841 and held annual fairs, usually at Cairo, though it was at Windham Centre in 1847 and at Catskill in 1858. Sometimes reports were optimistic; the 1852 fair drew 1,200 people. But on other occasions, as in 1854, reports were largely negative:

> . . . *it seems to us that Greene County is* always *behind her neighbors in every interest that pertains to the husbandman. Her people do not seem to understand or appreciate the great object of agricultural gatherings.*[337]

The final word on the 1854 fair was that "the swine, and other exhibitions which we will not now enumerate, were decidedly swinish in many respects."[339]

Still, Greene County farmers sought out the fair year after year for opportunities to exchange ideas and information, and especially to examine new equipment. Speakers sometimes brought valuable ideas. One of the most prominent was Horace Greeley, who spoke in 1858. According to tradition he addressed a skeptical audience on "How to Make Farming Pay," recommending the sub-soil plow. One farmer questioned him, arguing that such methods were impracticable in Mountaintop soils. Greeley raised his eyes and simply said, "Raise sheep!" and went on.[340]

Threshing oats in Prattsville
Photograph, late 19th century
Collection of Zadock Pratt Museum

One of the most important benefits of the 19th century agricultural fair was the popularization of labor-saving machinery. In the picture, Grandma Brandow, A.D. Brandow, Vernon Ballard, Mr. Stickles, and Bruno the Dog are using horse power to operate a threshing machine; both gadgets were exhibited at fairs.

By the last quarter of the century, such fairs had become public entertainments. DeLisser observed in 1894:

> *It has been found necessary, however, in these latter days, to introduce amusements, such as racing, balloon ascensions, wheelbarrow and bicycle races, etc., in order to attract larger crowds, whose admission fees go toward defraying expenses and paying the awards.*[341]

Harness racing at Cairo Fair
Photograph, 1891
Collection of Robert Uzzilia

County fairs quickly discovered "attractions" were necessary to build attendance.

At least three local fairs began after the Civil War. The Catskill Agricultural and Horticultural Association organized in October 1866 and

purchased 15 acres at Jefferson where they erected buildings and laid out a half-mile track. Fairs were held there from 1867 through 1874. The Prattsville Agricultural and Horticultural Association operated fairs from 1881 to 1918. The 1893 fair featured an all-night dance as well as a cattle show; in 1910 the attractions included a balloon ascension with a torpedo act, a moving picture show, a merry-go-round, trotters, and the Prattsville cornet band. Harness racing was also featured at the fair of the Coxsackie Fair Grounds Association, organized in 1883, which held an agricultural fair each August beginning in 1884.[342]

The Cairo fair continued until the Depression; it is believed the 1936 fair was the last. An attempt was made to revive it in 1983, and a small but festive community-based event was held for several years.[343]

CHAPTER 30
FARMING MECHANIZES

*H*enry Whittemore, writing about Cairo in 1884, emphasized the historical importance of stock raising in that town, and noted the beginnings of change:

> *The general rotation of crops has been the usual method of farming here, and, until within the last few years, not much attention has been given to the raising of specific varieties of fruit, farm, or garden products.*[344]

Long before dairying became Greene's most successful specialization, cattle and sheep raising had a brief time of importance. Raised in the higher grazing lands, they were driven east to market: in 1847, 26,687 cattle and 53,638 sheep were ferried eastward across the Hudson, not all of them Greene County livestock, of course. Many poorer farmers in the "highlands" concentrated on sheep farming which, in 1884, was "still carried on to a large extent." But the business fluctuated widely due to variations in the price of wool. At the time of the War of 1812 wool was highly profitable, and the purebred Merino sheep prized by more prosperous farmers. The number of sheep shorn in Greene County jumped from 32,641 in 1820 to 47,561 in 1825. But it began to drop after that with declining wool prices, except for increases during the Civil War and again between 1875 and 1880. As late as 1902, several flocks of sheep were driven to Coxsackie Landing en route to the New York market.[345]

Zadock Pratt was an early and articulate voice for dairying as a specialization under these same conditions. In 1847 he advocated a wholesale shift to dairy on the Mountaintop:

> *The country is admirably adapted for grazing, both for cattle and sheep, and the finest sweet grass and cold springs, offer as great facilities for making excellent butter, as the world affords.*[345]

Pratt's own farm at Prattsville was something of a model, but developed, he claimed, "without any extravagant outlay." Milking from April 1 to December 1, he kept about 50 cows, mostly native cattle with a few nearly full-blooded Devons. His operation was extremely frugal as well as clever: buttermilk was carried from the dairy to the piggery in underground logs, and

Hauling milk to Prattsville creamery
Photograph by Harvey S. Peckham,
Prattsville
Collection of Zadock Pratt Museum

Once the railroad reached Greene
County, most farms were able to
market fluid milk to a creamery, which
either manufactured butter or re-
shipped the fluid milk to the city
markets.

water from the yard was turned out onto the lowlands for irrigation at the same time the yard's manure was used for fertilizer.

The butter was churned in ordinary barrel dash churns by water power. "After churning, the butter is thoroughly worked in the ordinary manner, and one ounce of Ashton's fine salt to the pound worked through it, and when hard, packed in white oak firkins, and kept in a cool dry place."[347]

While Pratt's purpose was to reclaim the hemlock lands with pasture and meadow of prosperous small farms, he was by no means a pioneer dairyman on the Mountaintop. Butter was the first product of those farms and had always been shipped down the Hudson. It increased from 1.2 million pounds in 1845 to 2.2 million in 1900, after which creameries took over the task, so that ten years later only 300,000 pounds of butter were made on the farm.

Cheese was less important in Greene County, and decreased rapidly. In 1845 production was 123,000 pounds, dropping to 21,000 a decade later and only 1,330 pounds in 1875.

Meanwhile the number of milch cows in the county remained virtually constant at between 12 and 15 thousand. Statistics for fluid milk beginning in 1855 suggest that a quantity was being shipped by farmers near the river landings to New York City markets; 75,000 gallons of fluid milk were sold in that year, but the figure did not exceed 100,000 gallons until after 1880. Twenty years later it had multiplied tenfold and was just under a million gallons. About 10 percent of the 1900 production was sold; the remainder was made into butter or cheese on the farm, or in a cooperative creamery. Fluid milk sales were stimulated both by refrigeration methods and by the expansion of rail lines. Other factors in the growth of dairy were four discoveries of the Victorian period: the condenser in 1856, Pasteurization in 1860-64, the DeLaval cream separator in 1878, and the Babcock butterfat

Haying with oxen at Ingalside Road,
Town of Greenville
Photograph, c.1895
Collection of Harriet Rasmussen

Threshing using a steam engine,
Prattsville
Photograph, late 19th century
Collection of Zadock Pratt Museum

"Trading work" among farmers was on
the decline after the Civil War, but
steam engines travelled from farm to
farm and required cooperative labor to
operate.

tester in 1890.[348] Another late introduction to dairying was the silo, about 1875; in 1882 there were only 92 in the United States, though experiment stations were actively promoting them for dairy farms.[349]

Creameries—factories, usually in rural areas, for the production of butter and cheese—were rare in nineteenth-century Greene County. Cheese factories were developed just before the Civil War and increased rapidly late in the war due to a scarcity of labor. They drew milk from a four- or five-mile radius, and had some distinct advantages: they saved labor, they produced better quality and quantity cheese, and their product could demand 1-2 cents more per pound at market. But they were not common in Greene.

The Durham Creamery Association was organized as a stock company in 1869 and made butter and cheese, but was not considered a profitable investment; it was abandoned. The 1875 census enumerated only one such factory in the county. Its nine patrons milked 90 cows, and it produced 12,500 pounds of cheese and 2,627 pounds of butter. By 1900 virtually all cheese was made in factories and one-third of butter was produced by creameries but, in Greene, they were just becoming important at that time.[350]

Dairying varied widely around the county. In Hunter, where "little farming is done," Edwin C. Holton wrote in 1884, "There are a few engaged in dairying, but only to supply the hotels with milk." Yet just down the Schoharie Valley at Lexington, as many as 65 cows were kept by "some of the more ambitious dairymen," who used "modern facilities, such as coolers, power-churns, butter-workers, etc."[351]

Marketing patterns are not easy to reconstruct, but the easiest, cheapest method of shipment was used. Thus, the steamboats were the primary method in the river towns, presumably with competition from the West Shore railroad after 1883. On the Mountaintop, the Ulster and Delaware provided most of the transportation for dairy products. Some evidence suggests that there were district agents who took charge of shipping; a Grapeville item in the *Recorder* noted that "Owing to the blizzard, Mr. Powell was unable to make his regular trip to Albany last week with butter and eggs."[352]

Pork packing had been so important a part of the early Catskill Landing economy that it should not be surprising to find nearly 22,000 hogs in the county in 1825. They fed themselves on acorns and butternuts; as the dairy industry grew they benefitted from the availability of whey, and native breeds were gradually replaced by better breeds. But the hog, in competition with Midwestern pork, declined continuously after 1845 and later was raised only for home use.[353]

By the century's end, there were ever broader shifts underway in Greene County agriculture. The peak of farming in Greene County was reached in 1880. In that year, 3,032 farms included 240,734 acres of improved land, nearly 58 percent of the county's total area. (Including unimproved lands, 85 percent of the county was in farms.) Acreage of the small grains—wheat, oats, barley, rye, and buckwheat—had not begun its precipitous decline; in fact, buckwheat and oats, as well as corn, were close to their maximum acreage since statistics were first collected in 1845.

But by 1890 signs of decline in the extent, if not the profitability, of farming were quite evident. In one decade, 233 farms had been abandoned. Up to 1880, farmers had settled on soils too poor or too distant from markets to offer anything better than a meager livelihood. DeLisser commented in 1894, "The occupation of farming does not seem to be extensively followed in many parts of the county." And a Jewett historian noted:

> *During the 1890s . . . the hillside farms became less profitable, for much of the land was not suitable to cultivation by the farm machinery that was becoming a necessity, and many farms were abandoned. The location was too rural, too inaccessible, to attract many summer boarders.*[354]

Profits from farms were increasingly generated by dairy, hay and fruit, and farmers were concentrating their holdings on the better lands. In the

Barn raising at Goslee Cottage, Jewett Heights
Photograph, 1912
Collection of Richard and JoAnne Makely

The timber frame barn was still being built early in this century, "raised" by crews of friends and neighbors.

Hay barracks
Photograph, early 20th century
Collection of the Greene County Historical Society

This photograph is not further identified, but it suggests that hay barracks, a form of storage originally brought from Holland, were still in use in Greene County several generations ago. A few, now used to shelter tractors, are still standing in northern New Jersey.

Aerial view of Ashland
Postcard by A.B. Munson, 1913
Collection of the Greene County
Historical Society

Although the poorers soils and steeper
slopes were already reverting to forest,
this view of Ashland shows it as a
farming village surrounded by open
land in every direction.

Lexington Bridge
Postcard, c.1910
Collection of Larry Tompkins

lowlands, the baling of hay for shipment to New York and other markets had
become a profitable endeavor; it peaked in 1875 at 96,000 acres but it
remained high for decades. Rye straw, too, was much in demand in the city.
On the Mountaintop, dairying increased, aided after the century's turn by
creameries. And in a few towns, notably New Baltimore and Coxsackie, fruit
growing emerged as a specialty. ❧

CHAPTER 31
FRUITS AND VEGETABLES

*L*aura Merwin Peck remembered a time before apples were grown in Jewett:

The writer can well remember the first apple she ever saw—one apiece for all the children, and perhaps as many for the parents, were bought at Schoharie Kill, now Prattsville, and brought home as a grand prize and luxury. After a few years the young apple trees, raised from seeds brought from Connecticut, began to bear a very few apples.[355]

Even in low-country Cairo, the first orchards were not planted until about 1795, when David Brewster and Joseph Shepherd brought stock from Connecticut.[356]

Apples were initially grown for home use. Many varieties originated in New York State; of the eleven important ones in 1850, the Swaar was developed near Esopus before the Revolution and the Jonathan came into being in Woodstock about 1800.[357] Fruit growing for market remained a rarity until the middle nineteenth century. From 1825 to 1860 fruit growing was pursued extensively on gentlemen's estates; but until transportation improved to the degree that most farmers could ship the bulky and delicate fruit to distant local markets, it remained unprofitable.[358] It could be pressed and shipped as cider but that, like distilling, was affected by the temperance movement. Frederick Nelson DuBois (1829-1915) remembered cider making on the Catskill farm of his boyhood:

In the Fall of the year when apples were ripe, all hands, including the children, were set to work picking cider apples (fifteen to twenty wagon loads) and putting them in a bin in the cider house. Then a horse would be hitched to the mill and enough apples ground up for one pressful. The press was made up of different layers of ground apples formed in a box and held together by layers of long rye straw. These layers could be piled up maybe six feet high and covered with long heavy oak planks. Then two big screws were brought down on the pile, pressing the cider into a large homemade oaken tub holding several barrels. This was a time for us boys to enjoy all the sweet cider we could drink. . . . All this was great fun during the ten days or two weeks the cider making lasted.[359]

Orchard workers, Cairo vicinity
Photograph, c.1910
Collection of the Greene County
Historical Society

Between 1850 and 1860 commercial orchards began to increase rapidly. Available statistics do not distinguish between apples grown for market and apples for home use, but there is a clear increase in production between 1855, with 192,184 bushels, and 1865, when 332,719 bushels were produced, an increase of 72 percent in a decade. One farmer, Moses Bedell of Stanton Hill, expanded his orchards after 1875, growing apples, plums, peaches, pears, cherries and quinces.[360]

Several of the other fruit crops were modestly important. In 1865 Greene County produced 1,677 bushels of plums which, though a small quantity, amounted to 36 percent of the state's crop. Twenty years later Henry Brace observed that pears and strawberries were grown in the rich agricultural district between Catskill and the Embought.[361] Census statistics for grapes are spotty, but vineyards seem to have peaked twice, in 1875 and 1935.

The growth of fruit farming stimulated three small, locally based industries: barrel manufacturing, fruit evaporators and other processing plants, and cold storage facilities.

One of several cooperages was T.B. Allcott's barrel factory in Coxsackie, founded in 1874. It employed between six and twelve and, "During a successful fruit year, upwards of 60,000 barrels are made and sold." Briggs and Son, Athens, produced fruit barrels in the late 1890s.[362]

Two evaporators were in operation in the early 1880s. At Prattsville, Ackerly's opened September 1, 1883 and employed 25 hands. It could process 200 bushels daily. The Norton Hill Fruit Evaporator was operated at the same time by Gardner and Hunt. A third operation, Van Wie and Delamater of Coxsackie, begun about 1897, had eight apple paring machines and three drying kilns. It burned in 1910. Jennings and Delamater's evaporating works at Freehold manufactured and evaporated cider by steam power.[363]

Cold storage preserved the crop, making it possible to release apples to the market when the demand was greatest and the prices high. A cold storage house was opened in Coxsackie in 1897; it held 1,600 barrels.[364]

Much of the fresh fruit was shipped by boat to commission merchants in New York, who sold it and remitted the proceeds less a commission to the farmer. While we don't know how much of the apple crop was shipped overseas, several 1896 news items show that improved transportation permitted some export of apples by Greene County farmers. Over 2,000 barrels had been shipped to Europe by Frank Sickles, a Coxsackie apple dealer, and a Liverpool agent was actually present in the county for some time.[365]

Market gardening was, like orchards, dependent upon improved transportation. In 1880, statistics are first given for the value of vegetables sold, at which time it was under $11,000. Ten years later it had doubled to more than $22,000. The *Examiner* described one such operation:

> *James and D.W. Saunders are shipping large quantities of garden truck to Pittsfield, Mass. It is a great pleasure in the early morning just as the sun is breaking over the eastern hills to see their trucks with immense loads of green stuff, congregate at the ferry slip for the first trip over.*[366]

Cornell Vosburgh of Athens, the Saunders' brother-in-law, founded the most important truck farm in the county in 1882. In 1896 he took to Catskill "a load of the finest musk melons" ever seen in the village and, the following year, he was shipping "fine tomatoes" to New York.[367]

Some of the production was canned, primarily at E.H. Lounsbury's Coxsackie factory. In operation by 1884, it employed 50 to 80 people in season. Most of its processing was sweet corn brought in by nearby growers, husked by a force of girls and run through a cutter and a filler, which filled 10,000 cans a day, but it also produced canned peas and apples.[368] ❦

CHAPTER 32
FOREST PRODUCTS

*T*he early years of indiscriminate destruction of forests ended with the disappearance of the hemlocks between 1845 and 1855. The forests began the long process of regrowth. Greene County's higher elevations were reforested by the end of the century. But even during the worst years several small industries made good use of the trees and, as the century moved on, Greene County woodsmen discovered other profitable businesses based on the forest.

Although lumber is frequently listed among shipments from the river ports in the early part of the century, it was relatively costly to ship and, as the forests receded from the river, it ceased to be significant. Potash and shingles were easier to transport.

Potash production seems to have increased until about 1825, when there were 20 asheries in the county, mostly in Durham, Greenville, Hunter, Lexington and Windham. In 1835 and 1845 only three remained, all on the Mountaintop.

Sawmilling in Greene County peaked a bit later, as the forests receded and the Mountaintop became almost denuded about 1835. At that time there were 144 sawmills in the county, of which 34 were in Windham and 35 in Hunter. Long-settled Athens, by contrast, had none in that year. But by 1845, sawmills had decreased to 112, and in 1855 there were 62. There were still 48 sawmills in 1865 employing 54 men and 5 boys, and producing pine, hemlock, spruce, maple and oak lumber. Many were small operations performing custom work; sawmills averaged only $490 a year in sales, while gristmills averaged $7,262.

Improved technology, by which a single mill could produce far more than in the past, contributed to the decrease as well. In 1865 one sawmill was a new steam-powered model, and 15 employed circular saw blades. The Losee mill of Greenville is an example. Built in 1792-1793, it was rebuilt by the grandson of the original owner in 1878 with a turbine and a steam engine. Its new machinery included two lathes, a planer, an upright drill, two circular saws, a hub and spoke machine and a pail lathe; this broad-based operation produced, among other things, "Smith's Excelsior Patent Butter Package."[369] Wooden furniture, tools, and boxes were produced from the early years of Mountaintop

Jerome Crandell's Sawmill, Big Hollow
[Maplecrest]
Photograph, c.1900
Collection of Larry Tompkins

A typical sawmill on the Mountaintop.
Left to right: Walter Barnum, Ebbie
Newcomb, Frank Hanley, Jerome
Crandell, Manley Mallory, Calvin
DeLong, Howard Crandell.

settlement, though they reached an industrial scale only as tanning declined. From the account book of Zephaniah Chase of Jewett, we know that he made coffins, chairs and tables between 1787 and 1804. Stephen Johnson of the same town built a wooden dish mill at a very early date and made wooden bowls and trenchers. Ambrose Chapman of Windham made chairs and hayrakes in 1820.[370]

Clear-cutting of hemlock began first in the Town of Hunter, so its second-growth hardwoods reached maturity earliest.[371] About 1835 the chair-making business began to develop there. Samuel Chichester employed 40 men to make cane and wood seated chairs. The business expanded for over half a century. The 1855 census recorded five chair factories in Hunter with 60 employees. The business seems to have peaked in 1880 when 610 people worked at chairmaking, 368 of them children and youths. In 1884 there were four large chair factories in Hunter, employing 68 men in production and 200 women and children caning seats. The newest was H.S. Lockwood and Company's factory at Edgewood, opened August 1881, which included a saw mill and chair stock manufactory, as well as 11 tenements for the workers.[372] The extension of the railroad up Stony Clove in 1882 was particularly beneficial to the chair factories.

Other Greene County hamlets manufactured wooden products of various kinds. Anson's well-curb and bucket factory at Forge [Purling] moved to Palenville in 1882, where he employed eight; buckets were also manufactured at Freehold from 1840 on, and in many small village and crossroads cooper shops.[373]

Windham was a center of wooden goods by the 1840s. Heman and Jared Matthews came from Southington, Connecticut in 1824, bringing with them machinery for making shaving boxes. In 1839 Jared and Elbert Matthews

Logging near Haines Falls
Photograph, c.1900
Collection of Mountain Top Historical
Society

The team, belonging to Elmer Pelham,
consisted of "Prince Henry" and
"Teddy Roosevelt." The woodsmen are
Arthur Moore, driver, with Ed France
and Harm Hommel.

acquired a millsite on the Batavia Kill and began manufacturing buttons, shaving boxes, and wooden combs. They transferred the lease in 1845 to John Soper, who continued the operation as a turning mill for shaving boxes. His production was 1.5 gross daily; at a finishing shop nearby, three girls inserted small looking glasses in the lids.[374]

In 1848, a wooden comb factory in the same town employed six men and six women, producing 550 gross of combs weekly from 1,700 feet of hard maple timber. Broom handles were also produced in Windham during this period.[375]

With the increase in tourism in the last quarter of the century, wood-turning shops produced vast quantities of wooden souvenirs, particularly in the towns of Hunter and Cairo and at Palenville. Bowls, vases, napkin rings, cufflinks, round jewelry boxes, rolling pins, lazy susans and walking sticks were carried back to the city as mementoes of the summer vacation. While never employing very many residents—most shops were one-man operations—they were highly visible reminders of the wood resources of the Catskills.

In 1879 Chester E. Whitcomb started his wooden fancy-goods manufactory in Cairo known as "Souvenirs of the Catskills." He produced fancy vases, napkin rings, alpenstocks, and other items. At about the same time E.B. Howard of Tannersville supplied "fancy wooden ornaments, made from native woods, from a small bazar."[376]

DeLisser recorded his observations in 1894:

> . . . pausing at Barton's mill, to see the souvenirs of the Catskills, 'turned out of native wood by native skill,' as the legend reads. Curious things they are (the souvenirs): mountain sticks as pretty as they are useless; inkstands, paper-cutters, and letter pails, and a host of other articles of every conceivable suggestion and embodiment of an active imagination, stimulated by that manna in the wilderness, the dollars of the 'summer people.'[377]

Steam sawmill at High Rocks
Photograph, c.1900
Collection of Durham Center Museum

An example of a small, portable rig set up in the woods.

Chair factory at Hunter
Photograph, before 1895
Collection of Mountain Top Historical Society

Four large chair factories in the Town of Hunter produced furniture from native lumber in the late 19th century; this was probably the largest, and burned in 1895.

Souvenir production continued through the middle of the twentieth century. Lester and Clinton Story at Freehold made wooden turned souvenirs between the World Wars; Clinton made Catskill goods while Lester catered to the Adirondacks. Edward Buff at Hannacroix, who died in 1929, sold his work at a seasonal store in Ellenville. Today a new form of wooden souvenir is carved with chain saws; one of the best such carvers has his shop at Lanesville.[378]

By the turn of this century, substantial stands of forest had grown back and, in the Town of Hunter, a modern lumbering operation began in 1903. In that year the Slawson brothers of Canisteo, New York bought 2,000 acres at the head of the West Kill, predominantly maple but with birch, beech and ash intermixed. Later sold to Tenant-Richards and then to the Fenwick Lumber Company of Fenwick, West Virginia, the operation used a mile-long inclined tramway which carried the logs to the sawmill at Edgewood. Fenwick, which employed many Hungarian immigrants, ceased cutting in 1917.[379] Contemporary to Fenwick was the excelsior mill on the present site of the Hunter Mountain ski area; it burned in March 1907.[380]

The Christmas tree business was something of a specialty in Hunter. In the first half of the century, though not yet "Christmas trees," balsams from Hunter were transplanted to Long Island and New York City. During the 1830s and 1840s, the custom of the Christmas tree was established in America; in 1851 Mark Carr of Hunter sent two wagonloads of balsam firs from Catskill Landing. With the extension of the railroad, shipment became easier; Stephen Vining shipped "several thousand" Christmas trees in 1897 and, in 1900, thirty carloads of balsams were sent from Hunter.[381]

Edible products of the forest included walnuts—in 1803, about 1,000 bushels were shipped from Catskill—and black spruce essence, for beer making, from the west part of Catskill Town.[382] Maple sugar, however, was the sweetest forest product on the Mountaintop.

Boiling syrup on the Mountain Top
Photograph, c.1900
Collection of Mountain Top Historical
Society

At first, farmers used an iron kettle suspended over a fire, expanding to an open furnace with a grate. Boiling pans (roughly three by six feet and six inches deep) were in use about 1850, and 15 years later partitioned pans gained favor. About 1880 modern evaporators came into use.[383]

Maple sugar production jumped nearly fourfold to 163,000 pounds between 1855 and 1865, since the Civil War affected the availability of cane sugar, but it continued to increase, peaking at 295,000 pounds in 1875 and 1890.

Meanwhile, maple syrup was becoming more popular. Census takers did not list syrup until 1875, after which it increased gradually to a 1920 peak of 28,000 gallons. Halcott residents proudly reported that Vermont syrup buyers said, "We buy some of our best quality syrup in Halcott."[384]

The twentieth century trend has been towards syrup production, packaged by the producer to eliminate adulteration, and away from maple sugar, which is now a specialty item. While 229 farms produced syrup in 1925 (about 10 percent of Greene's farms), only 28 farms tapped trees in 1964. Since that date statistics are unavailable.

In this century cordwood has been an important product; in 1924 nearly 31,000 cords were cut in Greene County. Gradually, the forest has covered most of the Mountaintop and much of the valley farmland as well. The clearing process of the early nineteenth century was virtually reversed by the early twentieth century: some farmland on active farms was allowed to revert to woodlot, many farms were abandoned, and clearing essentially stopped. In a five year period (1920-24) only 43 acres in the county were cleared of forest.[385]

CHAPTER 33
FISHING

*T*he Hudson River provided a living for many Greene County residents during the last century. Fishing, though little documented, supplemented the diet from first settlement and provided a commercial opportunity, probably after 1790. Clark Brown said, in 1803, that "shad, bass, herring, sturgeon, pike, trout [and] perch" were caught in the Hudson.

Hiram Bogardus, writing in Beers, suggests that New Baltimore was primarily a fishing community until Sherman began building boats there in 1815. Hamburg-on-Hudson, a hamlet at the mouth of the Corlaer Kill on the Catskill-Athens town line, "was wholly a fishing hamlet." In 1930, "some fishing with large nets [was] still done from there."[386] But these were only the most visible fishing communities.

Elsie and Barbara Van Orden of the Embought have written a fine account of Greene County fisheries, particularly for carp, from their own experience and the memories of elderly residents:

Fishing provided work, food and cash for men in this area. In spring, after the ice disappeared and while the tide was out, fishermen would don their hip boots and go out on the mud flats to stomp down or remove water lilies, bogs and weeds, thus cleaning up the area; this was to protect their nets. The Embought Bay and the shoreline up and down the river were staked out to indicate each individual's territory. The men usually respected each other's boundaries. Two types of nets were used: a set net for carp, and a haul seine for smaller fish. Separate fishing licenses were required for each.

Early in the season, in May, the haul seine was used, placed in the stern of a net boat and run in an oval position at high tide. One end was pulled up toward shore to catch fish within its confines. Small fish such as herring, bullheads and eels were caught in this manner; they were sold locally.

* * *

In June the set nets were used for carp. The set net was longer—1500 to 2000 feet. It was rowed out in a circular fashion and the fish were picked up when the tide receded. The men stood in the mud and shallow water and lifted out each carp which weighed anywhere from five to thirty pounds. Smaller fish were released.

The fish car was a wooden box, 14 x 8 x 2 feet, shaped like a scow at the front, so that it would be towed easily. The whole thing was slatted with 1-inch cracks to allow the free flow of water.

* * *

When full the fish cars were towed to the edge of the little channel and anchored. Two or three times a week the fish boat would come down the river, weighing and collecting fish as it went by. The carp were placed in dry wells and shipped to New York.[387]

Herring fishing was pursued from Athens to a considerable degree; about 1835, 3,000 barrels of salted herring were shipped from Catskill.[388] Sturgeon fishing, too, was important, particularly from 1875 to 1920 when the fish and its roe (caviar) were processed at Catskill and shipped to New York. Edward Wells of Coxsackie was a shad fisherman who sold direct to farmers who bought 100-500 shad from him and dressed and salted them for their own use.[389]

Growing up on Brick Row in Athens early in this century, John Kisselburgh knew the importance of the river fishing to his family: "My father's gun, steel traps, and fishlines provided a few extra dollars and a great many meals."[390] But the days of commercial fishing were numbered by the time technology was brought to bear on it, as the Van Ordens relate:

. . . tank trucks picked up carp from fish cars moored along the shoreline. A dealer named Solomon hauled carp from the Embought in a new Diamond T truck with brass radiator. Finally cracked ice was used to pack the fish for hauling to New York, with trucks leaving at nightfall to travel through the cooler hours and arrive at Fulton Street at dawn. As the river became polluted, carp were held in fresh water ponds along the shore for about six weeks and fed cracked corn to remove impurities. Prices finally dropped to a nickel a pound and commercial fishing came to a halt after World War II.[391]

The gradual cleansing of the river since the 1960s has improved the fishing. Today, a very small number of Greene County residents derive income from commercial fishing. ❦

CHAPTER 34
ICE

A century ago thousands of Greene County men worked in the annual ice harvest, when the 3-5 a.m. shift, "the 'morning extra' men carried lanterns and the lights danced on the river like fireflies."[392] The harvest ceased generations ago, but we have the recollections of one of the last who worked on it. Morris Tischler was 12 years old when he helped his father and grandfather fill an ice house about 1922:

This harvest created work for many men drawn here from all over the County. If it snowed I remember watching the men drive big, flat, horse-drawn scrapers (with handles for steering) to push the snow into great piles or dump it into huge holes cut through the ice for the purpose.

The ice-marker, also horse-drawn, could be adjusted to size. It cut into the ice one-half to three-quarters of an inch deep, then other men followed with single horse-drawn planes, back and forth, until the cut was four to six inches deep, according to the thickness of the ice at the time.

The first cakes were sawn and chipped out to get a fresh water path to the ice house. The ice saw was about seven feet long, including the wooden handle. The ice-chopper was a long bar with a knob on top and a flat, four-to-five inch blade with triangular teeth.

Once a canal was opened to the ice house the ice was chopped into squares and pushed by men with ice poles and tongs through the channel of clear water to the ice house elevator. At that point it was drawn up the long slide into the ice house. As the house filled the slide was raised higher and higher until the last layer was in.[393]

The American ice industry began when Bostonians shipped ice to the West Indies in 1805; New York City joined in shortly afterward. In February 1828 the sloop *Ancona* first loaded ice at Coxsackie and took it to New York. In 1847, 13,000 tons of ice were shipped from Catskill to New York.[394]

Workers at H.F. Dernell Ice Tool
Company, Athens
Photograph, before 1910
Collection of Athens Museum,
courtesy of Lynn Brunner

The Dernell shop shipped its ice tools
around the world. Left to right: Ethan
Brandow, Charles and Fred Eichhorn,
Harry Van Loan and Percy Brandow.

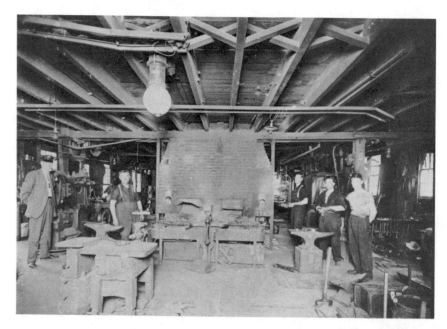

Greene County's profitable involvement began about 1850 when Hiram
Van Steenburgh hired empty warehouses at Coxsackie Lower Landing and
attempted to store ice there in large quantities. The other towns became
involved: New Baltimore built its first icehouse in the winter of 1853-54, the
Independent Ice Company located at Athens in 1854, and Catskill's first
icehouse was built at the Point in the same year.

A few more were built in the years following; and the first icehouse at
Smith's Landing [Cementon] opened in 1868. The business went through wild
price fluctuations. A small ice crop was followed by high prices, which resulted
in overbuilding and overharvesting; this drove the price down, resulting in
increased demand, only to fuel the cycle again.[395]

During one of these cycles the ice industry in Greene County exploded. In
the decade beginning 1873, New Baltimore's capacity expanded from 27,000
tons in one icehouse to 267,000 tons in eleven icehouses. Athens reached a
total of nine icehouses holding 283,000 tons by 1884, and Coxsackie had 15 ice
houses with a capacity of 401,000 tons. A number of large ice houses at
Catskill belonged to the Knickerbocker Ice Company of New York. Even tiny
Smith's Landing had five houses with 221,000 tons capacity. Between Catskill
and Albany six thousand men joined the harvest each winter.[396]

The winter months were a time of slack employment in Greene. Many of
the ice cutters were brickmakers from the brick yards "which are idle in the
winter." Others came from farms in the country. In New Baltimore, "Ice
boarders flood the town at the present time." Even schoolboys sometimes
helped. Isabella Rainey of Athens remembered when "we closed the school two
weeks in winter so older boys could work on the ice."[397]

The hard work during the 10- to 20-day harvest resulted in some $10,000
going into circulation along the upper Hudson. Much of this was in scrip—in

the 1870s Moses Bedell of Stanton Hill recorded that "Vine and Charley bought wood—then paid me in ice checks $4.00"—but it was a welcome infusion of funds. In Athens creditors would say, "I'll pay you in ice cutting!"[398]

Others worked in the summer, "breaking it out" and loading the ice on barges for shipment to New York City. Storage and shipping each cost twelve cents a ton, and half the ice melted during handling, but for generations it was a profitable business for the river towns.

An industry developed in Greene County to supply tools and equipment for ice cutting. With the exception of the "Champion" snow scraper and the "Champion" crust breaker, manufactured by Coxsackie's Elias Gates in the 1890s, the tools were made by the Dernell firm. Herman F. Dernell came to Athens in 1858 and began general blacksmith work and the manufacture of ice tools. He soon specialized in implements for the ice industry. He added a steam engine to the shop and soon, with the closing of an older firm he had worked for, he became the largest manufacturer of ice tools in the United States, employing 20 hands in 1884.

Between 1880 and 1917 H.F. Dernell and Company issued an illustrated catalogue. Over sixty different implements were offered and buyers ordered through the catalogue from England, Germany, Sweden, Norway and Russia. With the shift to ice manufacture, the firm closed in 1927.[399]

Most ice was lifted into the ice houses by "endless chain elevators driven by 25-35 horsepower engines." In 1884 all but one of the New Baltimore houses used steam power. A. and B. Wiltse of Water Street, Catskill, perfected and manufactured this ice elevating machinery, and built steam engines as well.[400]

The ice harvests improved as the century ended: four million tons were harvested in 1898-99, and the winter of 1900-01 was called the "largest and

Knickerbocker Ice House, Catskill Creek
Photograph, c. 1914
Collection of the Greene County Historical Society

finest to date." About 1900 Every and Eichhorn of Athens built one of the last of the great ice houses.[401] But Hudson ice cutting was threatened by the growing problem of sewage from Albany and Troy which was released into the river. Increasingly people sought ice cut on inland lakes or pristine rivers in Maine. Only on South Lake, where the Ulster and Delaware harvested, did Greene County participate in the sale of lake ice.[402]

Artificial refrigeration finally ended ice-cutting. Ice was increasingly manufactured under sanitary conditions. Then, the affordability of the household refrigerator eliminated the need for the iceman and his huge blocks of ice. By the end of the first quarter of the twentieth century the industry was in rapid decline, and by 1950 it was extinct. Many ice houses burned: frame structures with sawdust insulation, they were dry as tinder. Others became mushroom plants.[403]

Ice cutting at Rogers Island
Photograph by Paul Park, Catskill,
c.1910
Collection of the Greene County
Historical Society

CHAPTER 35
CLAY

Greene County's resources included extensive clay banks, plenty of firewood for firing kilns, and cheap river transportation to market. For a time these resources were used by a small but important Athens pottery manufactory. They later contributed to the Hudson River brickmaking industry, which reached its zenith in the late nineteenth century.

Nathan Clark (1787-1880) came to Athens in 1805 with his brother-in-law, and for eight years they produced earthenware. After 1813 stoneware was Clark's exclusive product. In 1820 he employed six men and ran six potters' wheels, producing pots, jugs, jars and pitchers.

Clark developed an unusual system for expansion:

> *It was his custom to select from among his apprentices those who were the most skillful, and when their terms of apprenticeship expired, to set them up in business by starting a branch pottery in some other part of the state, and putting them in charge. Many worthy young men were helped by him into business.*[404]

By this method subsidiary potteries were established at Kingston, Cornwall, Lyons, Rochester, Oswego and Mount Morris.

The business passed through several reorganizations. Ethan S. Fox became Clark's partner in 1829 and bought him out in 1838, but sold the business back to Clark, whose son Nathan, Jr. then ran it from 1843 until his 1891 death. During the Civil War era production was particularly high.

Nathan E. Clark, the third generation, took over in 1892, but in the following year it became a cooperative under the ownership of Thomas and Edward Ryan. It closed in 1900.[405]

The only related industry was the Excelsior Pottery and Drain Tile and Pipe Works on West Water Street, Catskill. Founded in 1865, it employed six to 20 men, producing 1,000 tons of hollow brick annually.[406]

By far the greatest user of Greene County clay was the brick industry in the river towns. It is impossible to pinpoint the date when brickmaking for the market began, but by 1820 there were at least 10 large brickyards. Eight were at Athens, but those at Coxsackie and Catskill each employed 14 men and, as such, were the largest producers. Amongst them, the 10 yards employed 84 men and 16 boys, not to mention the oxen which ground up the clay, and they shipped some 5,640,000 bricks to the New York market.

Numbers increased as the years passed. By the 1830s Coxsackie's Middle Landing was the site of 20 yards which manufactured 50 million bricks a year, employing 25 sloops.[407] Some idea of the volume can be read in a letter from Henry Adams of Coxsackie to his brother in New York City:

> *I have this morning Rec'd yours of the 21st Inst in which you wish to inquire how many and at what price brick could be procured here on contract. I have seen a number of manufacturers. O.T. Wright has two million bricks on hand, 800,000 of which are front [face] brick. He will take $7.50 and $5.50 [per thousand.] Hallenbeck has 900,000, Vosburgh and Wolfe 500,000, Hubble has sold his to Bartlett & Van Schaick yesterday at $7 and $5. At the upper landing there are about one million all of which can be got except what is sold, with the privilege of all they make to the first of June or July next—there are about three million at Athens—and a considerable number at Catskill are good brick.[408]*

Workers at Clark Pottery, Market Street, Athens
Photograph, c.1892-1900
Collection of Athens Museum, courtesy of Lynn Brunner

From 1813 to 1900 the Athens pottery produced stoneware. Ed Ryan, co-owner, and John Hallenbeck are in the doorway. The hive-shaped kiln is visible behind the building.

In 1855 Greene County had 22 brick manufactories and was third in the state in production, after Rockland and Westchester Counties. Five brickyards at Athens in 1860 employed 120 men for five months.

Two brickyards at Smith's Landing [Cementon and Alsen] developed somewhat later. The yard near Alsen was owned and worked by French Canadians who mostly left the area when the yard closed in the 1880s. At Cementon some African-Americans were employed as brickmakers.[409]

In 1890 the Catskill Shale Brick Company began producing a new type of brick. Seven years earlier the Elmira Shale Brick Company developed this new variety, tough and hard but not brittle. It used harder stony deposits, rather than the soft plastic clays of common or mud brick.

Deposits of red Chemung shale were found near the Cairo branch of the railroad, and there were clay banks along the tracks nearer the village. The little railroad benefitted: in 1898 shale and clay accounted for 70,000 of the 74,000 tons of freight carried on the little line.

This brick manufactory was not a pleasant neighbor. In 1896 residents complained about gas and smoke from its chimneys.[410] But in 1901 the bottom dropped out of the market and production ceased for five years. When it resumed in 1906, the yard operated as Eastern Paving Brick and Tidewater Paving Brick. Again in 1910 there were bitter complaints about the plant's dense smoke; its chimneys were simply built higher. But after 1912 production declined.[411]

Common brick also declined in the new century. In 1910 G.W. Washburn and Company operated eight machines at its Catskill plant, and B. Goldin and Son operated six in the same village, while W.W. Rider Jr. of Athens, in business since 1875, used four machines. A state study in 1913, however, tallied seven common brick operations in Greene County, producing 26 million brick.[412]

Shale Brick Works, Catskill
Postcard, c.1910
Collection of the Greene County
Historical Society

Beginning in 1890 the Catskill Shale Brick Company produced a new kind of brick.

Two firms were operating in Athens five years later: Gladfelter's and Joseph Mayonne's. In 1925 Mayonne, which had a plant at Glasco, Ulster County, set up in Catskill as well. But in 1929 imported Belgian brick was offered for sale at less than those of local manufacture. With the crash, the

Washburn Brickyard, West Side,
Catskill
Photograph, c. 1915
Collection of Robert Carl

brick industry finally died. Mayonne struggled through the 1930s and then closed up shop.[413] The three Athens brickyards, according to John Kisselburgh, mostly "provided work for the Italian immigrants and the more hardy of the natives."[414]

The brick industry was also particularly important to Greene County's African-Americans. Early in this century the Athens brickyards lured Black workers from the South on a seasonal basis. Many found jobs in the brickyards, while others worked in construction, on the river, or in factories. Though they constituted a significant community throughout history—in 1869 Blacks founded an African Methodist Episcopal church in Coxsackie—most of their population growth has occurred since the 1920s as Southerners fleeing poverty arrived. Norman Lattimore, a Tuskegee graduate, recruited workers from the South for Catskill employers; today a less formal network of acquaintance and referral continues to bind Blacks in small towns to relatives and friends in the cities and in the South.[415]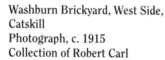

CHAPTER 36
FACTORIES

*T*he surplus of labor and capital which resulted from the rapid decline of tanneries encouraged small industry, particularly on the Mountaintop. In 1847 a report to the State Agricultural Society noted:

As the resources from which our tanneries have been supplied, began rapidly to diminish, capital is seeking investment through other channels. Manufactories are springing up on every hand, and amply rewarding investments that are made, and opening new markets for the proceeds of the farmer's labors.[416]

Manufacturing in Greene County has never been particularly strong. Despite the variety and dispersal of small mills and factories throughout the nineteenth century, they never contributed to the economy on a scale with farming, shipping, ice cutting, or tourism.

Windham was a good example. O.B. Hitchcock wrote in 1884, "It had a late beginning and a slow but steady growth. The decadence of the manufacturing communities has left it the rural metropolis of the western Catskills."[417] In 1850, as Richard Wiles has shown, 159 men and 62 women of Windham worked in manufacturing ladies' satchels, shaving boxes, button moulds, combs, paper and other goods. Manufacturing declined somewhat by 1860. But, Wiles notes, "It was more frequently true . . . that business and economic activity was short-lived with rapid turnover either due to changing market conditions or poor business management."[418] In a similar vein, Henry Whittemore of Cairo noted, "With the exception of those that were started to supply the demands of an agricultural population, these [manufactories] have not been a permanent success, owing to the difficulties of transportation, and other incidental causes."[419]

Yet all through the nineteenth century and into the twentieth, shops, mills and small factories employed hundreds in the river towns and along the creeks and country roads of the inland towns. Wooden goods were probably the most important of the products. During the mid- and late-nineteenth century a number of industries came and went, while others developed slowly into more significant aspects of the county's economy. Foundries, woolen and cotton mills, a few paper mills, and pistol and gunpowder factories all contributed to the postwar economy.

The earliest foundries in the county were at Catskill and Madison [Leeds], and both seem to have begun by making iron ploughs. The Catskill Foundry, founded in 1808, was a broad-based shop, the secret of its survival until 1952. In the last quarter of the nineteenth century the Wiltses produced their steam-powered ice-elevating machinery there. It also provided specified parts and repairs for the nearby brick and cement industries. A second foundry began operating in Catskill in 1880, the Imperial Facing Mills; its 11 employees produced foundry facings.[420]

Oak Hill was another center of the early iron industry. Perhaps its earliest foundry was the one begun in 1833. It burned in 1865 and in the following year it moved to the river as the "Coxsackie Malleable and Grey Iron Company"; its 75 employees made castings and fittings. The Campbell and Scofield foundry, sold to Sheldon Cherritree in 1844, made the "Dutcher Plow No. 2" in its early days; in 1884 it produced the "Climax" plows and a hardware line. A third foundry, established by Calvin Adams in 1854, made coffee mills, corn shellers and door hardware; as late as 1884 it employed 20-30 hands.[421]

Foundry work also began in Windham when Alonzo and Bolivar Newbury began manufacturing the Newbury Printing Press, along with agricultural tools, in 1854. Like the Oak Hill foundry which relocated at Coxsackie, the Newbury plant would benefit from river transport and readily available moulding sand; with the advent of steam power, millsites on mountain watercourses were no longer essential. The Newburys moved to Coxsackie in 1866 where they employed 10 men and continued production of printing presses as well as a patent paper cutter and steam fittings and castings. Alonzo sold out to Bolivar in 1881, who later sold to Albert C. Hotaling; meanwhile Alonzo acquired the Malleable and Grey Iron Company and built a new foundry at West Coxsackie which employed 22 people. It burned in 1899.

Coxsackie businessmen recruited the Kennedy Valve Company about 1890. This large factory employed 100, but about a decade later inadequate rail siding space was given as the excuse for its move to Elmira, taking about 100 families with it.

About 1900, Coxsackie attracted American Valve, which also employed about 100, manufacturing brass and iron "gate valves." The firm built a new plant in 1919. During much of the twentieth century, Coxsackie was home to five more metals plants: Walter Brothers, Cooper Roller-bearing Trolley Wheel Company, Union Wheel and Manufacturing Company, Albrass/Scully Foundry, and State Wire and Cable.[422]

Several relatively small cotton and woolen mills grew up during the decline of the tanneries; six woolen mills were reported in the 1865 census. Those in Ashland suffered, and closed, because of their inland location, which caused high transportation costs. Morss' cotton factory built at Red Falls near Prattsville in 1848 was of course under the same disadvantage, but survived

Oak Hill Manufacturing Co.
Photograph c. 1867
Collection of Douglas and Sancie
Thomsen

until 1881, sometimes employing 50 women and 30 men. At Palenville, the woolen mill of Teale and Lawrence was operating in 1830, and rebuilt after an 1858 fire. It was still working in 1884, with five employees producing bats, flannel and satinets using water power. In 1867 there was a small woolen factory at the west end of Cairo hamlet.[423]

Despite Greene County's abundant water power, the only real milltown was at Madison, established by 1827 as "Mill Village" but renamed Leeds in the same year. In 1844 Harris and Harding purchased a millsite there and, within two years, built a steam-powered woolen mill which employed as many as 150; at the time of the 1850 census there were 35 male operatives and 65 female. According to tradition, "hundreds of experienced workmen were brought over from Leeds, England" and renamed the place in honor of Richard Hardwick. The 1850 census, however, lists Germans, Swiss, Irish, Scottish and native-born factory workers, along with five who were English-born.[424]

The mill struggled along through the 1850s. In 1857 some New York capitalists built a second, much larger mill to the east, 106 by 44 feet and four stories high. It went into operation in May 1859.[425] Three years later the first mill burned, but was rebuilt as the Leeds Waterville Manufacturing Company. When it became insolvent in 1874, it was sold to Alexander T. Stewart, the Belfast-born founder of the modern department store; the second mill was also purchased by Stewart in insolvency. Before his 1876 death he contracted for a four-story addition to the second mill.

The two mills employed as many as 550-700, making cloakings, shawls, cassimeres and robes. Leeds thrived:

Leeds was much larger then than now—a busy little village.
There were four temperance organizations, Odd Fellows, and a

139

weekly paper edited by George Warner; there were the humming clanking mills, and there were lines of houses down what was called Back street—big boarding houses—and close-set houses on Main street that held the families of the workers. At closing time and when the bells gave out their call there was a stream of humanity which filled the street.[426]

It also had a company store and, after 1878, St. Bridget's Church, to minister to the growing Roman Catholic population.

After Stewart's death his estate liquidated his holdings. On January 1, 1881 the second mill closed; the first mill closed a year later. Hundreds lost their jobs, and most left the area. Services at St Bridget's were discontinued for many years. The mills stood gaunt and empty for more than a generation. The second mill burned in 1918, and the first mill was taken down three years later.[427]

Catskill Village also had several mills. The Harris Manufacturing Company began making woolens in 1864, employing 175 hands, and after 1881 the Hop-O-Nose Knitting Company of West Catskill produced 100 dozen shirts and drawers a day, utilizing 120 hands and a steam engine.[428]

Paper manufacturing got an early start and survived for many years but never became a major industry in Greene County. The Hope Mill in "The Glen" near Catskill employed only five in 1885, but operated 24 hours a day with its two 180-pound engines driven by water power. It produced bonnet and press board.[429]

Croswell's mill at New Baltimore, converted from a gristmill to paper manufacturing by 1826, employed three in 1855. It produced wrapping paper and wallpaper, and closed in 1897.[430]

There were other, smaller papermills at various times: that of the Hitchcock brothers at Big Hollow [Maplecrest] operated for about five years at mid-century, making straw binders' boards and straw wrapping paper; another at Woodstock in Cairo town, begun by Isaac and Charles Hoffman and revitalized by Charles J. Cave in 1881, also making wrapping paper; and there was a mill at Coxsackie, "when in operation," in 1893.[431]

Gunpowder and pistols were a well-known product of the Town of Catskill after the Civil War. Winthrop Laflin built a powder mill near High Falls on the Cauterskill in 1837. Later its owners were Laflin, Smith and Boice.

No one was surprised, we can be sure, when the powder mill blew up on a number of occasions during its history. In 1847 the *Catskill Democrat* reported that three men were "blown to atoms." Yet it was rebuilt; in 1865 the mill produced 18,000 kegs of gunpowder worth $85,000 and shipped them from Saugerties landing in kegs produced at Palenville. After a final explosion, probably in 1875, the firm moved to New Jersey.[432]

Meanwhile James Reid was manufacturing his "Knuckleduster" nearby on the Cauterskill. This barrelless revolver, patented in 1865, had an elongated

cylinder so that the front of the chamber acted as the barrel. A patented knuckle guard could be used as "brass knuckles."

Reid bought a burned-out mill and millsite on the Cauterskill two miles west of Catskill in 1864 and built a 25 by 50 foot gun factory, along with a gristmill and 19 houses for workmen. By the time he began production in late 1868, he had fitted it up with seven lathes, a drill, a polishing machine, and plating baths. Reid failed about 1884 due to economic depression and the slackening of gun sales at that time.[433] ❧

Stewart Mill, Leeds
Photograph by Paul Morrison, Catskill, 1903
Collection of the Greene County Historical Society

CHAPTER 37
STONE

*M*any Greene County residents from early days to the present have worked in stone quarries and sand mines. The market for this buried treasure has been subject to changes in technology and in fashion but there has always been a demand for some of Greene's geological resources.

The richest of these is the belt of Silurian-Devonian carbonate rocks, commonly called limestone, which runs parallel to the Hudson in the ridge of hills called the "Kalkberg" or Lime Hill. Settlers made use of this stone from the beginning; the Dutch and German settlers of the four river towns built many of their farmhouses and some of their village houses out of limestone chunks available without quarrying. About 2 percent of Greene County's houses in 1855 were stone, and most of these 100 buildings were in Catskill, Athens, Coxsackie and New Baltimore. Some marble deposits were found in the limestone; in 1804 a plan was formed to work a marble quarry in Catskill owned by Timothy Green.[434]

The most consistent use of the limestone was for lime. Burned in kilns to break it and purify it, the stone provided flux for the iron industry, a component of plaster, a component of masonry mortar and an enriching agent for farmlands. In 1855 Greene County had four plaster mills and four lime kilns. One of these lime manufactories, situated three miles west of Catskill, was founded in 1833 and was still operating in 1884, with seven employees.[435]

Bluestone occurs both in association with limestone and separately. This smooth, handsome sandstone was used for sidewalks, coping for ornamental walls and mantels, and many other purposes. In the 1830s an industry developed to quarry the bluestone for construction use, originally for urban sidewalks but later for water tables, sills and lintels on brick buildings. Bluestone was quarried in the western part of New Baltimore, and at various places in the Town of Catskill, particularly near High Falls and Smith's Landing [Cementon]. The slabs were stacked on the docks along the river in the winter. Even in Hunter flagging stone was quarried, once the railroad on the Mountaintop made shipping economical.[436]

The bluestone industry peaked between 1870 and 1895. In 1870 16 quarries employed 57 men and produced stone worth $25,760. Four years later Griffin's quarry at Palenville was advertising flagging, curb, gutter, cross-walks, platforms, sills, lintels and coping of "Catskill Mountain Bluestone."[437] In 1895 a newspaper account predicted continued demand:

> *The soil of the Catskills holds within its embrace material from which great cities of the future will be built. From beneath these barren stony hillsides, so sterile as to be useless save for pasturing a few sheep, will, before the end of the century, come forth in installments millions of tons annually of material sufficient to build a city at the mouth of the Hudson.*[438]

But the widespread use of bluestone ended suddenly about 1900, following the rise of Portland cement, a product which gave great prosperity to the Smith's Landing neighborhood. Local builders continued their use of limestone; stone from George W. Holdridge's quarry a mile west of Catskill village was used in many of the village's structures in the late nineteenth century and was still being quarried in 1930.[439]

Meanwhile another industry developed in the Coxsackie area thanks to the presence of high-quality sand deposits. Foundries which cast brass and iron required large amounts of fine sand to form the moulds. Albany moulding sand was the finest, but Coxsackie sand, found under the flats in and near the village, was almost as desirable. In both cases it had been deposited during the Ice Age by the glacial Lake Albany.

Thomas Bell purchased the moulding sand under 43 acres of the Stephens Farm near Four Mile Point in 1886. He built a boardinghouse for his employees and a long dock on the river. The dock provided a platform for two-wheeled, horse-drawn dump carts. These, when loaded with moulding sand, were taken to the end of the pier and were dumped into barges using a hinged platform.

Bell's business became New York Sand and Facing Company. Meanwhile, also in the 1880s, Michael Dolan leased sandlots, wharf space and railroad sidings at Coxsackie and entered business, incorporating in 1902. The company offered to ship "all kinds of Coxsackie and Albany Moulding Sand, fire sand and fire clay by rail or water in carload or boatload lots."

Other sand firms were Whitehead Brothers and Claude DeFrate of Coxsackie and the Whitbeck Company of New Baltimore. Only Whitehead survived the Depression.[440]

Through the 1880s improvements were being made in the quality of Portland cement and the methods used in its manufacture. In 1895 New York State produced 59,000 barrels of Portland cement and nearly four million barrels of natural cement. By 1905 the quantities were nearly equal at over two million barrels each, but five years later Portland had taken the lead and natural cement amounted to only 8 percent of production.

Portland proved equal to or better than bluestone for many purposes. Industrialists learned that the same region from which bluestone had been shipped offered them limestone beds adjacent to deposits of the clays necessary to provide alumina and silica to the Portland mixture. Since these deposits were close to the river and to the West Shore railroad, shipping costs could be kept to a minimum.[441]

The cement industry at Smith's Landing [Cementon] was initiated by the incorporation of Catskill Cement Company by two Catskill businessmen. The first meeting was held in Jersey City, New Jersey on August 9, 1899; in August 1900 it made its first shipment. The firm built a plant, private docks, a private siding and, in October 1901, housing for the workers who came from many countries, but especially from Croatia in the Austro-Hungarian Empire. Capacity was increased from 350 barrels daily to over 1,000 barrels by 1909. In 1906 the post office at Smith's Landing was officially changed to Cementon to celebrate the booming industry.[442]

In the same month that Catskill Cement shipped its first product—August 1900—a group of German investors formed the Alsen American Portland Cement Company. They built a plant just north of the first one; the Alsen railroad stop was added in November 1901. Alsen, too, built a dozen workers' homes; in 1907, District No. 17 was established to provide a school in the hamlet.[443]

By means of cement plant jobs many families, newly arrived in America, established themselves in a new country. But news stories from the first decade of operation reveal the great risks. In 1902, Marko Luekich was ground to death in a conveyor at the Catskill plant. Julius Colwick was killed in 1905 when he was buried in a bin of cement at Alsen. In 1909 Frank Sanger was killed at Alsen, and George Doyle was ground to death at the Catskill works; and in 1910 Charles Roorke was smothered to death at Alsen.[444]

Workers at Pete and Uriah Haines' Quarry
Photograph by Alden Ticefeldt, Chichester, c.1890
Collection of Mountain Top Historical Society

One of many bluestone quarries in the county, Haines' was near Sphinx Rock on Prospect Mountain, above Haines Falls.

Machinists at the Alsen Cement Company
Photograph by P.R. Morrison, Catskill, June 15, 1920
Collection of Josie Zelusko

At Cementon and Alsen, cement manufacturing was almost the sole employer early in this century. Front row, lft. to rt.: (1) Gus Duffy (3) Frank Yannone; back row: (1) John Lucas (5) Frank Snyder (6) Jack Bannon.

The Seaboard Portland Cement Company bought land north of the other two plants in 1907 and began building a mill in 1912; by 1914 it was taken over by Acme. Within two years it was producing 600 barrels a day.

The 1920s were a prosperous time for Cementon. One of the chief reasons for this was the road-building program of the State of New York. At this time most state highways had concrete pavement and, it was said, much of it was composed of Acme cement. In the mid 1920s about a quarter of its product was shipped by boat to New York; the rest was distributed around New England and New York by rail.

Company buy-outs were frequent in the cement businesses. Catskill Cement was sold in October 1909 to Alpha Portland Cement Company of Easton, Pennsylvania, which rebuilt the plant and increased its capacity to 4,000 barrels a day by 1914, when it was exporting its product to South America due to the war in Europe. Alsen was next: in 1919 it came under American ownership and in 1925 was sold to Robert F. Johnson of Brooklyn. It later became part of the Lehigh Portland Cement Company. Acme was sold in 1926 to North American Cement Corporation. Later it passed through the ownership of Marquette and Lone Star; early in 1984, with 110 still on its payroll, it was sold to Independent Cement Company.[445] 🍀

CHAPTER 38
COMMUNICATIONS

*T*he development of communications in Greene County was a slow process, with post offices and the postal routes supplying them gradually increasing through the nineteenth century. By 1875 the telegraph became a practical, if costly, method of communication and the telephone followed soon afterward.

The new nation passed a comprehensive postal law in 1792 but most letters were sent privately for many years thereafter. There wasn't even a post office in Greene County until Catskill and Freehold were so designated on September 30, 1800. The central places of the county were added over the following decade: Windham in 1801, Loonenburg [Athens] in 1803, Cairo in 1804, Coxsackie in 1805, and Durham in 1808. These few important post offices were joined within the next 25 years by many more, including offices at remote East Kill, above East Jewett, and Sportsville, somewhere in the old town of Lexington.[446]

At first the mail was carried by boat and on horseback. In the earliest years William Faulkner "rode the post" with a mail pouch and a horn from Hudson to Lexington; a Mr. Cole went to the Catskill post office to pick up letters for his Jewett neighbors. Even in connection with post offices, letters might be carried only once a week, as they were from Prattsville to Griffin's Corners [Fleischmanns] by way of Halcott, before the railroad.[447] Congress authorized the use of railroads for mail shipment by declaring them "post roads" in 1838.

The expansion of rural mail service began in 1845 when the Star Route system was provided. This system linked smaller post offices with larger ones by an intricate (vaguely star-shaped) network of stage and other routes. Two years later the postage stamp made its appearance, and after 1855 it was mandatory.

Greene County's own congressman, Zadock Pratt, once introduced a resolution in Congress to *reduce* postage costs, then 25 cents, to a level that would reflect the true costs. Seven years later the measure was implemented; postage was reduced to an average of five cents, but subsidies made their appearance only six years thereafter.[448]

Windham, with some significant businesses but distinctly isolated, first "agitated" a connection to the outside world by telegraph in 1874. A subscription meeting in January 1875 launched the project, and by July there was a line through Beaches Corner, Hunter and Stony Clove. The Catskill, Cairo and Windham Telegraph Company organized a month later and completed its line in October. Both lines were later sold to Western Union, in 1881 and 1883. Shortly after the Windham connections were made, a Cairo and Durham Telegraph Company organized, and then a Greenville and Freehold Telegraph Company. These, too, became part of Western Union.

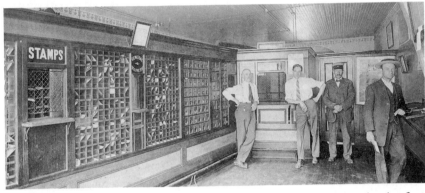

Coxsackie Post Office
Photograph, c.1918
Collection of the Greene County
Historical Society

At Catskill, which apparently had telegraph connections already, the first telephone service opened July 15, 1881 with 22 subscribers, including the Mountain House. Two years later the Catskill Telegraph and Telephone Company was sold to Hudson River Telephone Company.[449] Small, independent companies were the rule for many years.

Mail was always picked up at the post office until, in 1863, some cities offered door-to-door delivery. But rural free delivery was only an experiment when first tried in 1896. Six years later it was made permanent, and on May 1, 1903 rural delivery began from the Catskill post office. Coxsackie followed in October, and the larger rural post offices joined the program after that.[450]

Telephone service remained dependent upon trained operators until recent decades. The resort business was capable of throwing the systems into confusion. Louie Hyser recalled the Schoharie Telephone Company at Tannersville in the 1920s:

> At the time there were a number of big hotels here, they were all Jewish hotels and at night sometimes they'd have 3000 calls at one time and there was no way that they could handle them because there were only nine switchboard operators on duty at night and they'd be all night long trying to get those calls through. Most of the people came from New York and they all tried to call New York the minute they got into town. They just never did get the calls because the telephone company was so busy with calls and this is what interested the New York Telephone Company, because the local telephone company couldn't afford to put in the type of equipment needed to handle all these calls . . . [451]

New York Telephone bought out the Mountaintop system in 1928. They continued it as an operator system until 1966 when dial service began. ❦

147

CHAPTER 39
ELECTRICITY

 *A* revolution equally profound in its effects was the introduction of electric lighting, which began about the same time as telephone service.

Urban gas lighting systems were adopted by many cities and large villages during the mid-nineteenth century; in Greene County, only Catskill had gas lighting, put into service in 1858 by the Catskill Illuminating Company. In Coxsackie, some "progressive merchants" installed their own systems of acetylene illuminating gas during the last years before electricity was made available.[452]

F.N. DuBois attended a lecture in Catskill in 1841 by one of the village's teachers at which the electric light was demonstrated,[453] but practical use of the power source was not possible until the mid-1870s through the experiments of Edison and others. The Catskill gas company built an electric generating station in 1888 and made electricity available to consumers, though it only operated the plant between twilight and 1:00 a.m.[454]

Soon nearby communities acquired generating capability. Coxsackie's Kennedy Valve installed a single light in front of its plant and, in 1891, agreed to supply electricity for the village. A steam generating plant of the Coxsackie Electric Light and Power Company was built in 1899. The new service was advertised in the village newspaper:

> *Special offer—for only one cent—Try using electricity—you can get the equivalent of 16 candles for One Hour. We give liberal discounts for quantity and early payments. Send for our information sheets. End the century by doing a good thing.*

Athens acquired a steam plant in 1900, while water-power-generating plants were put in service at Hunter a few years later. Between 1905 and 1907 another was built at Woodstock. Fred Trumpbour built the first plant at Palenville, in 1903.[455]

Consolidation was an early trend, since interconnections between the tiny systems reduced prices and increased dependability. Coxsackie and Athens were absorbed by Upper Hudson Light and Power in 1901. Through further consolidations, Central Hudson Gas and Electric Corporation emerged in 1927.[456]

The availability of electricity in farming areas of Greene County lagged behind. Halcott Valley finally got electric lines in the fall of 1927. As late as

S.R. Hommel, Electrical Contractor
Photograph, c.1910
Collection of Mountain Top Historical
Society.

1925 only 60 percent of farms in the county reported electric service, but rural electrification advanced rapidly through the 1940s so that in 1950 98.6 percent of farms were connected.[457] 🐦

CHAPTER 40
MODERNIZING
TRANSPORTATION

*W*ith all the modern conveniences and vast changes in the way Greene County people earned their daily bread, the methods used to move people and goods remained fairly inconvenient after the Civil War. The slowness of the steamboats, the small number of railroad lines in the county, and the limits on horsedrawn conveyances all contributed to a sense of isolation. Highways, in particular, were terrible. Muddy in spring, dusty and rutted in summer and fall, they were comfortable to travel only when frozen and snow-covered so that sleighs might be used.

The improvements in roads actually pre-date the availability of the automobile by several years and were begun for a recreational device—the bicycle.

The bicycle fad hit the nation in the 1890s. Cycling clubs, open to both sexes, were organized in Coxsackie in 1893 and in Athens in 1896. The "Wheeling Club" of Catskill re-organized in 1896, when Tolley and Wynkoop of that village reported they were selling a bicycle a day. Even in remote Lexington there were 20 "wheelmen." Clubs sponsored competitive races and parades of decorated cycles.

But these affluent and influential advocates of the new sport found the public roads abominable, so they pressured town budget commissioners to set aside funds for "sidepaths," separated from the highway by a "verge" or grass strip. Six hundred dollars in pledges paid for "a splendid cycle path, 6 feet wide" constructed from Catskill to Palenville in the spring of 1899.[458]

Cyclists also published road books which reported on the conditions on the public highways. *The Standard Road-Book of New York State* reported only three "good" roads in Greene County in 1897: from Hunter to Haines Falls, from East Windham to Ashland, and from New Baltimore out to Coeymans Hollow. There were a few "fair" roads, and all the rest were "bad."[459]

The progress in electric power generation set the stage for an attempt to facilitate local passenger travel. Horse-drawn "bus" lines operated by I. Wheeler Brandow had provided local service in and near Catskill since 1882. Beginning in 1895 a number of trolley lines were proposed, mostly by investors outside the county since the financial troubles of the Catskill

Mountain Railroad made local investors cautious. Initially, the Catskill, Cairo and Windham Street Railway incorporated, but it reorganized two years later as the Catskill Electric Railway Company. Its first section from Catskill Point to Jefferson commenced operation September 20, 1900. In its first year it carried 176,595 passengers but lost $2,957. It was extended to Leeds by 1904.[460]

In the meantime other lines were proposed, and it was thought that a Coxsackie to Greenville line would get underway. In 1903 the Catskill company projected an extension to Middleburgh in Schoharie County, and an Albany and Catskill trolley company formed. There was discussion of a line to Oneonta and another to the Mohawk Valley.[461] One attempt to increase trolley ridership was the construction of an amusement park. Rip Van Winkle Park on Catskill Creek east of Leeds opened by 1908. Soon after the line became insolvent. A year later, in 1910, a new franchise was granted to Catskill Traction Company, which filed for an extension to Oak Hill. It was granted permission to build to Cairo, but was unable to finance it. By 1917 the line was entirely bankrupt, and it was torn up.[462]

As it turned out, the automobile, rather than the trolley, became the dominant mode of transportation in the new century. The horseless carriage was still a curiosity in 1895, when only four were registered in the United States, but there were 3,200 just four years later, and in 1900 the number had jumped to 8,000.

In that year, Greenville reported "the first automobile ever seen in this vicinity" when Miss Helen Gould motored through en route to Roxbury; Augustus J. Phillips of Kingston drove a 7.5 horsepower locomobile up

Trolley car on Main Street, Catskill
Photograph, c.1900
Collection of Robert Carl

Leeds Bridge and Trolley
Photograph, c.1905
Collection of Larry Tompkins

through Platte Clove.[463] Soon millionaires were seen driving automobiles through Greene County on their way to their mountain cottages.

Despite the early adoption of the automobile by persons of wealth and influence, there was plenty of prejudice and hostility against it. Elka Park had a prohibition against automobiles until 1906. And as Windham reported in 1908:

> *The first auto this season passed through Windham on Tuesday. It succeeded in upsetting the stage, throwing out a passenger, and in going at a 16-mile clip. Of course the driver stopped at the hotel and explained how he always gave the road, slowed down or stopped when a horse appeared frightened.*[464]

Building the State Road, Durham
Photograph, July 1926
Collection of Durham Center Museum

Commercial uses were found for the automobile beginning in the 1910s. The first motorized bus service seems to have been Henry J. Albright's Mountain View Coach Lines which made daily trips from Coxsackie to Albany in 1916; his wife followed behind in a car if there were extra passengers.[465] Ten years later Albright was making three runs daily to Albany, and he had been joined by six other small companies: Yannone's to Leeds, Smith's to Cementon (five trips daily), Garrison's to Tannersville, Alle's from the Day Line boats to Prattsville and beyond, and Kelsey's from the Day Line boats to Cornwallville, Oak Hill and Durham.[466]

Morris Tischler remembered the competition by boardinghouses which had their own vehicles to meet the trains and boats:

> Some boarding houses sent their own conveyances,—some still horse-drawn in the 1920s, but most had their own motor carry-alls which met the boats. My parents had their own vehicles for their "Golden Hill House." One was a seven-passenger six-cylinder 1926 Studebaker sedan which sometimes carried as many as eleven people squeezed in or on one another's laps, Drivers for competing boarding houses contended so vigorously and noisily for arriving vacationists that the village fathers enacted an anti-noise ordinance. That generated a forest of signs held high overhead which soon became weapons necessitating police regulation.[467]

The New York City to Catskill auto bus made its first trip in the early summer of 1927 and, in December, began running to Albany.[468] As the introduction of buses seems to have lagged behind pleasure cars, so did the use of motor trucks, which affected farming at least as much as automobiles did passenger travel. Cornell Vosburgh of Athens, a market gardener, acquired a truck in 1916. Carrie (Spaulding) Ingalls of Greenville wrote in her diary on February 19, 1917: "Stanley and Ransie went to Albany to pay $100 on our truck," and a few days later, "The men came with our truck."[469] This was a Federal, purchased from Ivan Hannay of Westerlo. Once trucks were in use, teamsters like Truman Ingalls were no longer limited to hauling produce to the landings or to West Shore Railroad depots; many began to carry produce direct to Albany market, or to sell direct in other ways.

With the advent of motorized vehicles, road building was forced to catch up. Paving of village streets had been desirable—to reduce summer dust— even before automobiles, but it seems that Catskill did not do so until 1910.[470] On the other hand, town roads were entirely unpaved and were maintained by road crews consisting of the taxpayers of the district. Burgess Howard remembered his first experience working on the road:

> My first job was working on the Onteora road when I was in my tenth year. The town levied a poll tax of one dollar or a day's work on the road. My father gave me a hoe two feet taller than I, and sent me to work out his road tax. After walking a mile I met the superintendent of the Onteora road, Cyrus Showers who paid his tax by being the boss. He was six feet tall which made me feel mighty

G.M. White's bus service, Cairo
Photograph, c.1918
Collection of the Greene County
Historical Society

Helen Gould's auto at McCabe's drugstore, Greenville
Postcard, c.1905
Collection of Greenville Town Historian

Miss Gould was en route to Roxbury when she stopped at Greenville. Since a postcard was made of the event, we may assume the sight of an auto in Greenville was still exciting.

small. Any way after the laughter of the others had subsided he let me hoe the loose stones back in the ditch. The taxpayers revolted at such extravagance—throwing the stones back that had just been plowed out the ditches. I forgot my lunch and Cyrus divided his dinner with me and six o'clock we quit. I waded home through the mud in my bare feet in a May snow squall.[471]

Some of these roads were the early horse-and-wagon tracks across the ridges, and had declined in importance as early as the turnpike era. For example, in 1867 three roads crossed the ridge from Halcott to Lexington, in addition to a number of others crossing from Halcott to Delaware County, though even at the time they were called "difficult and unfrequented roads." The roads were unsuitable for automobiles and trucks and, in the 1920s, a new road was proposed from Halcott Center to the foot of the ridge in Lexington. It was never built. Again in 1983 the county highway map indicated the location of a proposed road from Johnson Hollow to the Little Westkill Valley.[472] At the present time automobile drivers from Halcott must pass through two other counties to reach the rest of the county.

Another mountain road was the one from the head of Spruceton valley through Diamond Notch to Lanesville; this was abandoned by the town board in 1924.[473] The Mink Hollow Road from Woodstock into Platte Clove had been used by Hunter's earliest settlers; in 1914 Elka Park's directors tried unsuccessfully to convince the town to improve it.[474] In general, the advent of the automobile meant not only improved surface conditions but the complete abandonment of roads which would be impractical or uneconomical to improve.

The real improvement in road travel occurred as a result of the state highway program of 1909, when an amendment to an 1898 highway law numbered five routes in Greene County as part of a statewide system. They were the river road (designated as state Route 3), the road from Catskill to the Delaware County line beyond Prattsville (Route 5A), the road from Cairo to the Albany County line beyond Durham (Route 5B), the road from Palenville to Haines Falls (Route 5C), and a section of the Schoharie-to-Grand Gorge road passing through Prattsville (Route 38).[475]

According to Gallt, "the first road" was built from Catskill to South Cairo, and extended to South Durham by 1914. The river road, "a trunk line," was built in 1912-1914.[476] Philip DuBois remembers its construction:

> *When we moved to Catskill the road to Athens was dirt. Some time later it was paved, and I heard that it would be an asphalt road. I asked the operator of the steam roller the color of asphalt. "Black,"* *he said, "but after it is covered with crushed stone, the road looks white."*[477]

It was not until about 1931 that Route 9-W as we now know it was built, diverting traffic away from the river towns. Route 145, though authorized in 1909, was also built about that time.[478]

Beginning in 1914 the present Route 23A was built through Kaaterskill Clove using prison labor. The convicts lived in a camp at Palenville while hewing the road out of the mountainside.[479] It took seven years to complete; a letter to the *New York Times* in late 1921 described it as "just completed" and commented:

> *Unfortunately, the road's financial history makes bad reading, having taken seven years to build at a total cost that is staggering. However, the results of convenience and pleasure to the territory served will be a lasting value.*[480]

The development of designated "trails" followed shortly after the building of the state highway system. These routes were created by commercial interests or municipalities along the way, and were essentially marking and

C.A. Schmiedell's Cozy Hollow cabins and filling station, Prattsville Postcard, c.1930
Collection of the Greene County Historical Society

Tourist cabins became common in the 1920s in response to automobile travel, and helped to draw people from the old-fashioned boardinghouse.

155

Point Lookout near East Windham
Postcard, c.1935
Collection of the Greene County
Historical Society

Point Lookout is still a tourist stop on
the Mohican Trail, which features the
spectacular view of the Catskill Valley.

marketing programs. Greene County interests marked two roads: the Rip Van Winkle Trail, now Route 23A, and the Mohican Trail, now Route 23. Attractive view books were distributed with information on attractions and accommodations.[481] With better state highway markings these "trail" programs declined although the names stuck. Along these routes were the heaviest concentration of the new, auto-dependent businesses—diners, gas stations and motor courts—all of which became a part of the landscape during the 1930s.

By the time the highway building program got underway, the impact of the automobile on railroad travel was evident. The Catskill Mountain Railroad, which operated seasonally and was never financially secure, reached its peak ridership in 1909 and began declining three years later. Although the Otis Elevating was reconstructed in 1903-1904 to permit direct transfer of cars from the Catskill line, it remained a losing proposition. On the Mountaintop, the narrow-gauge Catskill and Tannersville carried 11,000 riders per year to the standard-gauge Kaaterskill's 30,000.

The three interconnected railroads had no direct link with other railroads, only with the steamboats. With a decline in traffic on the Evening Line and competition from the auto as well as the direct Ulster and Delaware link to the Kaaterskill Railroad, the trio was doomed. Between May and August of 1915 they went into bankruptcy and, four years later, the lines were torn up for scrap.[482]

The Ulster and Delaware branch to the Mountaintop peaked slightly later in 1913, but dropped thereafter, especially during World War I. The line was acquired by the New York Central in 1932 but service to Haines Falls and Hunter was discontinued in 1940.[483]

Only the West Shore line continued operating through mid-century. In 1953 it still ran three trains daily in each direction stopping at Catskill and Coxsackie; the early train made additional stops at Alsen, West Athens and New Baltimore. Fare to New York City was $3.81.[484]

River travel continued to be significant and changed with the times. In 1898 Augustus Sherman was able to commute daily from New Baltimore to his Albany job as secretary of the State Prison Commission on the steamboat *Lotta*. Philip DuBois remembers that such steamboats also made other, unofficial stops at ice house docks.[485]

The river's freighting capacity was improved in the 1910s. John Kisselburgh recalls:

> *I remember the river before any sandpiles dotted it every few miles. It was a broad, open river with its marshlands or flats completely covered on high water. The middleground, where now the sand island extends from the lower village past the Brick Row to the old oil dock, was such a tidewater flat. It was thick with lily pads and wild rice, and provided excellent fishing along its edges and excellent duck shooting in the fall of the year.*
>
> *Then one summer, small boats went up and down the river, placing stakes with red and white markers on both banks and along the edges of the middleground and bays. Soon afterward crews came and spent a whole summer shooting angles back and forth across the channels—moving from the oil dock and on down the river. The groundwork was being laid for the dredging that created the sand islands all along the river. The Deeper Hudson was to become a reality. Ocean freighters were to go all the way to Albany.*[486]

Ferries, of course, remained important east-west links, though they were out of service in winter when the river froze over. DuBois remembers that "Business in my father's drug store in Athens was best when the Hudson-Athens ferry had shut down for the winter and the river had not frozen sufficiently so that the distance could be walked safely."[487]

Discussion of a bridge across the Hudson began in 1925 or 1926. A bill was introduced into the State Assembly in January 1930 to appropriate

The Athens ferry, *George H. Power*
Photograph, c. 1925
Collection of the Greene County
Historical Society

$450,000 for such a span, but was vetoed by Gov. Roosevelt in 1931 since he wanted the state to sell authority bonds secured by toll revenues. A bill to authorize it was passed January 1931 and signed by Roosevelt in March 1932. The preliminary plans for the bridge placed its approach on the Cole estate but the third plan altered the location slightly. The steel was erected between May 1934 and January 1935, and the Rip Van Winkle Bridge opened officially on July 2, 1935. No longer were travellers limited by the ferry schedule or the winter shutdown which closed river crossings.[488] The Catskill and Coxsackie ferries ceased operations soon afterward, but the Athens ferry ran until 1947.[489]

Steamboat patronage began declining about 1926, and accelerated during the Depression. The steamboat lines began running large deficits, and both Night Line and Day Line went into receivership in 1932-33. The Night Line ended service in 1939, but the Day Line continued, eliminating deficits briefly in 1942-43 due to increased passenger traffic during war rationing. The Day Line made its final regular New York-to-Albany trip on September 13, 1948.[490]

The Wright brothers flew their primitive "aeroplane" in 1903, but it was some years before planes were familiar to Greene County residents. Primitive airstrips were built in the years between the wars at various locations: Cairo, Prattsville, Platte Clove, East Jewett, Sunside, Kiskatom, and Ashland. The Prattsville strip was the site of the first fatal accident in the county when, in 1914, a plane overshot the field and flipped, killing a woman passenger.[491]

By 1930 Tannersville boasted the Rip Van Winkle Airways Airport, "one of the few mountain airports officially recognized east of the Mississippi." About six years later the first airmail went out of Windham in the care of pilot John Garraghan. After World War II an airport at Greenville, now defunct, was followed by ones at Cairo, Athens and Hunter.[492]

Since World War II most of the changes in transportation have been improvements in the highway system. The Hudson River Day Line made its final excursions to Catskill in 1952 and 1953, and the West Shore Division discontinued passenger service in 1958, continuing to the present only as a freight carrier. But 1953 and 1954 saw the construction of the New York State Thruway, built across the flats a mile or two back from the Hudson. First planned under Governor Lehman in 1942, it was delayed by the War; in 1955 most of the superhighway was in use across the state.[493]

Upgrading of the state highway system—which, in 1971, amounted to 18 percent of the county's road miles—continued, with the additional traffic fed by the Thruway rendering it more important. In 1960 Route 81 was upgraded to provide Greenville with good access to Coxsackie.[494] Route 23 was reconstructed from the river to Cairo in the 1970s as a four-lane, partially limited-access road which bypasses Catskill, Leeds and Cairo, and from there to East Windham it was relocated and widened as a two-lane road, bypassing Acra and South Durham; this project severely damaged main street commerce in the string of hamlets. Route 23A was improved to bypass Lexington hamlet, and substantial improvements were made on many other highways.

Warren Ingalls at the Ingalside
Landing Strip, Greenville. Photograph,
mid 1930s
Collection of Leona Rundell

A direct result of the dependence upon the autombile was the shift from village commerce to highway business. Under way in urban and suburban areas in the 1950s, this phenomenon made a late appearance in Greene County. Since 1970 a few small plaza-type shopping centers have been built, at Catskill, Cairo and Greenville. Perhaps a greater impact on local business has been that of the regional shopping malls, the first of which was Colonie Center in 1968. Gradually, retail trade has decreased in the villages, with some of the slack taken up by tourist-oriented businesses. ❧

CHAPTER 41
REFORMERS

*A*s the twentieth century began, the temperance movement was mature but still vital, and its creation, the woman's rights movement, was just making its appearance on the local level. Philip DuBois' aunt Hattie Brown was an example of the natural linkage between the two:

> *Her cause was prohibition and all progress toward it was followed carefully. When it seemed that males were thwarting the drive toward prohibition, women's suffrage seemed a likely facilitating step, so she became an early and energetical advocate of "votes for women."*[495]

The first record of local interest in woman suffrage was a study club formed about 1875. The next recorded event was an 1884 lecture by a Mrs. Blake, who was quoted in the *Examiner* as saying, "We do not wish to be men. God forbid!" Ten years later the New York State Woman Suffrage Association held a convention in Catskill's old opera house and, from that meeting, the Political Equality League of Catskill was organized in the spring of 1895. After several years of hard work, a Constitutional Convention failed to include their platform and the club lapsed at the end of 1898.

The movement was apparently dormant for a decade. In the spring of 1910 or 1911 a suffrage meeting was held at Catskill, and in September 1911 an informal club organized. An army of suffragettes marched through the village in January 1912, en route to Albany where they intended to petition the legislature to pass a bill for women to serve as poll watchers when suffrage reached the ballot.

The Equal Franchise League of Catskill organized in March 1914 and established headquarters on Main Street; in June, Carrie Catt spoke in the village. A league was also formed in Tannersville through the efforts of Onteora Park residents. In late summer the woman's rights advocates staffed a booth at the Cairo fair, reporting that a great number of people were reached who had no idea of the meaning of the slogan, "Votes for Women!"[496]

The level of apathy in the county is also reflected in a story about a suffrage worker who boarded one summer with Miss Emily Becker of Catskill while she was:

. . . working all over the county against what to her, seemed terrific odds: no one would take her seriously. She was well trained to oppose arguments but the people she tried to talk to were just not interested. If she had been more attractive it might have helped but in a day when puffs and curls were a must, her hair was pulled back in a hard bun and her tweeds and heavy shoes made her look as much like a man as possible. Such a contrast to Miss LaFolette in her sweeping black dinner gown and waved golden hair and the applause she received. Miss Dodge used to come back at night and weep on Miss Becker's shoulder and at the State Convention she broke down and was taken to a sanitorium. The indifference of Greene County was harder to take than downright persecution, then she could have felt like a martyr.[497]

Despite this indifference and, very likely, some outright hostility, woman suffrage became New York State law by a vote of the male electors in 1917 thanks to the hard work of Miss Becker, her guest, and the many other well-educated, determined women of the 1910s.

The progress of the temperance movement was not so clear-cut. Local laws sometimes restricted alcohol: Catskill had 15 persons in the liquor business in 1915 but no saloons, as they had been "voted out" several years earlier.[498] In other places heavy consumption among some groups of people had continued, although the temperance movement had made substantial inroads among many Protestant church members, some devout Catholics, and especially among middle-class people with pretensions of respectability and social status.

After Prohibition became law on January 1, 1919, alcohol consumption continued outside the law, giving rise to a vast underworld of producers, transporters, and dealers; much of the Canada-to-New York movement passed through Greene County.

Acra achieved a certain notoriety as the location of Jack "Legs" Diamond's country hideout. The New York City gangster, active in liquor and drug dealing, bought the place late in the 1920s at the suggestion of an associate whose mother ran a Cairo boardinghouse. His lavish expenditures and casual generosity earned him the respect of those whose judgments were influenced by easy money. Despite his reputation for buying the collusion of police departments, the Catskill and Cairo chiefs were incorruptible. Diamond survived a gangland-style assassination attempt at the Aratoga Inn in Cairo in April 1931; he recovered but, after a trial and conviction, he was shot to death in his bed just eight months later.[499]

Nearly a century old, Greene County's temperance movement was represented primarily by its chapters of the Women's Christian Temperance Union. In 1927 ten chapters had 297 members, one of the state's smallest county organizations, with members in Acra, Ashland, Cairo, Catskill, Coxsackie, East Durham, Hensonville, Maplecrest, Prattsville and Windham.

After repeal in 1933, there were those who continued to fight for temperance, but the WCTU was down to 143 members in six chapters four years later.[500] Despite continued anger over vehicular crimes by drunks and the rising hard-drug problem, the temperance movement today is virtually dead, buried by a shift in American political thought from the rights of the community to personal liberties.

Not all was progress in Greene County during the 1920s. That was also the decade of the Ku Klux Klan. It seems to have organized in Prattsville on October 25, 1925, and it claimed members in that community as well as Ashland, Windham and Catskill, with the river-town group possibly operating separately. A woman's affiliate, apparently called the "Ever Ready Club," organized in June 1926 and held a demonstration at Catskill in July at which a forty-foot cross was "lighted."

There is no evidence of overt acts by the group which, at its peak, was insignificant. The Prattsville chapter, called a "klavern," counted a grand total of 81 members but its average "klonklave" attendance was 15, reaching 43 on one occasion in 1927. By 1928 its attendance was in the single digits and its last recorded meeting was held that June.[501]

Centralization was another important progressive movement of the mid-twentieth century, although it had a deleterious impact on community identity.

Union Free Schools had been established in larger communities, beginning in the 1850s, and drew students from a number of districts. They often had graded classes and substantial buildings and, as educational expectations increased, they were seen in a more favorable light than the country district. Windham, for example, became a Union Free School in 1900, thereby adding high school grades.[502]

Country school districts exercised almost complete control over day-to-day operation, subject to minimal state requirements. But they were small and poor and isolated. Halcott's four districts, for example, had no high school near enough for its advanced pupils to attend until 1908, when a high school was built at Fleischmanns.[503]

Reformers began to seek ways to improve the system. In 1897 a law permitted districts to contract with other districts to educate their children. A Central Rural Schools act, passed in 1914, designated all monies from the composite districts and the Union Free School allocation to any consolidated school. Three years later the state required township-wide school boards; this measure was so unpopular it was quickly repealed.

In 1921 the State Education Department published an account of the consolidation attempt in which their bias in favor of centralization was obvious. The Department, the State Teachers' Association, and five rural-based organizations formed a Committee on Rural Schools. Their report appeared a year later and made a strong case for centralization.

By the Central School Law of 1925 the state promised to pay consolidated districts' transportation costs and 25% of the cost of new buildings, as well as some other costs through a complex formula.[504]

In Greene County rural schools closed gradually through the 1930s, both by centralization and by contracts which sent pupils to village districts. The 1931 Windham-Ashland-Jewett merger, for example, brought "to the people of this area the instructional advantages enjoyed by the schools of the cities." The district built "a new and modern fireproof building of brick and steel" in 1936.[505]

Greenville centralized in 1930, Hunter-Tannersville in 1931 (its new buildings opened in 1936), Cairo-Durham in 1939, and Coxsackie-Athens in 1947. The Climax school closed in 1954, when its students went to Coxsackie-Athens. Catskill, with its well-developed village school system, was a recipient of contract students from rural districts until its 1955 consolidation. In 1954-55 Catskill High School drew from 15 districts in the Town of Catskill and three in the Town of Athens, but four of the districts had their own elementary schools: Palenville with 57 pupils in grades 1-6,

Saloon at Prattsville
Photograph, 1904
Collection of Zadock Pratt Museum,
courtesy of Larry Tompkins

While temperance drew the allegiance of many Greene County residents, others patronized saloons such as this one.

163

Leeds with 63 in K-8, Cementon with 78 in K-8, and Alsen, which closed in June 1955 after a season with only one pupil. The other rural districts each sent between one and nine pupils to Catskill. This unwieldy system was then consolidated into a single Central School District.[506]

The last rural school in Greene County, Rocky Store at Hannacroix, closed in 1961, but the centralization mania continued a few years longer. In 1967 a proposal was advanced to merge Windham-Ashland-Jewett, Cairo-Durham, and Hunter-Tannersville. The proposal for a vast district went down to defeat.[507]

The culmination of this movement has been the present central school districts; where once there were hundreds of elementary schools and a few academies, Greene County today has nine elementary schools and six high schools. Another cooperative institution, Columbia-Greene Community College, opened in 1966 in a former Athens school, later building a campus in Columbia County.

One other educational institution, the Coxsackie prison, rose out of the progressive and reform movement of the early twentieth century. The state facility, intended to intervene in the development of juvenile criminals among boys over 16, was housed at the New York House of Refuge on Randall's Island. In 1933 the state purchased 720 acres of farmland west of Coxsackie for what was then the New York State Vocational School. It opened two years later, designed for 500 young men. At its opening, Commissioner Walter N. Thayer of the Department of Correction assured the audience with the stirring words: "I am convinced our problem is not altogether hopeless."

The institution has provided employment to many Greene County residents, particularly those of Coxsackie. It is now termed the Coxsackie Correctional Facility and offers high security. In the 1980s Greene Correctional Facility was built on the farm for less serious offenders.[508]

Greene County's only hospital was also a creation of the second quarter of the century. "Memorial Hospital of Greene County, Inc." formed May 20, 1926 to hold in trust some legacies intended for a general public hospital. The legacies were not adequate to establish a hospital so, in 1931, an agreement was made between the corporation and the county Board of Supervisors to build and operate a hospital. It opened, with a capacity of 24, on its site in Jefferson on August 10, 1933.[509] It merged in the late 1980s with the Hudson hospital as Columbia-Greene Medical Center. Recently, with the state health department's policy of discouraging small hospitals, the Catskill facility's use as an acute-care institution ended. Greene County citizens, alarmed by the possibility of traffic delays on the Rip Van Winkle Bridge and the distance to Albany and Kingston, fought the closure, and are hopeful that sale of the hospital building to a team of physicians will re-establish acute care. In the western end of the Mountaintop, Greene County residents often use Margaretville, Oneonta or Cooperstown hospitals. ❧

Nelida Theatre, Catskill
Photograph, 1912
Collection of the Greene County
Historical Society

High school plays and graduations,
vaudeville, motion pictures, and
lectures by distinguished people such
as Admiral Peary were held in this
converted skating rink, now the site of
the Community Theatre, 373 Main
Street, before it burned on January 1,
1917.

CHAPTER 42
INDUSTRY

*T*wentieth-century manufacturing in Greene County has shown significant departures from its evolution in the nineteenth century. By the turn of this century, the small village mills and shops were mostly a thing of the past, and manufacturing had concentrated in the river towns of Catskill, Athens and Coxsackie. In 1912 the state registered 56 factories in the county, of which only four small factories were on the Mountaintop. Prattsville and Windham, factory communities before the Civil War, had none. Catskill claimed 25 of the 56.[510]

The Depression closed many of the older factories in the river towns. The foundries were the one group that survived into the postwar period; in recent years all but one of the foundries have closed. The D.W. Travis foundry in the Village of Athens was acquired by Ralph Wormuth after World War II, and continues operations today on a new site as Wormuth Brothers Foundry.

A number of relatively small manufactories have opened over the past 50 or 75 years. In 1963 for example Greene County had 48 industrial establishments, of which 63 percent were in Catskill, Athens or Coxsackie; only seven employed 150 or more workers. Increasingly, in the last 20 years, they have located in decentralized locations.

American Valve Company was Coxsackie's anchor industry through most of the twentieth century. Incorporated in New Jersey in 1901, it began operation in the old Newbury plant. New buildings were put up in 1906 and again in 1920. American Valve manufactured both iron and brass valves and, in its early years, averaged 100 employees. It was providing 260 jobs in 1963, when neighboring Scully Foundry employed 35. When closure of the bankrupt American Valve was announced in the fall of 1986 only 95 jobs remained. The owners cited as causes of its failure the antiquated plant, low-priced imports, and the skyrocketing product-liability rates.[511]

The Catskill foundry, the oldest in the county having been founded in 1808, modernized in the twentieth century to service Corliss steam engines for firms around the East. During World War II it produced precision parts for the U.S. Air Force.[512]

By the turn of the century the weaving of cloth was no longer being performed in Greene County, but the three largest river towns soon began manufacturing ready-to-wear clothing. In 1912 the Union Knitting Company employed 381 at its two mills in Catskill, one producing wool sweaters and the other sportcoats.[513] The Athens Knitting Mill was organized by local investors in 1897 and a mill building was built in just two months that winter. The factory produced knit goods and employed both Athens and Hudson workers; the latter crossed by ferry or by rowboat. Later, as the Athens Manufacturing Company, the same building housed a handbag factory; in 1963 it employed 140.[514]

In 1963, 200 operatives worked in Catskill's Atlanta Lingerie and 45 in the same village's Helene Manufacturing Company, producing women's apparel. Athens' Atlantic Knitting, which opened in 1950, employed 80. In Coxsackie George Krauss employed 60 and Adamo Dress 20. Cairo's Mary Lou Manufacturing Company was a small shop with 25 employees.[515]

The surviving textile and clothing operations all closed during the 1970s and 1980s. Atlantic Knitting ceased operations in June 1982 when its owner moved his operation to North Carolina.

Boat building had a brief renaissance in the twentieth century before it, too, disappeared. The Athens Dry Dock began in 1909 with 25 employees; during the 1920s the Benter Boatyard was still in operation in Catskill. When the Dry Dock's owner, Michael Lenahan, died in 1941, it closed but, by 1943, the Imperial Life Boat and Davit Company was turning out a dozen lifeboats a week in Athens, employing 135 people.

After the war the property was sold and became Aerobilt Bodies, a Grumman subsidiary which manufactured aluminum alloy truck bodies. They built a new plant at West Athens and were the county's largest factory in 1963, with 328 on payroll. With the union coming in, Aerobilt moved to South Carolina in December 1981.

Workers at Coxsackie Malleable and Grey Iron Works
Photograph by E.W. Cook, Albany, c.1890
Collection of the Greene County Historical Society

Kennedy Valve Manufacturing
Company, Coxsackie
Engraving, 1897
From its "Price List."
Collection of the Greene County
Historical Society

Beginning in 1962 Allied Boat Company manufactured fiberglas boats in Catskill, among them the *Seawind*, a thirty-foot sailboat.[516] The marinas on Catskill Creek in Catskill, and in New Baltimore, sell new and used boats but no fabrication is done here at the present time.

Several other metal or technical factories have provided employment in Greene County. Metal lath was fabricated in Athens beginning in 1916. Coxsackie was home to Union Wheel and Manufacturing Company, incorporated 1909, which made polishing and buffing wheels, as well as State Wire and Cable, a small wire manufacturer in the postwar period. Coxsackie also made the "Superior," a motion picture projector for general use, beginning in 1922.[517]

By the late 1950s and early 1960s, a more technical class of manufacturing was making small inroads into Greene County. The American Thermostat Corporation employed 140 in Cairo, Becker Durham Inc. made radio speakers in East Durham with a work force of 120, and 30 workers at Stiefel Laboratories at Oak Hill produced medical soaps from 1946 on; a new plant at Durham opened in 1963.[518] In 1969 the "newest" addition to West Coxsackie was American Technical Industries, Inc., manufacturer of artificial Christmas trees.

The largest corporations in Greene County today include the ski areas as well as Stiefel, and aerospace-related DynaBil Industries of Coxsackie. A new entry in Greene County's economy is warehousing, drawn by moderate land prices and ready access to transportation; a few years ago United Stationers, a Chicago-based office supply company, built a large warehouse in Coxsackie.

CHAPTER 43
CHANGE ON THE FARM

*F*arming was relatively stable during the first two decades of this century and, in its crops and techniques, more closely resembled the late nineteenth century than the period between the World Wars. The number of farms declined 18 percent and the acreage of improved land declined 24 percent, continuing the slide begun after 1880 with the abandonment of the poorest and most remote mountain farms. Jason Clum of Clum Hill, Tannersville, remembered life before Greene County began "to run down hill":

> *In them days there was neighbors around us; workin' the farms their fathers had worked before them. There was hundreds of tons of hay cut where you won't find nothin' but second-growth trees now. And there was nice, comfortable homes, where there's nothin' now but old cellars choked with bushes.*
>
> *Then a man begun buyin' up the farms around here. I don't know what he wanted 'em for, because he ain't never done a thing with the land. But he bought it anyhow; and the families moved out, and went—I don't know where.*[519]

Charles A. Beach of the Mountain House noted the change, too, in his testimony against the street railway extension in 1910. He stressed the decline in population since 1865 and he said that farming was a declining source of revenue, giving way to a three-month summer boarding business.[520]

Lowland and mountain hayfields continued to supply the cities with vast quantities of hay, though down substantially from an 1875 peak; rye straw was also sent to city stables, but declined in twenty years by 42 percent. Many New Baltimore farmers, for example, shipped their hay and straw on Michael Dolan's "Farmers' Freighting Line Company," organized in 1907.[521] The mechanical developments of the post-Civil War era included many horse-drawn machines and some steam-powered ones that reduced labor costs and incidentally discouraged continued farming of the poorest lands. Farms typically used mowing machines and dump rakes; some had a hay tedder, which was a reaping and binding machine. Much of the threshing was done by threshers powered by steam engines.[522]

The number of milk cows changed little from 1880 to 1920. Fluid milk production peaked at nine million gallons in 1900; but sales of fluid milk rose from a million gallons in 1900 to 5-1/2 million gallons in 1910, dropping back to 3-1/2 million gallons in 1920.

Creameries had become an important link in dairy marketing. The first in Halcott was the Kingston Dairy and Ice Cream Company about 1888-1889. The Catskill Mountain Creamery shipped butter to commission merchants in Albany, New York and Brooklyn at least from 1889 to 1893. Coxsackie's creamery was new in 1897; Prattsville's incorporated in 1900.[523] Some creameries were cooperatives, such as the Locust Grove Creamery in Durham and the Lexington Co-op Creamery Association.

In 1918 the Locust Grove co-operative was still operating at Oak Hill. The Farmers' Creamery Company at East Durham and the Prattsville Dairy Company received milk, as did milk stations for Breakstone and Levine, and other New York producers, located at Hunter, Jewett Heights, Prattsville, North Settlement and Windham.[524]

Greene County's apple production peaked in 1910 at 630,000 bushels. Pears, peaches, cherries, plums and prunes, grapes, and even quinces were found in county orchards; Greene was important statewide only for pears, with 6 percent of the state's trees. Small fruits were also growing in importance, led by strawberries, though Greene had much less than one percent of the state's small fruit acreage.

John Kisselburgh recalls picking fruit as a boy in Athens:

As the years accumulated and we grew to be big boys, our summer days were filled with jobs. Before the school year was finished, strawberries were ripening on Harry Waters' farm. After school each afternoon and all day Saturdays we were on our knees gathering the luscious fruit, for three cents a quart. It was tedious work for impatient boys. . . .

Allen Moseman Farm, Little Westkill
Photograph, c.1910
Courtesy of Larry Tompkins

Little Westkill, a farming district of Prattsville, is valley land and still in agriculture. But as this pre-World War I photograph shows, it was relatively remote and some of its farms remained very old-fashioned.

As the season progressed, school closed and other fruit and vegetable crops matured in quick succession: raspberries (black and red), currants, cherries; and not long after them, string beans and peas at thirty cents a bushel. . . .

At a later date we joined the fruit pickers and helped harvest Clapp's Favorites, pears that ripened just before school opened in the fall. We picked for Garry Hollenbeck and Walt Herr for thirty cents a barrel. It was fun! . . . Sometimes we made twenty or thirty dollars in a summer.[525]

At this time the steamboat *Storm King* carried Coxsackie produce to market in New York, with a capacity of 4,000 barrels per trip.[526]

A smaller Mountaintop crop was potatoes. Their peak county production was 3,850 acres in 1875; about half that quantity was harvested in 1920, but it was sufficiently important economically to merit the organization of the Windham Potato Growers' Exchange in August 1917.[527]

Though the decline was still slow, the changes in the farm country were evident enough to spark a number of efforts to strengthen community and advance agricultural efficiency. The Patrons of Husbandry and Patrons of Industry were the most important of these before World War I.

The Patrons of Husbandry or "Grange" was founded in 1867 as a political and economic tool for farmers, primarily in the Midwest. It had lost its initial, political power by 1877, when Greene County's first Grange organized at Grapeville. From 1896 to 1900 there was a flurry of interest, with eight new organizations, at Jewett, North Settlement, Huntersfield, Little Westkill, Halcott Center, South Jewett, Ashland and Spruceton.[528]

The Grange had economic benefits—insurance plans, bulk buying, and other cooperative endeavors—and it offered its members cultural and educational benefits through lectures and programs. Most importantly, it provided a social outlet for isolated farmers at a time before radios or automobiles were common. Grangers attempted to keep the old cooperative spirit alive; the older folks had been raised on house- and barn-raisings, and most Grange halls were built by the members:

Smith Tompkins had a grove of hemlock from which he gave the rough lumber and James Hummel had a grove of oak from which he furnished the shingles. There was an old-fashioned bee and the labor was all contributed so that the only expense in the building to the [Huntersfield] Grange was the hardware, glass, etc. This was a two-story structure, the second floor to be the hall. The first floor was all enclosed, with stalls on the sides for stables, for in those days everyone drove horses.[529]

A similar organization, the Patrons of Industry, organized chapters in the valley towns about 1900. At Britt's Corners, Kiskatom, the Patrons of Industry dealt cooperatively in groceries, flour and feed, seed, meal, salt, etc., lapsing before 1915. But Patrons of Industry organizations at Staco, Climax and Hannacroix became Granges in 1918.[530]

By the end of World War I, with prices high, farming in Greene County had settled into distinct regional patterns. The Mountaintop was dairy country, with some potatoes and poultry in Windham. In the town of Hunter, "Farm products [were] largely used in providing for the summer guests." In the Catskill Valley moderate amounts of fruit were grown; Durham and Greenville were dairy towns, while Greenville and Cairo produced some small grains. Hay was grown throughout the valley. The river towns produced fruit, hay and grain; Athens, Coxsackie and New Baltimore also raised poultry, which was generally increasing.[531]

As in the nineteenth century, New York City was the principal market for Greene County farms, though produce went to Catskill and Hudson and the boarders consumed an increasing amount. The northeastern towns had begun to ship to Albany.[532]

During World War I, mechanization was still in the future. Only 16 farms had tractors and 28 had milking machines.[533]

Though the 1920s were a time of prosperity, the Depression hit the farmer long before the stock market crash. The abandonment of farms, especially the poorer ones on the mountaintop, accelerated, despite a small return flow from the cities during the worst of the Depression. The number of farms in Greene County dropped 26 percent in the 1920s and 1930s. The percentage of Greene County in farms (including unimproved land such as woodlots) dropped from 69 percent to 50 percent during this period.

Modernization hit the farm in the 1920s with the introduction of the tractor; at mid-decade one-third of Greene County farms had them. Roads were improved by scraping and with gravel; by 1938 25 percent of the farms were on paved roads. Electricity reached many farms. In 1930, Marion C. Albright, who farmed 167 acres in the village of Athens, had "forty separate and distinct electric machines and utensils in use on his farm and in his farm house, and he has a wealth of electric light, hence the place is commonly called the electric farm."[534] But even the small farm was likely to have a radio: 14 percent did in 1925.

Vernon Haskins of Durham Center remembered these times:

Seems like only yesterday that neighbors like Frank and Daniel Mackey and Everett Searing were making a good living on their 10-cow dairy farms. Maybe they didn't have a limousine, but they had a car that got them to town and back. Maybe they didn't have a TV, but neither did anyone else, then. They did have a radio and a 'phone as soon as anyone else, and they had three square meals a day.

Only three neighbors have been named, but they are typical of the general run of folks all up and down the valley. They were good neighbors, folks who had time to help one another buzz wood, thresh grain, or fill silo. They worked hard but they enjoyed life, too. Best of all, they were running their own business. Seems like now-a-days one must be big or get out of business. Sort of seems like business is running the farmer now.

In days gone by there was work for everyone right here at home, and we had time to visit one another once in a while; but shucks, now my neighbors commute 20, 30, maybe 40 miles to work. Seems to me they spend half their lifetime commutin' and half their wages on gas, oil and tires.[535]

Dairy farming remained important. The number of milk cows declined little over 20 years, while milk production increased 30 percent. Acreage in pasture and meadow was down to half its 1875 peak by 1935, with most of the loss in high elevations.

Creameries were larger and more modern. The Dairymen's League opened its new Catskill Creamery in 1925 and soon was processing the milk from 215 farms, at the rate of 300 forty-quart cans daily. The milk was weighed, pasteurized, put in sterilized bottles and shipped to New York every afternoon by fast express.[536] Ten such creameries in 1930 produced or processed milk, cream, butter, cheese, sour cream, soft cheese and skim milk powder.[537]

Specialty crops increased in value during the period. In 1930, market gardens sold $94,000 worth of produce. One of the major market farms was that of Cornell Vosburgh in Athens. Beginning in 1882 he developed a fine produce farm aimed at metropolitan markets. He took his farm wagon on the sunrise ferry to sell produce in Hudson, and he shipped specialty products such as fine tomatoes to New York City.

He was one of the first farmers to recognize the increased profit in roadside marketing. A crude log cabin at the head of his driveway was the first

Plowing with horses, Town of Greenville
Photograph, early 20th century
Collection of Greenville Town Historian

The tractor did not finally replace horses for plowing until during and after World War II.

173

farmstand, selling fruit and ice cream. In 1928 the Vosburghs built a stone structure in which they ran a tea room and sold chicken dinners and homemade pies.

The business shifted to nursery materials when the first greenhouses were built in 1931. Cornell's children James and Adelaide ran the business until the late 1970s.[538]

Fruit growing remained important during the years between the wars, although the production of the two major crops, apples and pears, both declined. Cairo was the center of fruit-growing, with 2,032 acres in 282 farms, but New Baltimore was close behind in acreage and had the largest individual orchards. Durham, Catskill, Athens, Coxsackie and Greenville each had more than 750 acres in fruit. Catskill's Edison Post Apple Products Company, incorporated in 1924, processed 100,000 barrels of apples into evaporated apples, cider and vinegar.[539]

A new specialty crop developed during the 1920s as the ice houses were abandoned. Alternative uses were sought for them, and it was found they were ideal for mushroom growing. Forty-two growers entered the business, at least eleven of them Cementon families; at Coxsackie and New Baltimore, the Knaust Brothers, Henry and Herman, became one of the world's largest growers of snow-white mushrooms. In 1937 Knaust built an addition and modernized:

> *The new plant was expected to increase the production to about 1,500 complete trays a day [27,000 pounds]. In the spring of 1938 the minimum daily production was estimated at 3,500 baskets and the maximum at 6,500. The new building contains 20 germinating rooms and one room is planted each day. The germinating trays, when ready, are taken to the icehouses, where they are arranged on both sides of the aisles in dark rooms with controlled temperature and where they remain until all the mushrooms have been picked. It takes six weeks from the time the germinating tray is prepared until the mushrooms can be picked and another six weeks until the tray has yielded all it can. The owners . . . market as many mushrooms as possible in baskets, with Chicago as about the limit in shipping distance. The surplus is canned in a factory belonging to the concern. . . .* [540]

Knaust Brothers employed 500 people in their new plant, and were believed to control 85 percent of the mushroom industry in the United States.

The poultry business grew substantially during the inter-war years. The number of chickens nearly tripled, while egg production increased 7 percent. With most poultry farms located in the Hudson Valley and Catskill Valley, Cairo was the center of the poultry business, having 285 farms raising nearly 20 percent of the county's chickens. White Leghorns and Barred Plymouth Rocks predominated. The summer demand was brisk for boardinghouses, though at Maplecrest a group of growers specialized in winter broilers.[541]

Small grains continued the rapid decline begun about 1880, until the period 1929-1934, when small gains in acreage were shown; but decreases resumed after that. The relative importance of the small grains—oats, buckwheat, rye, wheat and barley, in order of magnitude—remained essentially the same, except that a serious drop in rye after 1920 placed wheat in third place. Corn acreage was almost steady from 1910 to 1945, despite occasional dips during the period.[542]

Marketing of garden or "truck" produce, dominated by commission merchants for generations, was altered beginning in the 1920s. In addition to roadside stands, Greene County farmers sold to both chain and independent retailers, itinerants, the New York markets, and on their own retail routes. But regional markets developed after 1929, and the need for them was emphasized by low prices from 1931-34. The Capital District Regional Market at Menands was built by a farmers' cooperative in 1934; by 1943, Greene County farmers sold 80 percent of their vegetables and 19 percent of their fruit by value, in addition to poultry and eggs, flowers and plants, at Menands. Growers rented stalls in the market; other alternatives were the farmers' markets in Albany, Schenectady and Troy. The regional market was the outlet for about one third of the vegetables grown in the region.[543]

Farm co-operation was strong, particularly during the 1920s. Though the Grange was still active at the time of World War I, the war mobilization was "the greatest single factor" in the organization of the Farm Bureau here in 1917. The Bureau gave aid in the organization of co-operatives of farmers at Windham, Coxsackie and Athens in its first three years of existence. Among its other early programs were the eradication of bovine tuberculosis as well as fruit spraying services. It assisted in the formation of some of the farmers' associations and breeders' clubs which became important during the 1920s: Guernsey, Jersey and sheep breeders' clubs, the Dairy Improvement Association, and Dairymen's League, and the Horticultural Society of Greene County. At Cornwallville, a cooperative for "thrashing" grain formed in 1925.[544]

In 1924 the Pomona Grange sponsored the first Greene County Picnic or "farmers' picnic": "A Day When Country and City Kids, Old and Young Kids, Can All Lay Aside Care and Have a Good Time Together." Nine of the other agricultural organizations were also sponsors, including the Greene County Agricultural Society. It certainly suggests an attempt to reclaim the agricultural patronage the county fair had lost: a horseshoe pitching contest was a perennial feature of the picnic, which continued for several decades.[545]

Between 1930 and 1935, the number of farms increased by 11 percent, perhaps due partly to families returning to farming. Some bartering took place, too: the Schmidts of Leeds remembered that apples grown in the valley were swapped for potatoes grown on the Mountaintop. But the decade ended with a net loss of farms. Census statistics of 1940 show 187 abandoned or idle farms in the county; the poor condition of the land was cited as the cause for abandonment of nearly half the farms.[546]

The war effort brought new capital to agriculture, as well as an increased use of rubber-tired tractors and silo filling equipment. Agricultural technology was applied more and more by the farmers themselves. During the decade land in farms declined from 50 percent to 41 percent of the county; the number of farms declined 22 percent, the number of acres harvested 27 percent.

In the middle of the decade, as the war ended, some staple crops were higher than they had been five years earlier. Hogs doubled, chickens and eggs increased sharply, corn and the small grains were up substantially as were potatoes, the number of milk cows increased slightly and gallons of milk hit a figure last seen about 1910. Vegetable sales peaked at $98,000.

Apples and pears, however, in a decline since 1935, continued to drop, but most other fruits and berries also increased slightly from 1940 to 1945. The value of horticultural specialties sold, however, was the real success story of the decade: $4,868 sold in 1940 became nearly a million dollars in sales in 1945 and over two million in 1950.[547]

Modern facilities became the norm on Greene County farms. By the war's end 72 percent had running water, 87 percent had electricity, 90 percent had radios, and 61 percent had a telephone. Farms with tractors were up to 45 percent, and that statistic offers the clue for trends after the war.

By the end of World War II any farm that had not begun to mechanize was in danger of being left behind in the competition for profits. Increasing numbers of Greene County farmers worked off the farm for part of their income. In 1935 only 28 percent did so, working 24,797 days. While the percentage of farmers working "off" remained the same for years, the number of days they received pay off the farm increased rapidly: 60,723 days in 1940, and 83,122 days in 1945. But the percentage also began climbing after V-J Day. By 1949, 36 percent of Greene County farmers worked off the farm: paychecks exceeded farm income for 79 percent of the group.[548]

The 1950s and the 1960s were the period of rapid decline for Greene County farming. For one thing, the young farmers of the World War I era, the last to start out without tractors or large capital investments, were reaching retirement age and their farms were not sufficiently viable to pass on to the next generation. Electrical and mechanical power replaced human labor. In 1960s and 1970s large equipment proliferated: kicker bailers, haybines, forage wagons and more powerful tractors. In the mid 1960s creameries delivered a death blow to many small dairy farms when they demanded refrigerated bulk tanks be used for milk on the farm.

The number of farms declined a sharp 71 percent and the harvested acreage a like amount. At the start of the period 41 percent of the county was still in farmland, but only 19 percent remained in 1969.

In 1950, 41 percent of Greene County's 1300 farms were dairy operations, 16 percent were in poultry, and 1 percent in fruit. There were five farms each that raised field crops, vegetables, or cash grains. Many farms, of course were "general," mixed or unclassified.[549]

The period witnessed a major exodus of agricultural labor to off-farm jobs. By 1954 nearly half of Greene County farms depended upon off-farm income, with almost all of them exceeding farm income in their outside paychecks.[550]

With the decline in farms and land, the number of cows decreased a substantial 53 percent, although the weight of milk per cow continued to increase. There were six milk plants left in the county, three each on the Mountaintop and in the valley.[551] Corn acreage held its own, losing only 20 percent, but the small grains diminished to insignificance. Chicken and egg production began declining after 1954, with the chickens dropping faster than the eggs.

In the valley, mushroom plants continued to produce vast quantities. Only 22 farms were producing apples in 1969, a far cry from the 1,734 producers 40 years earlier. Peaches, pears and plums remained a side crop. Berries declined to a single acre on a single farm by 1974.

The number of farms in Greene County continued to decline in the seventies and eighties, though at a less precipitous rate—26 percent—since most of the non-viable operations were eliminated by the late 1960s. Hay held its own, while orchards declined from 22 to 17, with an even steeper decrease in acreage. Vegetable farms decreased from 16 to 11 but acreage increased substantially.

The number of cows continued to drop; the number of dairy farms has fluctuated between 45 and 50 in recent years. Sheep-growing saw an increase in the 1980s, with over twenty small sheep farms in the county.[552]

There are still about 250 farms in Greene County with an average investment of $200,000 in land and buildings. Each farm has on the average 222 acres. Total county land in farms is 68,000 acres or 17 percent of the land area. The New York State Agricultural Districts Law has provided a procedure for the creation of agricultural districts, of which there are four in Greene, totalling 28,907 acres. The largest areas of viable farmland today are the Embought, the Coxsackie Correctional Facility, Kiskatom Flats, western New Baltimore, Norton Hill, large parts of Durham, sections of Ashland, the Little Westkill, and the Halcott Valley.[553] ❧

CHAPTER 44
STATE LAND

*D*uring the years prior to World War I, public land became a part of Greene County's landscape. Greene County has a large percentage of its land in state forest preserve, and a New York City Water Supply aqueduct also traverses the county. The forces which created this vast public resource were set in motion while the Revolutionary War was still being fought.

In 1779 the new state passed the Act of Attainder, which confiscated all lands of the Crown and of Loyalists within the borders of New York. Five years later, "An Act to encourage the settlement of the waste and unappropriated lands within the state" established a procedure for the sale of state lands.[554] The word "waste" in the second act is significant, for it is emblematic of the low esteem wild forests were given at the time; but the two acts did create a bank of state lands.

Scientific farmers had begun to recognize the risks of clear-cutting forests, for in 1791 the Society for the Promotion of Agriculture, Arts and Manufactures recommended the study of a system of tree planting to reforest the small portions of the Adirondacks which had already been stripped bare of their trees.[555] In the Catskills the damages became visible as the tannery business boomed; aside from tannery pollution, the loss of forest cover caused the water temperature to rise and the fish in mountain streams to disappear. By the 1850s Americans, who were starting to engineer water supplies, began to recognize the importance of forests for that purpose.

In 1872 the State established a Commission of State Parks, which reported a year later on the need for "immediate protection," but was quickly forgotten. Yellowstone became the first National Park in the same year. During the late 1870s the price of timber soared, further threatening the surviving forests; and in 1883 an attempt to open Yellowstone to logging raised public concern.

The State took action soon after, for the Erie Canal was a major state asset and its navigability was threatened if it silted as a result of further depletion of the forests. The members of the Forestry Commission, a successor to the Commission of State Parks, reported in 1885 with the same recommendation as in 1872, though they thought the Catskills were a low priority because the "merchantable timber" was already gone. They reported:

The forests of the Catskill region are not unlike in actual condition those covering the hills which mark the southern limits of the Adirondack plateau. The merchantable timber and the hemlock bark were long ago cut, and fires have more than once swept over the entire region, destroying the reproductive powers of the forest as originally composed and ruining the fertility of the thin soil, covering the hills. The valleys have now, however, all been cleared for farms, and forest fires consequently occur less frequently than formerly. A stunted and scrubby growth of trees is gradually repossessing the hills, which, if strictly protected, may sooner or later develop into a comparatively valuable forest. The protection of these forests is, however, of less general importance than the preservation of the Adirondack forests. The possibility of their yielding merchantable timber again in any considerable quantities is at best remote; and they guard no streams of more than local influence. Their real value consists in increasing the beauties of summer resorts, which are of great importance to the people of the State.[556]

An act passed by the 1885 session created the state forest preserve; a constitutional amendment of 1892 designated it as "forever wild."

Meanwhile, political machinations brought Catskill lands into the preserve. An act of 1879 required counties to acquire all lands not sold for arrears of taxes, and to pay the state the taxes due. An Ulster legislator objected to this turn of events; he was elected to the Assembly, and he secured passage of a bill which repealed the 1879 law and conveyed Ulster County's surplus lands to the forest preserve.

In 1899 the state passed an appropriation of $50,000 "for the purpose of acquiring land to extend the forest preserve in the Catskills." Five years later

Burning of the Catskill Mountain House
Photograph, January 25, 1963
Collection of Edward G. West

In accordance with the New York State policy of "Forever Wild," when the Mountain House land was acquired by the State, the remains of the old hotel were destroyed.

The aqueduct under construction near Prattsville
Photograph, 1917-1924
Collection of New York Power Authority

The construction of the Shandaken Tunnel to carry the aqueduct from the Schoharie to the Esopus was one of the incursions of state government control into western Greene County early in this century.

the forest preserve land became a part of the Catskill Park, designated as a resource for public recreation though not necessarily state-owned like the preserve.[557]

Five bond issues in this century have permitted the extension of state-owned forest preserve land in Greene County. Funds expended through 1907 allowed the purchase of the east slopes of Stony Clove. A 1916 bond issue, in use through 1927, was used to purchase many of the high peaks. The 1924 bond issue secured 72,000 acres in the Catskills for an average price of $9.59, including the old Mountain House Park in 1930. The 1962 bond act, in use through 1971, bought 12,000 acres, averaging $37.10. And the 1972 bond act permitted the acquisition of 23,203 acres in its first decade.[558]

The growing thirst of New York City created another class of protected lands. In the spring of 1905 the state legislature created a state and municipal water commission, which presented its original report in October of the same year. It proposed that the Rondout and Schoharie watersheds be developed to supplement the Esopus, on which work began. The Catskill watershed was also part of the original plan: four reservoirs on the Catskill Creek at East Durham, Oak Hill, Preston Hollow and Franklinton were shown on the original 1905 plan but fortunately were never built.[559]

Esopus water was sent to New York City in 1915. In that year Gallt observed that the "great dam" on the Schoharie, 150 feet high, would wipe out forty large farms and the entire village of Prattsville some time in the following eight years. But the Board of Water Supply discovered—just in time for Prattsville—that by placing the dam at Gilboa, the watershed area would increase from 226 to 314 square miles and the storage capacity from 9-1/2 to 20 billion gallons; the Schoharie could yield 250 million gallons a day. The amended plan was approved in the summer of 1916, and the dam contract was awarded in June 1919.[560]

To move the water from the Schoharie to the Esopus, the Shandaken Tunnel was constructed betweeen 1917 and 1924. This 18.1 mile tunnel from the reservoir northwest of Prattsville through the Town of Lexington to Allaben, Ulster County, was the longest in the world of any kind at the time it was completed.[561] The Schoharie Reservoir, which inundated only a few acres of Greene County below Prattsville, was completed in 1927.

The Schoharie water project came at a time when Greene County was losing population dramatically. From 1910 to 1920 the county lost 15 percent of its population, and every town except Prattsville and Lexington—where water supply construction was happening—lost at least 10 percent. Prattsville and Lexington grew modestly, but then lost population during the 1920s.

The appropriation of land and land rights by the City of New York for its water supply came back to life in the late 1980s with the promulgation of new regulations which, some farmers claimed, would have required diapers on their dairy cows. An unusually strong grassroots movement, centered in Delaware County, secured a compromise from the city in 1992.

It was not the first time Greene County residents had organized to fight outside interests. The Association for the Preservation of Durham Valley came together in 1970 to fight a proposed transmission line from the Gilboa dam to Leeds. In the late 1980s, one of the most notable citizens' movements was the opposition to new landfills, made necessary when the old town dumps were declared dangerous. In Durham where a dump site had been identified hand-painted cartoon signs appeared on trees and telephone poles. The issue, which probably cannot be resolved to everyone's satisfaction, did spur a broad-based interest in and support of recycling, which began in 1989.[562] ❦

CHAPTER 45
RESORTS

*T*hough boardinghouses were scattered thickly all over the county at the end of World War I, the seeds of change were everywhere. The automobile grew in importance to American life through the decade, and during the 1920s it transformed the vacation business: in 1925 a Catskill newspaper reported, "No special demonstration marked Labor Day, but it is estimated that between 8,000 and 10,000 cars passed through Catskill."[563]

Guests were no longer willing to stay in one place, at least not without the provision of extensive recreational facilities. The change was slow but, through the 1920s and 1930s, the effect could be seen on the Mountaintop where there was less demand for food and hired help. Many Jewett residents moved away to find new means of employment. While Cairo charted continuous growth, and several other towns gained in the 1930s, most towns remained static. But Jewett lost 12 percent of its population during the decade.[564]

The large hotels, in particular, were affected. They had come into being to serve a predominantly Anglo-American clientele and, for generations, American "society" had summered at the Catskill Mountain House. Through the 1920s the Mountain House carried on, though there are signs that its fortunes were declining. About 1920 the Kaaterskill Hotel became the property of Harry Tannenbaum, who renovated it and carried it through "its most prosperous season ever," catering to the newer ethnic markets, but it burned a week after the close of its 1924 season in a fast, sensational fire.[565]

Meanwhile Jews who had favored Tannersville for almost 30 years were joined by Armenians, Greeks, Syrians and Italians, and boardinghouses in the Town of Hunter took on various ethnic identities. The Sunset Park Inn was one of the larger surviving institutions that made this shift; it catered to Armenians in its later years, and its last owner, after 1958, was Greek.[566] The Mountain House itself was leased to three brothers in the 1930s who revitalized it to some extent with a Kosher kitchen, making it a forerunner of the Sullivan County resorts of the postwar period.[567]

As ethnicity in the resorts increased, boardinghouse owners made desperate attempts to maintain the old character of their resorts. An advertising brochure for "Windham Township . . . Season of 1921" advised potential visitors that "Attendance . . . upon religious services of all Christian denominations may be enjoyed," which was a kind of code language to encourage Gentile trade, if not to discourage Jewish visitors. In Cairo, where dozens of boardinghouses were operating for generations, many had assumed distinct Italian or German identities during the 1920s and 1930s. Advertising usually carried the tag lines "Near All Churches," "Christian House," or "Gentiles."

Promoters were well aware of the threats to their businesses. A Cairo brochure published shortly before World War II observed that "Many people think they are having a vacation and all they do is rush from one place to another . . . " On a more positive note, the brochure described the attractions of Cairo:

> Cairo is situated in a fine farming section that assures you as a visitor, an abundance of fresh vegetables, pure milk, fruit, eggs and poultry. . . . The social life of Cairo and vicinity is one of its chief attractions. Interhouse dances, many of which are of the masquerade type, to which guests from other hotels and boarding houses are invited, form one of the popular evening pastimes.[568]

At the same time, there were new developments in Greene County's seasonal business. As agriculture declined further, farmers in the more prosperous farming districts took in boarders the way others had done two generations earlier. The northern tier of towns, especially New Baltimore, Greenville and Durham, saw the growth of their business, as Cairo expanded as a destination. Greenville in particular had few boardinghouses before World War I, but soon afterward it boomed. Gerald Ingalls, in a 1990 interview, described the growth of his Ingalside Farm resort at West Greenville:

> My dad . . . decided to become a farmer so in 1913 we moved here. My mother had taken boarders with my two aunts and in 1913 some of those people walked here to see if they could get a chicken dinner and of course got one. That decided them they could make a couple dollars and go into the boarding business. In 1914 they took a few and it graduated in 1920 when they did the house over taking about 20-25 people, quite a number then. In 1924, Ingalside burned down on Christmas Day. Then it was built over. My dad was a little ahead of his time—he put a rec hall in. He also had running water.[569]

Ingalside was one of the first of the large Greenville resorts; it was the first to put in a pool, in 1933. Ingalls remembers that the boarders were nearly all Irish.

Meanwhile, a few miles away, the boardinghouses at East Durham began to draw Irish New Yorkers. By the late 1920s the Ferncliff House established itself as an Irish resort, the forerunner of the many large Irish boardinghouses

Hayride at Willow Brook Farm
Photographed by Coursen of Cairo,
July 12, 1929
Collection of the Greene County
Historical Society

which began to dominate the village during the 1930s.[570]

The Police Recreation Farm and the Blarr Health Farm were also 1920s phenomena. In late 1920 the New York City Police Commissioner, looking for a place to send physically ill members of policemen's families, bought 332 acres near Elka Park and built a hotel, "Mountain Rest," with accommodations for 50 families; it burned in 1921 and was replaced the following year by a fireproof building. It served for over sixty years, though its name changed to the New York Police Centre. Today it is home to the Hutterian Bruderhof, a group of Christian communitarians based at Rifton, Ulster County.[571]

Catherine Maier Blarr, a naturopath and chiropractor, purchased a 110-acre farm at Medway and remodelled it into the Blarr Health Farm, offering exercise and wholesome food to 60-75 boarders at $16-$18 a week. It thrived until the end of the 1942 season when Blarr sold out; it is now Silver Lake Farm.[572]

The Depression affected Catskill tourism. George Meyer reported in 1937:

> . . . in the past five years times have been hard. Summer visitors were scarce. The region lacked modern hotels and business did not warrant their erection. For a decade, each year had seen two or three hotels destroyed by fire, or torn down to escape taxation. These were never replaced.[573]

But the newer-style resorts grew modestly, especially in the northern tier of towns. Other parts of the county remained untouched by the business. Oriana Atkinson noted that "in 1928 there were no boardinghouses in Oak Hill (nor today), but then there was a sizeable one on a side road . . . "and, a mile away, at her village of Durham, "we have no boarding houses and we like it that way."[574] Her preferences were clear. "One small town near us"—East Durham is strongly implied—"has gradually assumed a reputation for drunkenness and general cutupishness among the visitors."[575]

Through the 1930s dancing and drinking became a growing part of the attraction of many Catskill resorts. Jack Robinson, who had a five-piece band that played at Mountaintop resort hotels from 1931 to 1938, remembered these days:

> Just about every boardinghouse and hotel had a live band, although the Mountain House and Sunset Inn were the only ones left with concert music. We played eleven concerts and three dances every week from Memorial Day until a week past Labor Day. . . .
>
> Cairo, Leeds and Durham had forty hotels and bars with live music. East Windham had a seven-piece orchestra from Cornell, my alma mater. Osborn's in Windham always had a good band, too.
>
> Palenville was a lively place with dancing and a show at the Central House and a fine dance band at Intermann's at the foot of Palenville Mountain."[576]

The Catskill Mountain House struggled on through the poor economic climate and the changing tastes. A visitor in the summer of 1941 remembered an unforgettable image from that second-to-last season:

> [O]n the huge veranda of the hotel a twenty-piece band in blazoned uniforms of scarlet and gold played round after round of polkas and waltzes as elderly visitors sat in the shade of the nearby trees and a happy throng of swirling, chattering youngsters spilled from the veranda to the green swath of lawn along the mountain's edge. It was one of the last images of a long fading elegance, soon to be gone forever.[577]

After its final season in 1942, banker Milo Claude Moseman, who had assumed ownership during the Depression, did everything in his power to preserve the hotel pending its sale to a responsible agency or philanthropic institution. He opened negotiations with the State which, however, was interested only in land. A hurricane in November 1950 took most of the columns and, late in 1951, hoping to secure funds for restoration of the original building, Moseman sold the wings for salvage, and began feverish plans for its rejuvenation.

But nothing was actually accomplished. He died in 1958; four years later the State purchased the remnant of the Mountain House and its surrounding park. And on January 25, 1963, the New York State Conservation Department burned it to the ground.

As the boardinghouses and hotels declined and the resorts with bars, dancing, pool and tennis grew increasingly important, tourist attractions made their appearance in Greene County, catering to the visitors who now arrived predominantly by automobile. The Catskill Game Farm was among the

Waitresses at the Balsam Shade, Greenville
Photograph, Summer of 1943
Collection of Harriet Rasmussen

In the town of Greenville, boardinghouses expanded into elaborate resorts, such as the one which employed these local women. Left to right: Bernice Cameron, "Skip" Covenhoven, Mary Felter, and Doris Lamb.

Summer tourists on the street outside
Austin's Drug Store, now
26 Main Street, <u>Cairo</u>
Photograph, c.1913
Collection of Robert Uzzilia

The hack driver is Grover Parks.

first, begun by Roland Lindemann in 1933; it extended the tourist season by opening April 15 and closing November 15.[578]

After World War II, addressing the "tourist slump," a group of Saugerties and Mountaintop businessmen planned "Rip's Retreat" near Haines Falls. Organizing in October 1953 they managed to open it in May 1954, well in advance of the 1955 Thruway completion which was anticipated would bring tourists. Rip's Retreat was "essentially commercial but based on historical, educational and recreational features." It included a colonial village reconstruction with craft demonstrations. Rip was on hand "in the bewhiskered person of Samuel Logan Sanderson, onetime University of Pennsylvania professor turned actor," replaced in the third season by "Hypie" Hoyt of Hunter. As hard as it is to believe today, we are assured by a 1953 newspaper that:

> A bowling green will be located in the center of the area, with traditional drawfs [dwarfs] on hand to set up pins for young and old to try their skill at this old-time sport.[576]

"Rip's Retreat" operated through the 1960 season and was auctioned to the Nature Conservancy, which sold the land to New York State.[580]

More recently, Carson City near Lawrenceville and the Zoom Flume near Cornwallville have offered organized amusement to summer vacationers and other travellers.

Other visitors, though they avoided the attractions and were the least likely to stay at the great resorts, continued the Victorian tradition of mountain walks. The formation of Catskill Park, the purchase of forest reserve land, and the restoration of woods and streams, made the Greene County Mountaintop an ideal destination for the growing number of recreational hikers, campers, hunters and fishers, who used the automobile to increase their mobility. The State, in its development of Catskill Park, improved trails and provided shelters. It also licensed and regulated hunting and fishing. Fly fishing, suited for mountain streams, was introduced to the Catskills in the 1890s. The late Art Flick of Lexington helped to disseminate knowledge about the sport, and is acknowledged as the dean of Catskill fly fishermen.

During the postwar period there were again signs of change in Greene County's resort business. The peak years were 1945 and 1946, in each of which 500,000 persons visited Greene and Ulster.[581] Americans, relieved of the war's burden, took advantage of old familiar places and existing facilities. Once recovery was underway, new trends asserted themselves.

The motel began to replace the tourist court and the boardinghouse in the early 1950s. Since the Depression and the War had affected modernization, many of the newest resorts were then 25 years old, and seemed dated to the generation that had survived the war. As early as 1953 the developers of Rip's Retreat characterized the situation as a "tourist slump" and, in 1955, a study noted "The industry as a whole is not healthy . . ."[582]

Yet ethnic enclaves had prospered. East Durham was in its heyday in the 1950s, with Irish bands playing the pubs and dance halls along Route 145 and the country roads.[583] Germans and Italians still favored Cairo, Purling and Round Top, where Bavarian Manor was establishing a self-conscious German identity. The larger resorts around Greenville expanded, including Shepard's, Ingalside, and Baumann's. Pleasant View Lodge, Friar Tuck, and Sugar Maples all maintained strong bookings. Along the Rip Van Winkle Trail the kitchens advertised American, Jewish, Italian, German, Viennese, French, Scandanavian, Greek, Armenian, Polish and Hungarian food![584]

New York City remained the source of most guests in the 1960s, although a few resorts cited New Jersey and Long Island as their main markets. Secondary markets for Greene County's resorts included Boston, Rochester, and New England.[585]

Unemployment off-season remained a problem. A low 4.2 percent rate in August gave way to 15 percent in February.[586] ❦

CHAPTER 46
SKIS

*T*he revitalization of the Greene County resort industry rested upon a sport that was barely known before the War. Curtis Jones operated a ski run on his Rising Sun Farm near Climax starting in 1927. It was open to the public on weekends without charge, and Curtis and his wife Ethel sold hot dogs and homemade pies to the skiers. As many as 200 people skied there on a busy weekend.

In 1932 the Olympic Games were held at Lake Placid. The skiing competition stimulated interest in the sport, and construction of small ski areas was soon underway in the mountains of the Northeast. According to George Meyer, "For a long time there had been talk about winter sports in the Catskills, but nothing was ever done. Community spirit and leadership seemed to be lacking."[587]

About 1935 a group of Civilian Conservation Corps members built a few ski trails in Phoenicia, in nearby Ulster County. George Meyer again:

> *Before anyone knew what was happening, Phoenicia became a boom town overnight. New York City journals gave columns of publicity to the village. Planes flew up to rush back pictures for publication. The railroads started running special snow trains and Phoenicia, unprepared, was unable to cope with the crowds that flocked there. What few hotels the village had were filled and private homes were called upon to accommodate the visitors.*[588]

At this point Tannersville went into action. They purchased Rip Van Winkle Lake and obtained a WPA grant to dredge it for both summer and winter use. They quickly completed a 2,000 foot ski run behind the lake, and made plans for a toboggan slide and club house, all to be ready for the winter of 1938. It did not last long.[589]

By about the same time Cairo developed a series of open slopes and trails along with a rope tow and an open slope, and began to advertise skiing as one of its attractions. By 1950 the Cairo Chamber of Commerce had a Sports Committee, which began to develop plans; Haines Falls talked about constructing a slope; the "Rip Van Winkle Slope" at the Timberlane Ski Ranch at East Jewett offered a 450-foot rope tow and a 1200-foot drop.[590] The

Birdseye advertising view of
Timberlane Ranch, East Jewett
Lithograph, c.1948
Collection of Haines Falls Free Library

One of the county's first ski slopes is
noted on this cartoon-like view of a
Mountaintop resort.

Princeton Ski Bowl on Bearpen Mountain near Little Westkill was in operation
by the mid 1950s. Skiing cost $3 a day.[591]

In the late 1950s the State, recognizing the growing demand for skiing
facilities within an easy drive of the New York metropolitan area, began to
consider its options in the Catskills. Reports released in 1957 and 1958 were
pessimistic: the slopes were rocky, they were steep above 2,000 feet, and the
snow cover was less reliable than in the Adirondacks.

In Hunter, a group of businessmen were searching at the same time for
an idea which would boost the sagging economy. Local contractor Orville
Slutzky suggested a ski area. The community decided to offer a mountain to
any developer willing to create a ski area. They placed an advertisement in *The
New York Times*, and the ski columnist from the *Herald Tribune* wrote a story
about the extraordinary offer.

Backed by the Hammerstein family, the Slutzkys began excavation in the
spring of 1959. Hunter Mountain Ski Bowl opened in January of 1960, with
two Savio chairlifts and snowmaking already in place. The Hammersteins
failed after three years and, in 1962, Orville and his brother Israel took over
and built Hunter Mountain into a world-class resort: so much so, that the
name "Hunter Mountain" is under license in Japan. It is particularly known
for its large snow-making capacity.[592]

Nearby, in Windham, C.D. Lane suggested Cave Mountain to the State of
New York for a state-built recreation center in 1958. Before a decision could
be made, the Macomber family purchased it and opened Cave Mountain Ski
Slope in December of 1960. Three years later they sold out to the Sheridan
family, which expanded it as Ski Windham. In 1967 they created the private

Skiers at summit of Ski Windham
Photograph, 1992
Courtesy of Ski Windham

Windham Mountain Club, which excluded non-members from its slopes. As a result, many of the affluent families investing the steep fees in the club chose to build or purchase vacation homes in the town, creating further contrasts between Windham and Hunter. In 1981 the slope went public as Ski Windham, but it retained its good reputation for both skiing and facilities.[593]

The last of the three present-day slopes is Cortina Valley, developed by Aldo DiBelardino about 1977.[594] Among the three busy slopes, more than half a million skiers enjoy Greene County each winter. ❦

Skiers on slope at Hunter Mountain
Photograph, c.1965
Courtesy of Hunter Mountain

CHAPTER 47
HOME AWAY FROM HOME

*T*hough the residential parks had offered Mountaintop homes for purely seasonal use, this kind of non-resident ownership was insignificant in Greene County for many years. The decline in fashionability of the grand hotels and the rise of the automobile, along with the affluence of the 1920s, resulted in the creation of a number of vacation homes or even year-round country retreats by well-heeled Anglo Americans, foreshadowing the more universal appeal in the last quarter century.

Among the first of these retreats was a Neo-Grecian house on Clum Hill near Tannersville, built by Welles Bosworth, Rockefeller's architect, in 1910. Another was the "Castle" on Potic Mountain near Leeds. This 36-by-80-foot mansion, three stories with an attic, was designed by Wilfred Buckland and was built for the Grier sisters of Canada in 1913. Margaret Grier married Sir Ion Hamilton Benn, M.P. Later it was sold to Mr. William B. McGoldrick of the New York office of Pierce and Pierce Ltd., a London firm. It burned in the late 1970s. A third large summer residence was the huge stone house, "Bailiwick," built near Catskill about 1920 by the eccentric, Everett Shinn; he lived there only briefly.[595]

One of the grandest of the country retreats was the Colgate place at East Kill above East Jewett. A commercial stock farm established in 1886, it was purchased by Gilbert Colgate from the heirs of the original owners in 1916 and developed into the several-thousand-acre "Black Dome Farm." It passed to his son Robert in 1933. He continued the farm operation until his death, and his executors sold the land for Forest Preserve in 1976.[596]

Brooks and Oriana Atkinson also represented this movement of individuals into the country; they bought their place near Durham in 1928. She began her search through the Strout Farm catalogue:

I looked quickly into the Catalogue to find something in South Durham that an aged owner could no longer handle. All the aged owners in South Durham seemed to be sitting tight. But a place called "Oak Hill" in the same general vicinity seemed to be more open to persuasion. The Strout Farm agent in Oak Hill, N.Y. was a Mr. John Huyck. . . . [He] answered me politely and said he had a list of attractive places at unbelievably low prices in and around Oak Hill that he would be proud and happy to show me. . . . [597]

Liftside Condos, Hunter
Advertising brochure, 1993
Courtesy of Liftside Resorts, Inc.

After making her way to Oak Hill which, she discovered, had no rail service, she set off with Mr. Huyck in search of just the right run-down farm: preferably one, she said, with a view, and a little brook. Many had one or the other:

> She wants a brook, Mr. Huyck said, apologetically. "Brooks," the farmer told me, "is ALWAYS in hollers. Can't have a brook AND a view."[598]

The Atkinson place on Prink Hill near Durham was a 111-acre farm which "had not produced anything but thin haycrops for a long time." Brooks Atkinson, a critic with *The New York Times*, and his wife Oriana brought the farm back with fields of grass and clover, reforesting other portions with red pine seedlings from the state tree nursery.[599]

More modest attempts to provide vacation homes were made as well. Silver Lake at East Windham was being laid out in streets and sections by a Brooklyn company in 1926. Nearby, the Durso Brothers created about 51 lots on the State Road in 1929, mostly 50 by 100 feet. Neither of these developments amounted to much. But the trend was there. The population of the county, which had decreased 14.6 percent between 1910 and 1920 as more farms were abandoned, held steady during the 1920s, actually gaining 12 people. Cornwallville, which was largely bypassed by the boardinghouse business, is an example of a community that drew families as summer residents. William Borthwick's 1927 census of its residents noted about one-third of the houses were used only in the summer.[600]

The Depression halted the development of both grand country estates and the modest bungalow communities. A few people who had vacationed in the Catskills moved up for the duration of the Depression: Claude Soehl as an example. A mechanical engineer for the International Projector Company, he moved to Hensonville. He planted a large garden, did a lot of canning, ran a taxi service using his car, and worked part-time as a tinsmith at the local hardware store. But when conditions improved, he moved back to New York City.[601] Overall the county's population increased 8.2 percent during the decade.

Several new ethnic groups arrived in the 1940s and early 1950s and established footholds. A community of Norwegian pentecostalists from Brooklyn began building summer homes at North Lexington during World War II; by 1951 they had enough of a year-round population to support a church and a pastor. In that year the first Ukrainian family, the Kobziars, came to the Lexington and Jewett region. By 1961 the Ukrainian community built their spectacular Church of St. John the Baptist, serving primarily a seasonal community, although many Ukrainians too retired to the Mountaintop.[602]

Population increases chart the shift from resort life to second- and retirement-home buyers in the postwar years. The 1950s witnessed a 9.1 percent increase, larger than that of the 1930s, but in the 1960s the population growth slowed to 5.6 percent. It was in the 1970s and 1980s that retirement, commutation to Albany and Kingston, and a limited reflection of the "back to the land" spirit of the time resulted in 20 percent increases in each of the decades.[603]

The flashiest sign of this movement was the creation of Sleepy Hollow Lake, on the Athens-Coxsackie border, beginning in 1971. United States Properties bought 1,898 acres and carved out 1,651 lots and an artificial lake:

> *The first lots were offered for sale while work was still under way on damming Murderer's Creek to create a 323-acre lake. In the selling stages, people drove for hours to see a manmade lake and to accept the gifts, boatrides and entertainment promised in mailings. There was a menagerie, a chuckwagon, a nursery, and a man dressed in a Rip Van Winkle costume who handed out balloons when not sleeping under a tree or otherwise creating atmosphere.*[604]

Three-quarters of the lots were sold, mostly to residents of New York City and its suburbs, before liens were filed against the developer in June 1974. Only 26 houses were begun before the development collapsed, passing through a series of financial reorganizations. In 1984 *The New York Times* carried an advertisement for a "Lake Lot Liquidation Sale" at $3,900 each.[605] Today, an office just off site continues to market the lots in the functioning, though still embryonic, community.

In 1971 studies of migration and employment showed Greene County was no longer an isolated area with a resort-based economy. New York City and vicinity was the point of origin for 32 percent of the residents, and Albany for 4 percent; migrants from elsewhere numbered 27 percent of the population. Greene County provided employment for 67 percent of its people, but 18 percent went to Albany County, and 5 percent to Ulster. Small numbers went to Columbia, Dutchess, Schoharie, Delaware and elsewhere.[606]

The 1980s were the decade during which development proceeded unchecked. Prior to 1980 high interest rates held back both development and sales. In the early 1980s interest rates dropped, and urban residents from New York City and vicinity looked north where land prices were cheap relative to such traditional destinations as Vermont and eastern Long Island.

This interest was spurred by a new approach to land marketing by two out-of-state land sale companies, the Patten Corporation and Land Properties of America. They had working capital and expertise. They began to seek land to acquire and develop, and to aggressively market the land. Both entered the Greene County market around 1982-83, at which time only two towns in the county had zoning in place.

Several conditions affected their subdivisions. The Health Department must approve any subdivision with five or more lots under five acres in size: so many developments were divided into 5.1 acre lots. Long, narrow lots called "bacon strips" obviate the construction of additional roads.

The pace of development was relatively constant for the first few years, accelerating substantially in 1984, during which over 300 lots were created on the Mountaintop, a number exceeded a second time in 1986.[607]

In addition to these badly planned, traditional developments, the Town of Windham especially was the target of builders creating vacation condominiums. The Quads, for example, opened in 1985 with units selling at $70,500, but the hot market sent prices to $99,000 within two years before the market went bust near the decade's end. Early in 1992 unsold units were auctioned.[608]

When the 1990 census figures were released, it became obvious that Greene had been through a boom. It showed a higher percentage of growth than any adjacent county. Only Hunter lost population. In Coxsackie, which had recently acquired a Thruway interchange, population increased nearly 27 percent. Jewett, the target of much of the Mountaintop subdivision, jumped 29 percent, and Halcott, whose tiny population was augmented by retirees, went up 26 percent. And these numbers do not include the seasonal occupants of the many second homes.[609]

While business recession from 1989 through 1992 slowed development in Greene County, the evidence of recent history suggests that only effective planning and consistent, enforced regulations on development can prevent the imposition of a haphazard, suburbia-like patchwork of new construction in both valley and Mountaintop. Greene County stands at a crossroads. With nearly 350 years of European settlement, its character during the next century or more may be decided before the end of the decade. ❦

Notes

1. Beers, 17-19.
2. Beecher (1991), 12.
3. *GCHJ* 11:32; Parker, 567-68.
4. *Ibid.*, 567.
5. Brasser, 198-99
6. *Ibid.*
7. Juet, 31-33.
8. Kammen, 17; Beers, 301.
9. Myers, 22; Brasser, 205-06; Beers, 94.
10. Kammen, 16; Beers, 115.
11. Beers, 29,95,102,117,289.
12. Prout, 77,124; Vedder (1927), 23; Pinckney, 74; Beers, 318.
13. *Ibid.*, 265.
14. Greene County Planning Department, *Catskill Residential Parks,* 7.
15. Jameson, 206.
16. Beers, 24; for a more in-depth exploration of van der Donck's activity as sheriff, see Van Gastel, 69-70.
17. Beers, 87,106; Gehring, 387-88.
18. Cohen (1981), 52-53; Beers, 152.
19. *Ibid.*, 27.
20. *Ibid.*, 25-28,152.
21. *Ibid.*, 25-28; Evers, 24-37.
22. DHNY 3:905.
23. Beers, 86-87,96.
24. Beers, 87.
25. *Heads of Families,* 9,22,186.
26. Kelly, 31; Clark, 116.
27. *GCHJ* 4(1):3.
28. Beers, 113,118.
29. *Ibid.*, 380-81.
30. *Ibid.*, 294-95.
31. Evers, 113-14.
32. Haskins (1979), 3; Beers, 205-06,211.
33. *Ibid.*, 260; *GCHJ* 15:2.
34. Richard Smith, 13.
35. Shattuck, *passim.*
36. Beers, 30.
37. Ross, 46; Crowley, 49.
38. Albany Committee of Correspondence, GCHS.
39. Beers, 238.
40. Crowley, 148,157,210-11.
41. Beers, 114.
42. *Ibid.*, 103.
43. *Ibid.*, 217.
44. Reilly, 405-27.
45. Beecher (1977), 60.
46. Spafford (1813), 144-45,330.
47. Hedrick, 331.
48. Beers, 200.
49. *Rising Sun*, Mar. 22, 1794.
50. Rev. Clark Brown, "Topographical Description," GCHS.
51. *GCHJ* 11:12.
52. Products of Industry (1820), schedules.
53. Beers, 167.
54. Van Bergen, 21; Rev. Clark Brown, "Topographical Description," GCHS.
55. Beecher (1977), 15-26.
56. Hedrick, 158.
57. Beers 168; Vedder (1922):25; *Products of Industry (1820), schedules.*
58. Coffin; Geil; Census...for 1855, 351.
59. Van Bergen, 28; Vedder (1922), 28; Beers, 190.
60. Butterfield, 156.
61. Mitchill, "Sketch," 309.
62. Gordon (1836), 469.
63. *GCHJ* 8:1.
64. Beers, 395.
65. Danhof, 190.
66. *Ibid.,* 219,222.
67. Rochefaucault-Liancourt, 2:223.
68. Pinckney, 11.
69. Ringwald, 1; Beers, 138-39.
70. Weed, 4; Evers, 361; Buckman, 14.
71. Beers, 138-39. Gallt, p.207, says the first Catskill to New York boat was the *Frank*, c.1837.
72. Buckman, 34-35,54-55,65.
73. Ringwald, 93.
74. DuBois, 73.
75. Vedder (1922), 44,75;
76. Beecher (1991), 27,50.
77. Gallt, 359.
78. *GCHJ* 8:11; Beecher (1991):72.
79. Beers, 116-17.
80. Smith, 13.
81. Vedder (1927), 38.
82. Beers, 403.
83. *Ibid.*, 42; Beecher (1977), 1.
84. Winterbothan II:306.
85. Beers, 42.
86. *Western Constellation*, Oct. 10, 1800.
87. Erdmann, 3,5; Beers, 412.
88. Beers, 43.
89. Beers, 325; Bonafede, I:12.
90. Beers, 362.
91. Evers, 386.
92. Beers, 140,400-01.
93. DeLisser, 31-33.

94. Climax, 55.
95. Beers, 48.
96. *Ibid.*, 47,400-01.
97. *Ibid.*, 47,79; Gallt, 324; Holmes, 237.
98. Beers, 45; Beecher (1991), 29; Ackerman, 48.
99. Beers, 126,128; Vedder (1922), 80.
100. Beers, 124-25; *Western Constellation*, Feb. 16, 1801.
101. Beers, 116.
102. de la Rochefaucault-Liancourt, 2:226.
103. Hedrick, 139.
104. Beers, 124-26; Rev. Clark Brown, "Topographical Description."
105. Pinckney, 42.
106. Beers, 131.
107. de la Rochefaucault-Liancourt, 2:225-26.
108. *Products of Industry (1820), schedules;* Mitchill (1804), 110.
109. Pinckney, 52; Gallt, 218.
110. Vedder (1922), 56.
111. Products of Industry (1820), schedules; TNYSAS (1847), 14.
112. Andrew Backus, letter.
113. *Catskill Packet*, Aug. 6, 1792.
114. Beers, 245-46.
115. Beecher (1991), 22-24.
116. "Map of Coxsackie, 1797."
117. Beers, 242.
118. *Ibid.*, 165.
119. de la Rochefaucault-Liancourt, 2:219.
120. Beers, 168-69.
121. *GCHJ* 7:40. The meeting dwindled to nothing by 1890.
122. Spafford (1813), 128.
123. *GCHJ* 10:32-33; Beers, 374.
124. Heritage of New Baltimore, Supplement No. 5 (June 1984). The Orthodox meeting was "laid down" or discontinued in 1867; the Hicksites continued past 1877 but had been inactive for a long time before they were "laid down" in 1898.
125. Ackerman, *passim.*; Beers, 370-72.
126. *GCHJ* 10:26.
127. Gallt, 483.
128. Beecher (1977), 51.
129. Spees, 13.
130. de la Rochefaucault-Liancourt, 2:220.
131. Beecher (1977), 51.
132. Beers, 260.
133. *Ibid.*, 275.
134. Evers, 282-83.
135. Shattuck; Beers, 380-81; *Record* 73:116. "Pettavia," at the mouth of the Batavia Kill, appears on a 1760s map entitled "The Plan of the Western Country Abut 120 Miles Extent Each Way," Special Collections, NYSL, reproduced on the endpapers of Florence Christoph, *Upstate New York in the 1760s* (Camden, Me.: Picton Press, 1992). The date 1712, given for the settlement of Prattsville in published histories, is without foundation and apparently derived from the settlement of the lower Schoharie Valley by the Palatines.
136. Beers, 322.
137. Jennie Haines Dunn, papers.
138. MacGahan, 17.
139. Beers, 393; Rockwell, 268.
140. Beers, 345.
141. Prout, 33.
142. Woodworth (1966), 3.
143. Jennie Haines Dunn, papers.
144. Spafford (1824), 576.
145. Beers, 334; Ross, 130; Evers, 433.
146. *Examiner*, Feb. 15, 1896.
147. Beers, 318-19; Geil.
148. Lemuel Hitchcock, Maplecrest: Vedder (1927), 124; Curtis Prout, Windham, *Windham Journal*, Jan. 9, 1877; Perez Steele, Windham, Prout, 68.
149. This story is told in *Brief History*, 7; we have not yet identified its source.
150. *Windham Journal*, Jan. 9, 1877.
151. Prout, 81.
152. *Ibid.*, 116.
153. Census...for 1855; Beers, 201.
154. *Ibid.*, 395.
155. *Ibid.*, 201; Prout, 124.
156. *Ibid.*, 104.
157. *Ibid.*, 116.
158. *Catskill Packet,* Oct. 12, 1792.
159. Beers, 31-32.
160. Van Bergen, 117; Chadwick, 37.
161. Beers, 32-36.
162. *Ibid.*, 129; *Greene County Court House*, 1-6,12.
163. Beers, 32.
164. Shattuck, 49-54; Beecher (1991), 91.
165. de la Rochefaucault-Liancourt, 2:226.
166. Ackerman, 30.
167. Spafford (1813), 128, 167-68.
168. Beers, 373; *Products of Industry (1855), schedules; Products of Industry (1860), schedules;* Disturnell, 261.
169. Spafford (1813), 128; Spafford (1824), 90; Pinckney, 40.
170. Disturnell, 135; *Products of Industry (1850), schedules;* Beecher (1991), 91; deLisser, 129.
171. Disturnell, 66; *Products of Industry (1850), schedules;* Beers, 195; Athens, 29; GCHJ

4(1):1,10.

172. *Examiner,* Aug. 14, 1930, 48.

173. *Census...for 1855,* 358.

174. *Products of Industry (1860),* 369; *Products of Industry (1870),* 700; *Products of Industry (1880),* 302.

175. *Daily Mail,* July 14, 1975.

176. *GCHJ* 6(1):1; Beers, 143; *Products of Industry (1820), schedules.*

177. Beers, 372.

178. Spafford (1813), 50-51.

179. Beers, 208,215; *Products of Industry (1820), schedules.*

180. Spafford (1813), 50-51.

181. *Censuses of 1825, 1835, 1845, 1865.*

182. *Products of Industry (1860), schedules,* 369; Beers Ellis and Soule, plate 16; Beers, 196-99,386; Pinckney, 43; *Census...for 1855,* 404.

183. Beers, 209, 214.

184. *Examiner,* Aug. 14, 1930:12; *GCHJ* 11:12.

185. Beers, 209; *Products of Industry (1820), schedules;* Gallt, 232.

186. Welsh, 18-19.

187. McIntosh, 8-9.

188. Beers, 58; Prout, 45.

189. Spafford (1813), 50-51; Beers, 58.

190. Edwards, 78-80.

191. William H. Edwards, account.

192. Edwards, 78-80.

193. Pratt, 5-8.

194. A short biography of Pratt is found in Evers, 341-50.

195. Wiles, 59,66.

196. *Ibid.,* 66; Beers, 402; Beers Ellis and Soule, plate 15.

197. *Catskill Association.*

198. *Report of the Railroads Committee.*

199. *Census...for 1845.*

200. Beers, 48.

201. Helmer, 18.

202. Pinckney, 79; Helmer, 20; *Catskill Association.*

203. Samuel Noyes, letter.

204. *Report of the Railroads Committee,* 6-7.

205. *Catskill Messenger,* Mar. 19, 1840.

206. Helmer, 30-31.

207. *Op. cit.,* 27-35.

208. Pinckney, 56.

209. Gordon (1836), 472.

210. Pinckney, 69.

211. Jennie Haines Dunn, papers; Evers, 208.

212. *GCHJ* 5(3):9-10; Jennie Haines Dunn, papers; *The Hemlock,* Aug. 1991.

213. Evers, 394.

214. Woodworth (1966), 9.

215. *GCHJ* 5(3):9-10.

216. *Ibid.,* 2(3):5.

217. Harriet Crandall, diary, Dec. 20, 1863.

218. *Constitution, Bylaws, and List of Members of the Greene County Society in New York;* photograph by Coursen, 1924.

219. *Census...for 1875,* maps F-N inclusive.

220. Evers, 405 ff.

221. Ellis, 262.

222. Prout, 88.

223. *Halcott Valley;* Evers, 430-31.

224. *Ibid.,* 429.

225. *Ibid.,* 434.

226. "Chronicle of Fame and Fortune in Greene County."

227. Harriet Crandall, diary, July 30, 1864, Sept. 23, 1864.

228. *The Hemlock,* May 1983; letter, Pat Millen, Prattsville, N.Y.

229. Beers, 65-69.

230. McMurry, 90.

231. Myers, 18.

232. Evers, 92.

233. Spafford (1813):330; Myers, 33.

234. Myers, 31.

235. Evers, 288, 320.

236. Beers, 79.

237. Evers, 351-64; Myers, 31; see also Van Zandt, *passim.*

238. Myers, 36.

239. Evers, 362.

240. Paulding, 144.

241. Summarized from Van Zandt, 140-215; see especially Myers, *passim.*

242. Evers, 401.

243. *Ibid.,* 397.

244. Beers, 215,282-83,338-42,411,446-47.

245. Myers, 139.

246. Beers, 330.

247. *Ibid.,* 79; Helmer, 71.

248. *Resorts of the Catskills,* 109; Myers, 35. Evers examined editions of Van Loan dated 1879 to 1915.

249. DeLisser, 9; Ulster and Delaware Railroad, 185-92.

250. Beers, 300,302,304,374; deLisser, 130.

251. *Halcott Valley.*

252. Longstreth, 85-87; deLisser 64,80.

253. Beers 403; Atkinson 91.

254. *GCHJ* 1(2):3; Gallt, chron.

255. deLisser, 76.

256. Best, 15-16.

257. McAlpine, 3.

258. Harriet Crandall, diary, Mar. 25, 1864. See deLisle, 52, for Table 1, "Table of Opening and Closing of Navigation of the Hudson

River through to Albany: 1800 to 1860."

259. *GCHJ* 13:15.

260. *Ibid.*, 13:11-15.

261. Kisselburgh, 138; Gallt, 499.

262. *GCHJ* 6:13.

263. Evers, 462.

264. Beers, 331; Best, 15-16; Ingersoll, 164.

265. Longstreth, 127.

266. Helmer, 41.

267. Beers, 257; Best, 49.

268. Helmer, 57.

269. Beers, 81,89,115.

270. Evers, 482.

271. *Ibid.*, 552.

272. *Ibid.*, 659.

273. Evers, 387; deLisser, 62.

274. Evers, 478.

275. *Examiner*, Aug. 11, 1877, quoted in Evers, 478.

276. *Ibid.*, 316-17.

277. Goldstein, 60.

278. Schwartzbaum.

279. Gallt, chron.

280. Evers, 688-89.

281. Ingersoll, 165.

282. Evers, 689.

283. Greene County Planning Department, *Catskill Residential Parks*, 5,9.

284. *Examiner*, Nov. 2, 1889, quoted in Evers, 542.

285. *The Hemlock*, June 1987.

286. Brooks (1983):22.

287. *Ibid.*

288. McGahan, 31.

289. *Ibid.*, 37.

290. *Ibid.*, 59,68,92.

291. *Ibid.*, 142.

292. Greene County Deeds 362:835.

293. McGahan, 68.

294. *The Hemlock*, June 1985; *Daily Mail*, Jan. 11, 1980.

295. McKay, 8,46; *Catskill Residential Parks*, 9,14.

296. *Ibid.*, 37; McKay, 46,53.

297. McGahan, 142.

298. Beers, 170; Shattuck.

299. *Ibid.*, 282.

300. *Building Citizens*, 3.

301. Beers, 246.

302. Hill, 11,12.

303. Beers, 130; Rev. Clark Brown, "Topographical Description."

304. Beers, 116. This may well be "Macrober" who appears in Van Vechten's accounts prior to the war.

305. DuBois, 25.

306. Beers, 326-27,393; Jennie Haines Dunn, papers.

307. *Building Citizens*, 3-4,10.

308. Beers, 319.

309. *Ibid.*, 54.

310. *Ibid.*, 55.

311. *Ibid.*, 308,382.

312. *Ibid.*, 282.

313. Tompkins, 49; *Brief History*, 16.

314. Beers, 131; Gallt, 241.

315. Beers, 56.

316. Spafford (1813), 179; Beecher (1977), 45; Beecher (1991). 51; Gallt, 278.

317. Beers, 57. See also *Census...for 1875*, 266.

318. Catskill Mountain Assembly Grounds Association, *Certificate*; Van Bergen, 29-30.

319. Phinney, *passim.*; Gallt, chron.

320. Beers, 62.

321. Vedder (1922), 192.

322. *Ibid.*, 66.

323. Beers, 214,402.

324. *Ibid.*, 329.

325. *Ibid.*, 116-17.

326. Evers, 381; file on Greene County Temperance Society, GCHS.

327. Beers, 270.

328. *Ibid.*, 62.

329. *GCHJ* 7:1.

330. Catskill Board of Health, *Owners and Occupants...in the Village of Catskill*, June 12, 1884.

331. Vedder, 48; Beecher (1991), 52,95; Evers, 336.

332. Athens (1976), 184-86; GCHJ 2(3):2, 2(4):1, 14:15.

333. *Greene County Volunteer Firemen's Association, passim.*

334. Schneider, 223.

335. *Ibid.*, 235.

336. Beers, 64,208; Gallt, 71-72.

337. Beers, 59; Hedrick, 113.

338. TNYSAS (1854), 464-65.

339. *Ibid.*

340. TNYSAS (1858), 624; deLisser, 123.

341. *Ibid.*, 108.

342. *Ibid.*, 146; Beers, 122-23; Beecher (1991), 63; *Brief History*, 26; Prattsville Agricultural and Horticultural Association, *Premium List*, 1910.

343. Interview, Robert Uzzilia, Cairo.

344. Beers, 213.

345. TNYSAS (1848), 13; Beecher (1991), 74.

346. TNYSAS (1847), 640.

347. TNYSAS (1857), 89,93; *Report of the Commissioner of Patents*, 411-26.

348. Hedrick, 364.

349. *Loc.cit.*

350. Beers, 276; Brunger, 62,64; *Census...for 1875*, 435.

351. Beers, 331,351.

352. *Recorder*, Feb. 15, 1901.

353. Misner, 40.

354. deLisser, 9; Woodworth (1966), 14-15.

355. Prout, 121.

356. Beers, 207.

357. Hedrick, 389.

358. *Loc.cit.*; Beach, I:13.

359. *GCHJ* 13:31.

360. *Ibid.*, 7:17.

361. Beers, 118.

362. *Ibid.*, 252; *Examiner*, Aug. 7 and Oct. 23, 1897.

363. *Ibid.*, 302, 452; Beecher (1991), 70.

364. *Examiner*, Nov. 27, 1897.

365. *Ibid.*, Aug. 29, 1896, Sept. 19, 1896.

366. *Examiner*, Aug. 28, 1897.

367. *Ibid.*, Aug. 29, 1896, Sept. 25, 1897.

368. Beers, 252; Beecher (1991), 70.

369. Beers, 292.

370. *Ibid.*, 397; Evers, 439; Prout, 72.

371. Evers, 438.

372. Beers, 337.

373. *Ibid.*, 147,302.

374. *GCHJ* 1(3):1-2.

375. *Products of Industry (1850, 1860)*, schedules.

376. Beers, 215,340.

377. deLisser, 34.

378. Gallt, 361; *GCHJ* 3(2):6; *Heritage of New Baltimore*, Supplement No. 3 (June 1981); Horne, 35.

379. *Daily Mail*, Oct. 4, 1980, 5; *Windham Journal*, Feb. 5, 1981.

380. Gallt, chron.

381. Evers, 442-43; Kudish, 73; *Examiner*, Dec. 4, 1897.

382. Beers, 118; Rev. Clark Brown, "Topographical Description"; Horne, *Agricultural Production Chart*.

383. Brown, 376.

384. *Halcott Valley*.

385. Horne, *Agricultural Production Charts*.

386. Beers, 374; *Examiner*, Aug. 14, 1930, 13; Rev. Clark Brown, "Topographical Description."

387. *GCHJ* 3(1):4.

388. *Examiner*, Aug. 14, 1930, 13; Gordon, 472.

389. Ross, 140; Van Bergen, 19.

390. Kisselburgh, 20-22.

391. Barbara Van Orden, "Flashback," *Daily Mail*, Apr. 7, 1979, 4.392. Claude B. Whiting quoted in *Knickerbocker News*,

Oct. 31, 1949, B-4.

393. *GCHJ* 9:32.

394. Dewey Hill, 1-5; Beers, 253.

395. Dewey Hill, 24.

396. *GCHJ* 3(4):1, 12:7; Beers, 141,253,373,416.

397. Dewey Hill, 26; *GCHJ* 3(4):1; Isabella C. Rainey to John Kisselburgh, Dec. 12, 1964, quoted in Kisselburgh, 133.

398. QB 7:10; Athens, 108-10.

399. Beers, 189; Nellie McKnight, memo; Dernell, *passim*.

400. Ross, 142; Dewey Hill, 26.

401. Beecher (1991), 41; *GCHJ* 3(4):1; Athens, 108-10.

402. John Ham, "Ice Was Important Area Winter Crop," undated clipping, GCHS.

403. Kisselburgh, 26-27; Beecher (1991), 78-81; Dewey Hill, 35-39.

404. Chace.

405. *Ibid.*; Ketchum, 82-83; Beers, 185; *Census of Industry, 1820*.

406. Beers, 142.

407. Van Bergen, 57; Beecher (1991):60-62.

408. Beecher (1991):61.

409. Elsie and Barbara Van Orden, in Pavlak (1985).

410. *Recorder*, July 17, 1896.

411. Best, 155; Helmer, 73.

412. Newland, 22.

413. Kisselburgh 125.

414. Gallt, chronology; Kisselburgh, 125.

415. Beers, 137; Swain.

416. TNYSAS (1847), 639.

417. Beers, 394.

418. Wiles, 55,67.

419. Beers, 213.

420. *Ibid.*, 141.

421. *Ibid.*, 252,276; Beecher (1991), 82-85; *GCHJ* 15:12.

422. *Loc.cit.*; Beers, 252.

423. *Brief History*, 12; Beers, 384; Beers Ellis and Soule, pl. 13.

424. Chadwick, 19; Vedder (1922), 27; Kay, 136.

425. *Examiner*, May 21, 1859.

426. Vedder (1922), 32.

427. Beers, 144; *GCHJ* 11:13.

428. Beers, 141.

429. Bryan, 72.

430. Ackerman, 93,102.

431. *GCHJ* 2(4):8; Beers, 397; deLisser, 129.

432. Van Gelder, 220,225; *Catskill Democrat*, Nov. 3, 1847; Gallt, 234; *GCHJ* 4(2):9.

433. *Op.cit.* 3(2):1; Bowen, 105-26.

434. Agreement filed under Catskill/Backus at GCHS.

435. Beers, 141; *Census...for 1855*, 384-85.

436. Atkinson, 105; Evers, 561; *GCHJ* 4(2):8-9; Beers, 331,369.

437. Kudish, 70; U.S. Census Office, *The Statistics of the Wealth and Industry of the United States,* 3:781.

438. Atkinson, 105.

439. *Examiner,* Aug. 14, 1930, 50.

440. *GCHJ* 6:27-28, 13:7; Beecher (1991), 86-87.

441. Newland, 16; Evers, 574-75; New York State Museum, *Geology of the Catskill and Kaaterskill Quadrangle,* 239-42.

442. Catskill Cement Company, *Minute Book*; *Examiner,* Aug. 3, 1900,Oct. 19, 1901; Gallt, 151; Pavlak (1985).

443. *Athens News,* August 15, 1900; Pavlak (1991).

444. Gallt, chron.

445. Pavlak (1985); Gallt, 151; *Greene County Catskills,* 31; *Catskill Mountain Star,* Jan. 7, 1955.

446. Kay, 135-38.

447. Beers, 320,326,345.

448. *GCHJ* 9:7.

449. Beers, 138,408.

450. Gallt, chron.; Beecher (1991), 45.

451. Delap.

452. *Examiner,* Aug. 14, 1930, 31; Beecher (1991), 98.

453. Gallt, 215.

454. *Examiner, loc.cit.*

455. *Ibid.*; Gallt, chron.; Beecher (1991), 98-99.

456. Beecher, *loc.cit.; Examiner, loc.cit.*

457. *Halcott Valley*; Horne, *Agricultural Production Chart;* U.S. Bureau of the Census, *U.S. Census of Agriculture,* 1954, Part 2, I:67.

458. *GCHJ* 1(2):4, 14:17-18; Catskill Wheeling Club, *Programme of Races.*

459. *Standard Road-Book of New York State,* pl. 4,11.

460. *GCHJ* 9:33, 10:5,11.

461. Gallt, 89,281, and chron. Note Gallt erroneously places construction of the trolley line in 1890-92 and is to be read with great caution.

462. *GCHJ* 10:15-18.

463. *Ibid.,* 14:16; Evers, 684.

464. Undated clipping, GCHS.

465. Cary, 15.

466. Catskill Chamber of Commerce, *Greene County Catskills,* 32.

467. *GCHJ* 9:32.

468. Vedder (1927), 142.

469. *GCHJ* 4(2):2.

470. Gallt, chron.

471. Howard.

472. Beers, 318; Vedder (1927), 91; The *Hemlock,* June [1983].

473. Vedder (1927), 197.

474. McKay, 47.

475. New York State, Commissioner of Highways, *Report of the State Commissioner of Highways,* 495.

476. Kisselburgh, 108; Athens (1976), 19; Gallt, 94-95.

477. DuBois, 85.

478. Ackerman, 74-75; *Examiner,* Aug. 14, 1930, 68.

479. Gallt, 94-95; MacGahan, 24.

480. Undated clipping from *The New York Times* containing a letter of Frank H. Hutton dated Dec. 6, 1921, GCHS.

481. *The Mohican Trail,* view book, ca.1925.

482. Best, 127; Helmer, 81,111,113,117.

483. Best, 161.

484. New York Central System, *West Shore River Division Time Table.*

485. *GCHJ* 12:21; DuBois, 80.

486. Kisselburgh, 233.

487. *Ibid.,* 52.

488. Vedder (1927), 136; Athens (1976), 20; *GCHJ* 9:25.

489. Athens (1976), 28; letter, J. Theodore Hilscher.

490. Ringwald, 1,179,198,203.

491. *GCHJ* 8:31-34.

492. *Examiner,* Aug. 14, 1930, 82; *Brief History,* 6; *GCHJ* 8:33.

493. *Climax,* 53.

494. *Ibid.,* 15,30.

495. DuBois, 27.

496. Gallt, 174-79.

497. Decker, Emily Becker of Catskill.

498. Gallt, 234.

499. Levine, *passim.*

500. *Annual Report of the WCTU of the State of New York (1927) and (1937)*:176.

501. Ku Klux Klan, Prattsville, records.

502. *Windham Journal,* Oct. 22, 1936, 1.

503. *Halcott Valley.*

504. *Building Citizens,* 20-23.

505. *Windham Journal, loc.cit.*

506. *Centralization Brochure*; Climax, 65.

507. *Combined for the Best in Education.*

508. *Daily Mail,* July 25, 1935; Cary, 36.

509. *GCHJ* 7:29.

510. New York State, Department of Labor, *Industrial Directory,* 98-99.

511. *Examiner,* Aug. 14, 1930, 62; op.cit., May 12, 1906; *Knickerbocker News,* Aug. 23, 1986; *Greene County News,* Aug. 28, 1986.

512. *Examiner,* Aug. 14, 1930, 12; "blue form,"

on file at GCHS.

513. Catskill Chamber of Commerce, *Greene County Catskills*, 31.

514. *Greene County News,* Mar. 2, 1978; *Greene County Industrial Data Book*, 30.

515. *Data Book, loc.cit.*

516. *Data Book, loc.cit.*; Allied Boat Company, leaflet, Jan. 1, 1964, GCHS; *Examiner-Recorder,* Feb. 8, 1962, 1.

517. *Examiner*, Aug. 14, 1930, 63.

518. *Greene County Industrial Data Book*, 30-31.

519. *The Hemlock,* Apr. 1986, quoting Mary S. Mullett in *The American Magazine*, July 1927.

520. *GCHJ* 10:16.

521. Farmers' Freighting Line Company, Records.

522. *Halcott Valley.*

523. *Ibid.*; Catskill Mountain Creamery, *Records*; Beecher (1991), 44.

524. New York State, Department of Farms and Markets, *List of Creameries*, 24.

525. Kisselburgh, 196-98.

526. Beecher (1991), 50.

527. *Examiner*, Aug. 14, 1930, 26.

528. Alexander, appendix.

529. *Examiner,* Aug. 14, 1930, 28.

530. *Ibid.*, 28-29.

531. Van Wagner, 338-42.

532. *Ibid.*, 342.

533. *Greene County Farm Bureau News*, Feb. 1918.

534. *Examiner*, Aug. 14, 1930, 56.

535. Haskins (1959).

536. Catskill Chamber of Commerce, *Greene County Catskills;* Vedder (1927), 132.

537. New York State, Department of Agriculture, *List of Milk Plants and Establishments in New York State*, 38.

538. *GCHJ* 13:3; "Vosburgh-Carrington Home," manuscript; *Daily Mail*, Dec. 14, 1977, Apr. 6, 1990.

539. *Greene County Catskills*, 30; Vedder (1927), 177; see also Barbara Van Orden, "Caring for an Old-Time Orchard," *Daily Mail*, Mar. 10, 1979.

540. Pavlak (1985); *Knickerbocker News*, Jan. 16, 1950; *Greene County News*, Feb. 18, 1982; New York State Museum, *Geology of the Coxsackie Quadrangle*, 360.

541. *Examiner*, Aug. 14, 1930, 27; United States, Bureau of the Census, *Census Data Taken from Photostatic Sheets Received from the Census Bureau by M.C. Bond.*

542. *Ibid.*, table 9.

543. Nicholson, 1,3,4.

544. *Examiner*, Aug. 14, 1930, 26; Cornwallville Grange Thrasher Co-operative Association, Inc., certificate 1925. Called "Cornwallville Grain Thresher's Association" in Vedder (1927), 189.

545. *Fifth Annual Greene County Picnic*, July 29, 1928.

546. M. and M. Schmidt, interview; U.S. Bureau of the Census, *Abandoned or Idle Farms*, 122.

547. U.S. Bureau of the Census, *U.S. Census of Agriculture: 1945*, I, part 2, 66; *U.S. Census of Agriculture 1954*, I, part 2, 63.

548. *U.S. Census of Agriculture (1935)*, II, 65; *U.S. Census of Agriculture: 1945*, I, part 2, 35; *U.S. Census of Agriculture 1954*, I, part 2, 67.

549. *Ibid.*, 57.

550. *Ibid.*, 67.

551. New York State, Department of Agriculture, *List of Milk Dealers and Milk Plants in New York State*, 28.

552. *Greene County News*, May 8, 1986.

553. *Greene County Development Guide*, 28; Vincent Ladue, "Greene County Agriculture," June 1987.

554. VanValkenburgh (1985):2.

555. *Ibid.*, 4-5.

556. *Ibid.*, 17.

557. Evers, 338,551 ff.; Van Valkenburgh (1983), *passim.*; Van Valkenburgh (1985), 2,4-5,8,12,19,33,38,41.

558. *Ibid.*, 42,46,52,59,64.

559. New York City, Board of Water Supply, Map and Profile (1905); *Catskill Water Supply: A General Description*, 24.

560. Evers, 591; Gallt, 489; New York City, Board of Water Supply, *Catskill Water Supply: A General Description*, 24-28.

561. *Ibid.*, 28.

562. *Recycling Awareness II*, no. 1 (Feb. 1990).

563. Vedder (1927), 134.

564. *The Hemlock*, March 1982.

565. Evers, 302.

566. *GCHJ* 5(1):5.

567. Evers, 306-07.

568. *Cairo in the Catskills.*

569. Gerald Ingalls, interview.

570. Durham Town Historian, oral communication.

571. Morton, 9.

572. Ackerman (1976), 206.

573. George Meyer, "Rip Van Winkle Awoke in 1935," *Tannersville Topics Illustrated* [1937], 6.

574. Atkinson, 6, 108.

575. *Ibid.*, 107.

576. *The Hemlock*, April 1991, unpaged.

577. Van Zandt, 308.

578. Roland Lindemann, letter.

579. Clipping, unidentified Saugerties newspaper, Oct. 16, 1953, GCHS.

580. See also *Travel*, Oct. 1954, 24 ff.

581. *The New York Times*, July 1, 1954.

582. Seward, 22.

583. Buttons Ryan in *Greene County News*, July 28, Aug. 4, Aug. 11, 1977.

584. Posselt, 144-54.

585. Seward, 19-20.

586. *Ibid.*

587. *Climax*, 27; Meyer, "Rip Van Winkle Awoke in 1935," *Tannersville Topics Illustrated*, 7.

588. *Ibid.*

589. *Ibid.*; interview, Justine Hommel, Haines Falls.

590. *Cairo in the Catskills*; Mack, 81-85.

591. *Princeton Ski Bowl on Bearpen Mountain*, brochure.

592. Pepe, *passim*.

593. Clement; *The New York Times*, Nov. 17, 1974, *Special Ski Report*.

594. Interview, Justine Hommel, Haines Falls.

595. *The Hemlock*, Apr. 1986; Gallt 186; *Recorder*, Oct. 3, 1913; *Daily Mail*, Jan. 9, 1978; DeShazo, 131-32.

596. *The Hemlock*, June 1988;

597. Atkinson, 3.

598. *Ibid.*, 6.

599. *Ibid.*, 96-99.

600. Vedder (1927), 159; map, "Building Lots of Durso Brothers on the Windham Mountain, G.W. Goetchius, Surveyor, 1929," GCHS; W.S. Borthwick, papers.

601. Brooks (1984), 40.

602. Greene County Planning Department, *Greene County Development Guide* (1988), 3.

603. Horne, 11.

604. *The New York Times*, June 4, 1978, Real Estate, 6.

605. *The New York Times*, Sept. 16, 1984, Real Estate; *Greene County News*, Aug. 4, 1977.

606. Greene County Planning Department, *Citizens Questionnaire*, 23.

607. Miner and Steelman, 9-10.

608. *Glens Falls Business Review*, May 18, 1992, 1,24.

609. Greene County Planning Department, *Results of the 1990 U.S. Census of Population in Greene County*, 1991. 22.

BIBLIOGRAPHIC ESSAY

Over a century ago, J.B. Beers published his *History of Greene County, N.Y., With Biographical Sketches of Its Prominent Men* (New York: J.B. Beers, 1884; republished, Cornwallville: Hope Farm Press, 1969). Assembled as a subscription publication with material solicited from contributors in most of the county's towns, it suffered from many biases; but it is blessed by an attention to detail and a nearness to the period being recorded. Its county chapters, unfortunately, are less detailed than those on the towns.

Early in the twentieth century a number of small-format county "histories" were published. Each is filled with errors, although each also contains material not otherwise available. They are: J.A. Gallt, *Dear Old Greene County* (Catskill, 1915); J. Van Vechten Vedder, *History of Greene County 1651-1800* (Catskill, 1927; republished, Cornwallville: Hope Farm Press, 1985); and George H. Chadwick, the *"Old Times Corner": First Series* (Catskill: Greene County Historical Society, 1932), a collection of newspaper pieces. Both Gallt and Vedder include appendices with abstracts of current newspaper stories from the early twentieth century. Of the three, Gallt unfortunately appears to be almost consistently inaccurate for events he did not remember personally.

A superficial survey was published thirty years ago: Mabel Parker Smith, *Greene County, N.Y.: A Short History* (Catskill: Greene County Board of Supervisors, 1963). Though competent it is very brief.

In the spring of 1977 the Greene County Historical Society began publication of *The Quarterly Journal* (changed to *Greene County Historical Journal* with volume 6, 1982), cited as *GCHJ* in the notes. This slim publication has produced articles of the highest quality for fifteen years and is gradually building a valuable body of reference.

One book was virtually indispensable in writing this history: Alf Evers' landmark *The Catskills: From Wilderness to Woodstock* (Garden City, N.Y.: Doubleday, 1972). It has no equal for scholarship, comprehensiveness and readability, and was my constant companion in writing certain portions of this book, particularly on the nineteenth century.

An anniversary edition of the *Examiner*, Aug. 14, 1930, not only contains topical history of varying accuracy but provides superb documentation of Greene County in the period following World War I.

TOWN HISTORIES

The town chapters in Beers represent the earliest systematic collection of Greene County town history.

Few others were published for ninety years. Exceptions are J. Van Vechten Vedder, *Historic Catskill* (Catskill, 1922, republished, Astoria: Fawcett, 1991) and Robert Henry Van Bergen, *Ye Olden Time*, ed. by Francis A. Hallenbeck (Coxsackie, 1935).

The bicentennial produced a flurry of books and booklets, most of them derivative from earlier publications. However, *Athens: Its People and Industry* (Athens: Bicentennial Commission, 1976) and Elizabeth B. Ackerman, ed., *The Heritage of New Baltimore* (New Baltimore: Bicentennial Commission, 1976), are above average, and reproduce many excellent photographs.

In the past decade Joseph Pavlak has privately published *Smith's Landing...Cementon* (Catskill, 1985) and *Alsen* (Catskill, 1991), full of vivid recollections, photographs, and the working-class history of those little villages. Finally, Raymond Beecher's *Under Three Flags* (Hensonville: Black Dome Press, 1991) updates and corrects the history of Coxsackie with his usual superb research, though recent years are unfortunately omitted.

The three major residential parks in Hunter have been well-chronicled. The best publication is John A. MacGahan's *Twilight Park: The First Hundred Years* (Yarmouth, Mass.: Allen D. Bragdon, 1988), though Christine G. McKay et.al. did very well with *There's a Place Up in the Mountains: A Centennial History of Elka Park* (Elka Park: Elka Park Association, 1989). See also Greene County Planning Department, *Catskill Residential Parks: Summer Retreats from the City* (Cairo: The Department, 1986).

PERSONAL NARRATIVES

We are fortunate to have four superb nineteenth century documents which are personal recollections rather than narrative history. For the Village of Catskill we can read Henry Hill, *Recollections of an Octogenarian* (Boston: D. Lothrop, 1884), and James D. Pinckney, *Reminiscences of Catskill* (Catskill: J.B. Hall, 1868), both of which are full of vivid and early material. Henry Hedges Prout's *Old Times in Windham* (Cornwallville: Hope Farm Press, 1970) was originally published serially in the *Windham Journal,* February 18, 1869 to March 31, 1870; it is a fine source about the settlement of the Mountaintop, much of it in the words of the last survivors of the settlement period. Finally, William H. Edwards, ed., *William Edwards 1770-1851* (Washington, 1897), contains extensive detail on the Hunter tannery written by its founder and his son. Many publications of Zadock Pratt might also be included here, though Alf Evers suggests that they were written for him, not by him.

For the twentieth century we have too little in print. Orianna Atkinson's *Not Only Ours: A Story of Greene County, N.Y.* (Cornwallville: Hope Farm Press, 1970) is a rather charming and witty story by a woman who came as a summer resident in the 1920s; but one wonders how someone so self-consciously urbane managed to integrate into the community. An equally literate but less pretentious writer is John W. Kisselburgh, whose *Shadows of the Half Moon* (New York: Vantage Press, 1972) is a really extraordinary story of growing up in Athens before the Depression, by a man with a mind for detail and an entertaining writing style.

Philip DuBois' equally fine recollections of his boyhood at Catskill were recently published as *A Catskill Boyhood* (Hensonville: Black Dome Press, 1992).

SPECIFIC SUBJECTS

A number of very good studies of specific subject areas are available.

Only one scholarly article on social and economic history has appeared: Richard C. Wiles, "Windham," *The Hudson Valley Regional Review* 2(1985):54-72.

Transportation has been extraordinarily well-researched, especially by railroad aficionados. Gerald M. Best, *The Ulster and Delaware: Railroad Through the Catskills* (San Marino, Calif.: Golden West Books, 1972) chronicles the line up the Esopus Valley with some attention to the Hunter and Kaaterskill spurs. William F. Helmer, *Rip Van Winkle Railroads* (Berkeley: Howell-North Books, 1970) covers the Greene County railroads thoroughly. Several articles by Raymond Beecher have dealt meticulously with transportation issues, including one on the Saratoga and Hudson River Railroad and another on the Rip Van Winkle Bridge; they have been published in the Greene County Historical Journal. Finally, Donald C. Ringwald, *The Hudson River Day Line* (Berkeley: Howell-North, 1965) studies that steamboat line.

Three excellent books deal with Greene County as resort: Roland Van Zandt, *The Catskill Mountain House* (New Brunswick: Rutgers, 1966, republished, Hensonville: Black Dome, 1991) is a scholarly study of the fabled hotel. *Resorts of the Catskills* (New York: St. Martin's Press, 1979) contains essays by Alf Evers, Betsy Blackmar, and others, on the architecture and social history of the Catskill resorts. It was originally published as an exhibition catalogue. Also a catalogue was Kenneth Myers' richly-illustrated *The Catskills: Painters, Writers and Tourists in the Mountains 1820-1895* (Yonkers: Hudson River Museum, 1987). Winter sports have only recently been discussed by Carol Clement in "Early Tracks: A Brief History of Skiing in the Catskills," *Kaatskill Life* VI:4 (Winter 1991-92) 14-21.

The only published oral history to date is Maryann Delap's *Mountain Laurels* (1981), which lacks pagination and publication data but does contain several fine interviews. Similar interviews have been published in the Mountaintop Historical Society's fine *Hemlock* (1978-), which also lacks volume and page numbers and dates of issue in most cases. *Climax Recollections* (Coxsackie, N.Y.: Greene County Historical Society, 1992) makes good use of oral material.

R. Lionel deLisser's *Picturesque Catskills: Greene County* (Northampton, Mass.: Picturesque Publishing Company, 1894, republished, Cornwallville: Hope Farm Press, 1967) is not a good source for history, but is a very good eyewitness report.

The many articles by Elsie and Barbara Van Orden, mostly on the history of the Embought and neighboring communities, which were published in the *Daily Mail*, are unusually fine work and deserve to be collected and republished.

COLLECTIONS

Greene County has rather few museums with historical collections; those that exist are unusually rich.

The Vedder Memorial Library of the Greene County Historical Society is a vast collection of published and unpublished material. It holds virtually all the published materials on Greene County. Particularly noteworthy is its huge and growing manuscript collection.

The Durham Center Museum at East Durham also has a large manuscript collection, including several hundred business ledgers.

The Mountaintop Historical Society maintains its collection at the Haines Falls Library. In addition to the usual books, it has some valuable unpublished materials.

The Zadock Pratt Museum at Prattsville also has some important manuscript materials.

Greene County, in common with the rest of New York State, has a system of municipal historians. As a rule, their holdings were not examined; however, the work of Donald Teator in Greenville promises to result in a superb town history in the future and was useful in the research for this book.

Sources Consulted

PUBLISHED

Ackerman, Elizabeth B. ed. *The Heritage of New Baltimore.* New Baltimore, N.Y. : Bicentennial Commission, 1976.

Alexander, L. Ray. *100 Year History of the New York State Grange.* Washington, D.C.: National Grange, 1973.

Allied Boat Company. N.p., Jan. 1, 1964. [Leaflet.]

Athens: Its People and Industry. Athens, N.Y.: Bicentennial Commission, 1976.

Atkinson, Oriana. *Not Only Ours: A Story of Greene County, N.Y.* Cornwallville, N.Y.: Hope Farm Press, 1985.

Beck, R.S. *Types of Farming in New York.* Cornell University Agricultural Experiment Station, no. 704. Ithaca, N.Y.: Cornell University Agricultural Experiment Station, 1938.

Beecher, Raymond. *Letters from a Revolution.* Coxsackie, N.Y.: Greene County Historical Society, 1973.

————. *Out to Greenville and Beyond.* Cornwallville, N.Y.: Hope Farm Press, 1977.

————. *Under Three Flags.* Hensonville, N.Y.: Black Dome Press, 1991.

Beers, F.W. *Atlas of Greene County, N.Y.* New York: Beers, Ellis and Soule, 1867.

Beers, J.B., ed. *History of Greene County.* New York: J.B. Beers and Co., 1884.

Best, Gerald M. *The Ulster and Delaware: Railroad through the Catskills.* San Marino, Calif.: Golden West Books, 1972.

Bonafede, Patricia. *Cultural Resources Survey Report: Route 23A Palenville to Haines Falls Greene County.* Albany: New York State Museum, 1980.

Bowen, Taylor G. *James Reid and His Catskill Knuckledusters.* Lincoln, R.I.: Andrew Mowbray Inc., 1988.

Brasser, T.J. "Mahican." In *Handbook of North American Indians*, vol. 15, edited by William C. Sturtevant, pp. 198-212. Washington, D.C.: Smithsonian Institution, 1978.

Brief History of Windham-Ashand-Jewett-Prattsville. Windham, N.Y.: Windham-Ashland-Jewett-Prattsville Bicentennial Committee, 1976.

Brooks, Doris West. *Short Stories and Tall Tales of the Catskills.* Vol. 1 and vol. 2. 1983-84.

Brooks, Loretta. *Along the Hudson: Sketches of Childhood Life in a Catskill Town.* New York: Exposition Press, 1959.

Broughton, John G.; Davis, James F.; and Johnson, John H.. *Geology and Mineral Resources of the Middle and Lower Hudson Valley.* Albany: New York State Museum, 1966.

Brown, Nelson C. *Forest Products: Their Manufacture and Use.* New York: John Wiley, 1919.

Bryan, Clark W. *The Paper Mill Directory of the World.* Holyoke, Mass.: Clark W. Bryan and Co., 1885.

Buckman, David Lear. *Old Steamboat Days on the Hudson River.* New York: The Grafton Press, 1907.

Building Citizens: A History of Public Schools in Otsego County. Cooperstown, N.Y.: Smithy-Pioneer Gallery Publications, 1988.

Butterfield. Roy L. "The Great Days of Maple Sugar," *New York History.* 39 (1958):151-164.

Cairo in the Catskills. Catskill, N.Y.: Examiner-Recorder Print, c.1939.

Cairo, Town of. *Economic Base and Population Study.* Cairo, N.Y.: The Town, 1971.

Carlsen, Laura Pine. *All of These Things.* North Newton, Kans.: Mennonite Press, 1974.

Cary, Peter, et al. *Coxsackie on the Hudson.* Coxsackie, N.Y.: Bicentennial Commission, 1976.

Catskill Association Formed for the Purpose of Improving the Town of Catskill. New York: Mitchell and Turner, 1837.

Catskill Board of Health. *Owners & Occupants . . . in the Village of Catskill.* Catskill, N.Y.: The Board, June 12, 1884. [Handbill.]

Catskill Chamber of Commerce. *Greene County Catskills.* 1926.

Catskill Examiner. *Picturesque Catskills.* Catskill, N.Y., 1948.

Catskill Mountain Assembly Grounds Association. *Certificate.* n.d.

Catskill Wheeling Club. *Program of Races.* Catskill, N.Y., Aug. 20, 1897. [Program.]

Celebration of the Completion of the Water Works System in the Village of Athens. Athens, N.Y., 1927.

"Census of the State of New York for 1825." In: *Journal of the Senate of the State of New York.* Albany, N.Y.: E. Croswell, 1826.

Census of the State of New York for 1835. Albany, N.Y.: Croswell, Van Benthuysen and Burt, 1836.

Census of the State of New York for 1845. Albany, N.Y.: Carroll and Cook, 1846.

Census of the State of New York for 1855. Albany, N.Y.: Charles Van Benthuysen, 1857.

Census of the State of New York for 1865. Albany, N.Y.: Charles Van Benthuysen and Sons, 1867.

Census of the State of New York for 1875. Albany, N.Y.: Weed, Parsons and Company, 1877.

Centralization Brochure. Catskill, N.Y.: Catskill Schools, 1955.

Chadwick, George H. *The "Old Times Corner": First Series.* Catskill, N.Y.: Greene County Historical Society, 1932.

Chase, Emory A. *Local Historical Gleanings.* Catskill, N.Y., 1910.

Christman, Henry. *Tin Horns and Calico.* New York: Henry Holt, 1946.

Clark, D.W. *The World of Justus Falckner.* Philadelphia: Mecklenburg Press, 1946.

Clement, Carol. "Early Tracks: A Brief History of Skiing in the Catskills." *Kaatskill Life,* vol. 6, no. 4 (Winter 1991-92): 14-21.

Climax Recollections. Coxsackie, N.Y.: Greene County Historical Society, 1992.

Coffin, Margaret. *The Fabulous Butlers of Brandy Hill.* N.p., 1953.

Cohen, David S. "How Dutch Were the Dutch of New Netherland?" *New York History* (Jan. 1981):43-60.

——. *The Dutch-American Farm.* New York: NYU Press, 1992.

Combined for the Best in Education. N.p., 1967. [Leaflet.]

Constitution, Bylaws and List of Members of the Greene County Society in New York. New York: The Society, n.d.

Cooperative Extension. *Community Concerns as Expressed by Mountaintop Property Owners.* Cairo, N.Y.: Cooperative Extension, 1975.

——. *1970 Non-Resident Landowner Study.* Cairo, N.Y.: Cooperative Extension, 1971.

Coxsackie Chamber of Commerce. *Shoppers in Coxsackie: A Group Study.* Coxsackie, N.Y.: Coxsackie Chamber of Commerce, 1955.

Crowley, James A. *The Old Albany County and the American Revolution.* Troy, N.Y.: Historian Publishing Company, 1979.

Danhof, Clarence H. *Change in Agriculture: The Northern United States, 1820-1870.* Cambridge, Mass.: Harvard University Press, 1969.

Delap, Maryann. *Mountain Laurels.* N.p., 1981.

DeLisle, Kenneth R. *The Hudson River Mail 1804-1858.* Albany, N.Y.: Albany Institute of History and Art, 1959.

DeLisser, R. Lionel. *Picturesque Catskills: Greene County.* Northampton, Mass.: Picturesque Publishing Company, 1894.

Dernell, H.F. and Co. *Descriptive Catalogue and Price List of H.F. Dernel and Company's Ice Tools.* Albany, N.Y.: C.E. Houghtaling, 1890.

DeShazo, Edith. *Everett Shinn 1876-1953: A Figure in His Time.* New York: Clarkson N. Potter, 1974.

Disturnell, J. *A Gazetteer of the State of New York.* Albany, N.Y.: J. Disturnell, 1842.

DuBois, Philip H. *A Catskill Boyhood.* Hensonville, N.Y.: Black Dome Press, 1992.

Durham, Town of. Bicentennial Commission. *A Bicentennial Booklet.* Oak Hill, N.Y.: Big Acorn, 1976.

Edwards, William H., ed. *Memoirs of Col. William Edwards.* Washington, D.C.: Printed not Published, 1897.

Ellis, David M. *Landlords and Farmers in the Hudson-Mohawk Region 1790-1850.* Ithaca: Cornell University Press, 1946.

Erdmann, David G. "The Susquehanna Turnpike." *The Catskills* Winter 1973: 4-11.

Evers, Alf. *The Catskills: From Wilderness to Woodstock.* Garden City, N.Y.: Doubleday, 1972.

Examiner (Catskill, N.Y.) Centennial Edition. Aug. 14, 1930.

Fifth Annual Greene County Picnic. N.p., July 29, 1928. [Leaflet.]

Fuller, Wayne E. *The American Mail: Enlargement of the Common Life.* Chicago: University of Chicago, 1972.

Gallt, J. A. *Dear Old Greene County.* Catskill, N.Y., privately printed by the author, 1915; republished, Cornwallville: Hope Farm Press, 1986.

Gehring, Charles T. *Fort Orange Court Minutes 1652-60.* Syracuse, N.Y.: Syracuse University Press, 1990.

Geil, Samuel. *Map of Greene County, N.Y.* Philadelphia: E.A. Balch, 1856.

Goddard, Ives. "Delaware." In *Handbook of the North American Indians,* vol. 15, edited by William C. Sturtevant, pp. 213-39. Washington, D.C.: Smithsonian Institution, 1978.

Goldstein, Herbert S. *Forty Years Struggle for a Principle: The Biography of Harry Fischel.* New York: Bloch, 1928.

Gordon, Thomas F. *Gazetteer of the State of New York.* Philadelphia: printed for the author, 1836.

Greene County. *Recycling Awareness,* II, no. 1 (Feb. 1990).

Greene County Board of Supervisors. *Greene County Industrial Data Book 1963-64.* Catskill, N.Y.: Greene County Board of Supervisors, 1963.

Greene County Court House: Its Diamond Jubilee 1910-1985. Catskill, N.Y.: Court House Diamond Jubilee Committee, 1985.

Greene County Development Guide. Cairo, N.Y.: Greene County Planning Department, 1988.

Greene County Historical Society. *Greene County Historical Journal.* Vol. 1, no. 1 (Spring 1977-date).

Greene County Industrial Data Book. N.p., 1963-64.

Greene County Planning Department. *Catskill Residential Parks: Summer Retreats from the City.* Cairo, N.Y.: The Department, 1986.

———. *Citizen Questionnaire.* Cairo, N.Y.: The Department, 1971.

———. *Environmental and Scenic Resources and Historic Inventory Supplement.* Cairo, N.Y.: The Department, 1971.

———. *Highway Study.* Cairo, N.Y.: The Department, 1971.

———. *Results of the 1990 U.S. Census of Population in Greene County.* Cairo, N.Y.: The Department, 1991.

Greene County Volunteer Firemen's Association: One-Hundred Years of Fire Service History. N.p.: The Association, 1989.

Halcott Valley 1851-1976. Halcott: Town Board, 1976.

Hall, Henry. *The Ice Industry of the United States, with a Brief Sketch of its History.* Reprint. N.p.: Early American Industries Association, 1974.

Haskins, Vernon. *James Barker the Patroon.* East Durham, N.Y.: Durham Center Museum, 1979.

——. *Yesteryear.* Oak Hill, N.Y.: Big Acorn Press, 1959.

Hauserman, Tim and Miner, Tom. *The Catskills For Sale.* Arkville, N.Y.: Catskill Center, 1984.

Heads of Families at the First Census of the United States Taken in the Year 1790: New York. Baltimore: Genealogical Publishing Company, 1971.

Hedrick, Ulysses P. *A History of Agriculture in the State of New York.* Albany, N.Y.: N.Y.S. Agricultural Society, 1933.

Heritage of New Baltimore. Supplements.

Helmer, William F. *Rip Van Winkle Railroads.* Berkeley: Howell-North Books, 1970.

Hill, Dewey D. and Hughes, Elliott R. *Ice Harvesting in Early America.* New Hartford, N.Y.: New Hartford Historical Society, 1977.

Hill, Henry. *Recollections of an Octogenarian.* Boston: D. Lothrop, 1884.

History of the Organization of the First Presbyterian Church of Durham, N.Y. Durham, N.Y., 1934.

Holdridge, George W. *Reminiscences of George W. Holdridge.* N.p., n.d.

Holmes, Oliver W. "The Stage-Coach Business in the Hudson Valley," *New York State Historical Association Quarterly Journal* 12(1931):231-256.

Horne, Field. *Mountaintop and Valley: Greene County Folk Arts Today.* Hensonville, N.Y.: Black Dome Press, 1991.

Hough, Franklin B. *Gazetteer of the State of New York.* Albany, N.Y.: Andrew Boyd, 1872.

Howard, Burgess. *A Native Descendant of the Pioneer Settlers of the Tannersville-Haines Falls Region.* Tannersville, N.Y.: By the Author, n.d.

Ingersoll, Ernest. *Illustrated Guide to the Hudson River and Catskill Mountains.* Chicago: Rand McNally, 1910.

Jameson, J. Franklin. *Narratives of New Netherland 1609-64.* New York: Charles Scribner's Sons, 1909.

Juet, Robert. *Juet's Journal.* Newark, N.J.: The New Jersey Historical Society, 1959.

Kammen, Michael. *Colonial New York: A History. New York:* Charles Scribner's Sons, 1975.

Kay, John L. and Smith, Chester M., Jr. *New York Postal History: The Post Offices and First Postmasters from 1775-1980.* State College, Pa.: American Philatelic Society, 1982.

Kelly, Arthur C.M. *Baptismal Records Athens, N.Y. 1704-1899.* Rhinebeck, N.Y.: privately printed by the author, 1974.

Ketchum, William C. Jr. *Early Potters and Potteries of New York State.* New York: Funk and Wagnalls, 1970.

Kisselburgh, John W. *Shadows of the Half Moon.* New York: Vantage Press, 1972.

Ladue, Vincent. "Greene County Agriculture." *Catskill Center News,* June 1987.

LaMont, T.E. *Classification of Land in Greene County.* Dept. of Agricultural Economics and Farm Management, N.Y.S. College of Agriculture. A.E. 267. March 1939.

Levine, Gary. *Anatomy of a Gangster: Jack "Legs" Diamond.* South Brunswick, N.J.: A.S. Barnes and Co., 1979.

Longstreth, T. Morris. *The Catskills. New York:* Century, 1918.

MacGahan, John A. *Twilight Park: The First Hundred Years.* South Yarmouth, Mass.: Allen D. Bragdon, 1988.

Mack, Arthur C. *Enjoying the Catskills.* New York: Funk and Wagnalls, 1950.

McAlpine, William J. *Reports and Estimates for a Ship Canal and Basin from Albany to New Baltimore.* Albany, N.Y.: Weed, Parsons and Company, 1853.

McIntosh, Robert P. *The Forests of the Catskill Mountains, N.Y.* Cornwallville, N.Y.: Hope Farm Press, 1977.

McKay, Christine G., et al. *There's a Place Up in the Mountains: A Centennial History of Elka Park.* Elka Park, N.Y.: Elka Park Association, 1989.

McMurry, Sally A. *Farms and Farmhouses in Nineteenth Century America: Vernacular Design and Social Change.* New York: Oxford University Press, 1988.

Melish, John. *Travels through the United States of America.* London: privately printed for the author, 1818.

Meyer, George. "Rip Van Winkle Awoke in 1935." *Tannersville Topics Illustrated* 1937:6-7.

Miner, Tom and Steelman, Bill. *The Mountaintop Subdivision Study: A Report on Land Subdivision, 1980-86.* Arkville, N.Y.: Catskill Center, 1987.

Mitchill, Samuel. "A Sketch of the Mineralogical History of the State of New York." *Medical Repository,* First Hexade I, No. 3 (1798):293-314.

——, and Miller, Edward. "Remarks on the Yellow Fever at Catskill, 1803. *Medical Repository,* Second Hexade II(1804):105-121,232-242.

Mohican Trail. N.p., ca. 1925. [View book.]

Morton, Dora Vann. *New York Police Centre: A Short History.* Cornwallville, N.Y.: Hope Farm Press, 1972.

Mountaintop Historical Society. *The Hemlock.* Irregular. I (1978)-date.

[Murdock, David.] *The Scenery of the Catskills.* Catskill: J.B. Hall and Son, [1846] 1872.

Myers, Kenneth. *The Catskills: Painters, Writers, and Tourists in the Mountains 1820-1895.* Yonkers, N.Y.: Hudson River Museum, 1987.

Newland, D.H. *The Mining and Quarry Industry of New York State.* New York State Museum, Bulletin 178. Albany, N.Y.: New York State Museum, 1914.

New York Central System. *West Shore River Division Time Table.* N.p., Sept. 27, 1953. [Railroad timetable.]

New York City. Board of Water Supply. *Catskill Water Supply: A General Description.* New York: The Board, 1926.

——. *Map and Profile.* New York: The Board, 1905.

New York State Agricultural Society. *Transactions.* Cited as TNYSAS.

New York State, Department of Agriculture. *The Fruit Industry in New York State.* Bulletin 79. Albany, N.Y.: The Department, 1916.

——. *The Sheep Industry in New York State.* Albany, N.Y.: The Department, n.d.

——. *List of Milk Plants and Establishments in New York* State. Bulletin 236. Albany, N.Y.: The Department, 1930.

——. *List of Milk Dealers and Milk Plants in New York State.* Bulletin 401. Albany, N.Y.: The Department, 1961.

New York State, Commissioner of Highways. *Report of the State Commissioner of Highways.* Albany, N.Y.: J.B. Lyon, 1920.

New York State, Department of Farms and Markets. *List of Creameries, Cheese Factories, Milk Stations, Condensed Milk Plants and Powdered Milk Plants in New York State.* Bulletin 112. Albany, N.Y.: The Department, 1918.

New York State, Department of Labor. *Industrial Directory.* Albany, N.Y.: The Department, 1912.

New York State Museum. *Geology of the Catskill and Kaaterskill Quadrangle.* Bulletin 331. Albany, N.Y.: The Museum, 1942.

——. *Geology of the Coxsackie Quadrangle.* Bulletin 332. Albany, N.Y.: The Museum, 1943.

Nicholson, V.H. *The Capital District Regional Market at Menands.* Dept. of Agricultural Economics, N.Y.S. College of Agriculture. A.E. 423. Ithaca, N.Y.: The Department, 1943.

Olsen, Margaret Radcliff. *East Windham, New York.* N.p., 1989.

Overbaugh, Francis. *The Hotel Kaaterskill: Clippings from the Past.* N.p., n.d.

Palatines of New York State. N.p.: The Palatine Society, 1953.

Parker, Arthur C. *The Archaeological History of New York.* New York State Museum, Bulletin 237-238. Albany, N.Y.: The Museum, 1922.

Paulding, James Kirke. *The New Mirror for Travellers; and Guide to the Springs.* New York: G.C. Carvill, 1828.

Pavlak, Joseph. *Alsen.* Catskill, N.Y.: privately printed by the author, 1991.

——. *Smith's Landing...Cementon.* Catskill, N.Y.: privately printed by the author, 1985.

Pepe, Paul E. *The Sleeping Giant.* Hunter, N.Y.: Hunter Mountain News Corporation, 1993.

Phinney, William R. *Maggie Newton Van Cott.* Rye, N.Y.: United Methodist Church Commission on Archives and History, 1969.

Pinckney, James D. *Reminiscences of Catskill: Local Sketches.* Catskill, N.Y.: J.B. Hall, 1868.

Posselt, Eric. *The Rip Van Winkle Trail.* Haines Falls, N.Y.: Arrowhead Press, 1952.

Pratt, Zadock. *Description of the Prattsville Tannery.* New York, 1847.

Prattsville Agricultural and Horticultural Association. *Premium List.* Prattsville, N.Y.: The Association, 1910.

Priest, Josiah. *The Low Dutch Prisoner: Being an Account of the Captivity of Frederick Schermerhorn.* Albany, N.Y.: privately printed by the author, 1839.

Princeton Ski Bowl on Bearpen Mount. Prattsville, N.Y., n.d.(ca. 1955). [Brochure.]

Prout, Henry Hedges. *Old Times In Windham.* Cornwallville, N.Y.: Hope Farm Press, 1970.

Report of the Commissioner of Patents for the Year 1861: Agriculture. Washington, D.C.: GPO, 1862.

Report of the Railroads Committee Upon Several Petitions for Legislative Aid to the Canajoharie and Catskill Railroad, 1838. Cornwallville, N.Y.: Hope Farm Press, 1973.

Resorts of the Catskills. New York: St. Martin's Press, 1979.

Ringwald, Donald C. *Hudson River Day Line.* Berkeley, Calif.: Howell-North, 1965.

Rochefaucault-Liancourt, Duke de la. *Travels through the United States of North America.* London: R. Phillips, 1799.

Rockwell, Rev. Charles. *The Catskill Mountains and the Region Around.* New York: Taintor Brothers, 1867. Reprint,Cornwallville, N.Y.: Hope Farm Press, 1973.

Ross, Claire and Kozacek, Edward R. *Greene County, N.Y. '76 Bicentennial Overview: Beginnings and Background.* Catskill, N.Y.: Enterprise, 1976.

Ryan, Buttons. "East Durham in the Roaring 20s." *Greene County News,* July 28, 1977.

——. "East Durham in the 40s and 50s." *Greene County News,* Aug. 4, 1977.

——. "East Durham in the 60s and 70s." *Greene County News,* Aug. 11, 1977.

Salomon, Julian H. *Indians of the Lower Hudson Region: The Munsee.* New City, N.Y.: Historical Society of Rockland County, 1982.

Saunders, A. Fred. "Memories of Steamboat Days on the Hudson 1884 to 1907. *American Neptune* 18 (1958): 223-234.

Schneider, David M. *The History of Public Welfare in New York State 1609-1866.* Montclair, N.J.: Patterson Smith, 1969.

Schwartzbaum, Bertram E. *Congregation Anshi Hashoran 1899-1974.*Tannersville, N.Y.: 1974.

Shattuck, Marquis E. "Entries in the Account Book of Teunis Van Vechten 1753-82." *Detroit Society for Genealogical Research Magazine* 16(1953):49-54.

Slutzky, Israel. *History and Remembrances, Diamond Jubilee, May 21, 1989, Congregation Anshe Kol Yisroal.* Hunter, N.Y.,1989.

Smith, Mabel Parker. *Greene County, N.Y.: A Short History.* Catskill, N.Y.: Greene County Board of Supervisors, 1963.

Smith, Richard. *A Tour of Four Great Rivers.* Edited by Francis W. Halsey. New York: Scribner, 1906.

Spafford, Horatio Gates. *A Gazetteer of the State of New York.*Albany, N.Y.: H.C. Southwick, 1813.

———. *A Gazetteer of the State of New York.* Albany, N.Y.: B.D. Packard, 1824.

Spees, S. Granby. *Memorial Celebration Comprising the Address Delivered on the Occasion (of Greenville's Centennial).*Saratoga Springs, N.Y.: 1872.

Standard Road-Book of New York State. Boston: W.L. Chase and Co.,1897.

Sutch, Gerald E. *The Civil War: The Town of Prattsville, and the Neighboring Greene, Delaware and Schoharie County Area.* Cornwallville, N.Y.: Hope Farm Press, 1986.

Swain, Charles B. *First Annual Black Culture Festival in Greene County.* Catskill, N.Y., 1978.

Tompkins, Flora. *Ashland Collegiate Institute and Musical Academy.* Cornwallville, N.Y.: Hope Farm Press, 1979.

Tourist for 1836. New York: Harper and Brothers, 1836.

Ulster and Delaware Railroad. *The Catskill Mountains.* Kingston, N.Y., 1908.

United States, Department of the Interior, Census Office. *Eighth Census (1860). Manufactures of the United States in 1860.* Washington, D.C.: GPO, 1865.

————. *Ninth Census (1870). The Statistics of the Wealth and Industry of the United States.* Washington, D.C.: GPO, 1872.

————. *Report of the Manufactures of the United States at the Tenth Census.* Washington, D.C.: GPO, 1883.

————. *Report of the Products of Agriculture: Tenth Census (1880).* Washington, D.C.: GPO, 1883.

————. *Reports on the State of Agriculture: Eleventh Census (1890).* Washington, D.C.: GPO, 1896.

————. *Census Reports: Twelfth Census (1900): Agriculture.* Washington, D.C.: GPO, 1902.

United States, Department of Commerce, Bureau of the Census. *Thirteenth Census (1910): Agriculture.* Washington, D.C.: GPO, 1913.

————. *Fourteenth Census (1920): Agriculture.* Washington, D.C.: GPO, 1922.

————. *Fifteenth Census (1930): Agriculture.* Washington, D.C.: GPO, 1932.

————. *U.S. Census of Agriculture (1935).* Washington, D.C.: GPO, 1936.

————. *Sixteenth Census (1940): Agriculture.* Washington, D.C.: GPO, 1943.

————. *U.S. Census of Agriculture: 1945.* Washington, D.C.: GPO, 1946.

————. *Abandoned and Idle Farms.* Washington, D.C.: GPO, 1943.

————. *U.S. Census of Agriculture: 1950.* Washington, D.C.: GPO, 1952.

————. *U.S. Census of Agriculture 1954.* Washington, D.C.: GPO, 1956.

————. *U.S. Census of Agriculture 1959.* Washington, D.C.: GPO, 1961.

————. *1964 U.S. Census of Agriculture.* Washington, D.C.: GPO, 1966.

————. *1969 Census of Agriculture.* Washington, D.C.: GPO, 1972.

————. *1974 Census of Agriculture.* Washington, D.C.: GPO, 1977.

————. *1978 Census of Agriculture.* Washington, D.C.: GPO, 1981.

Van Bergen, Robert Henry. *Ye Olden Time.* Edited by Francis A. Hallenbeck. Coxsackie, N.Y., 1935.

Van Gelder, Arthur P. and Schlacter, Hugh. *History of the Explosive Industry in America.* New York: Columbia University Press, 1927.

Van Valkenburgh, Norman J. *The Forest Preserve of New York State in the Adirondack and Catskill Mountains: A Short History.* Schenectady, N.Y.: Union College, 1983.

————. *Land Acquisition for New York State: An Historical Perspective.* Arkville, N.Y.: Catskill Center, 1985.

Van Wagner, Edith, ed. *Agricultural Manual of New York State, Arranged by Counties.* Department of Farms and Markets Bull. 133. Albany, N.Y.: The Department, n.d.

Van Zandt, Roland. *The Catskill Mountain House.* New Brunswick, N.J.: Rutgers University Press, 1966; republished, Black Dome Press, 1991.

Vedder, J. Van Vechten. *History of Greene County. 1651-1800.* Catskill, N.Y.: County Historian, 1927.

————. *Historic Catskill.* Catskill, N.Y.: privately printed by the author, 1922.

Weed, Thurlow. *Life of Thurlow Weed, Including His Autobiography and a Memoir.* 1882.

Welsh, Peter C. *Tanning in the United States to 1850: A Brief History.* Washington, D.C.: Smithsonian, 1964.

Wheeler, Candace. *Yesterdays in a Busy Life*. New York: Harper, 1918.

Wiles, Richard C. "Windham." *The Hudson Valley Regional Review*. 2(1985):54-72.

Winterbothan, William. *An Historical, Geographical and Philosophical View of the United States of America*. New York: J. Reid, 1796.

Women's Christian Temperance Union. *Annual Report of the WCTU of the State of New York*. N.p., 1927, 1937.

Woodworth, Olive Newell. *East Kill Valley Genealogy*.Cornwallville, N.Y.: Hope Farm Press, 1974.

——. *Methodism in the Catskills*. East Jewett, N.Y.: Methodist Church, 1966.

SOURCES CONSULTED: UNPUBLISHED

Adams, Calvin. *Daybook*. 1835-42. Manuscript in New York State Historical Association, Cooperstown, N.Y.

Albany Committee of Correspondence. *Transcript of Minutes* 1775-78. Manuscript in GCHS.

Backus, Andrew. *Letter*. July 16, 1815. Backus Papers, John Hay Library, Brown University, Providence, R.I.

Borthwick, W.S. *Papers*. Manuscript in GCHS.

Brown, Rev. Clark. *Topographical Description of Catskill in the State of New York*. 1803. Transcript of original at Massachusetts Historical Society. In GCHS.

Brunger, Eric. *Changes in the New York State Dairying Industry*. Ed.D. dissertation, Oswego State Teachers' College, 1943.

Catskill Cement Co. *Minutes*. 1899. Manuscript in GCHS.

Catskill Mountain Creamery. *Records*. 1889-93. Manuscript in GCHS.

Chace, Paul G. *Many Worthy Young Men: Nathan Clark's Potters in New York State*. 1970. Manuscript in GCHS.

Chronicle of Fame and Fortune in Greene County. 1973. Manuscript in GCHS.

Coxackie, Map of. 1797. In Secretary of State Papers, New York State Archives, Albany, N.Y.

Crandell, Harriet. *Diary*. 1863-64. Transcript in GCHS.

Cross, Thomas R. *The Greene County Resort Industry*. 1978. Manuscript in GCHS.

Decker, K. "Emily Becker of Catskill." Manuscript in GCHS.

Dunn, Jennie Haines. *Papers, especially notebooks on the settlement of Hunter*. Manuscript in New York State Historical Association, Cooperstown, N.Y.

Edwards, William H. *Account dated Dec. 22, 1896 at Coalburgh, W.Va*. Manuscript in Mountain Top Historical Society, Haines Falls, N.Y.

Erdmann, David G. *The Susquehanna Turnpike in Greene County, N.Y., 1800-1901*. Manuscript in GCHS.

Farmers' Freighting Line Company. *Records*. Manuscript in GCHS.

Green, Timothy. *Agreement to work marble quarry owned by him*. 1804. Manuscript in GCHS.

Greene County Clerk. Deeds.

Horne, Field. *Agricultural production chart prepared from U.S. and New York State agricultural census reports*. Manuscript in GCHS.

Ingalls, Gerald. *Interview, July 18, 1990*. Manuscript held by Greenville Town Historian, Greenville, N.Y.

Ku Klux Klan. *Records of Prattsville Klavern*. 1925-28. Manuscript in New York State Library, Manuscripts and Special Collections Section, Albany, N.Y.

Kudish, Michael. *Vegetational History of the Catskill High Peaks*. Ph.D. diss., SUC Forestry at Syracuse, 1971.

Lindemann, Roland, Catskill Game Farm. *Letter to C.E. Dornbusch.* January 27, 1966. Manuscript in GCHS.

McKnight, Nellie. *Memo.* Mar. 29, 1930. Manuscript in GCHS.

Noyes, Samuel. *Letter from His Cousin Charles He(nty?) at Catskill.* April 30, 1836. Transcript in GCHS.

Reilly, John T. *The Confiscation and Sale of the Loyalist Estates and its Effect Upon the Democracy of Landholding in New York State 1779-1800.* Ph.D. dissertation, Fordham University, 1974.

Schmidt, M. and Schmidt, M. *Interview by Lois Howser.* 1973. Transcript in GCHS.

Seward, E. Harris. *A Study of Current Trends in Resort Facilities and the Vacation Image of Greene County, N.Y.* 1965. Manuscript in GCHS.

Strong, Selah. *Weavers' Account Book.* 1779. Manuscript in GCHS.

United States. Bureau of the Census. *Census Data Taken From Photostatic Sheets Received from the Census Bureau by M.C. Bond.* 1935. 2 v. Mann Library, Cornell University.

United States, Bureau of the Census. *Products of Industry. Schedules,* Greene County. 1820.

———. *Products of Industry. Schedules, Greene County.* 1850.

———. *Products of Industry. Schedules, Greene County.* 1860.

———. *Products of Industry. Schedules, Greene County.* 1870.

———. *Products of Industry. Schedules, Greene County.* 1880.

———. *Population Schedules. Schedules, Greene County.* 1850.

Van Gastel, Ada. *Adriaen Van der Donck, New Netherland and America.* Ph.D. dissertation, Penn. State University, 1985. "Vosburgh-Carrington House." Manuscript in GCHS.

Mahican and Lenape placenames are not included. Many other European-American placenames can be identified using deeds and other records less readily available.

ASHLAND, formed from Windham and Prattsville, Mar. 23, 1848.

Ashland p.o., name changed Apr. 20, 1848. Previously:
    Scienceville p.o. 1823-48.
East Ashland: appears on 1867 map.
Four Corners, locality.
West Settlement. Previously:
    Richmond Corners: appears on 1867 map.

ATHENS, formed from Catskill and Coxsackie, Feb. 25, 1815.

Athens, incorp. village 1805, p.o. 1810, name changed from: Loonenburgh p.o. 1803-
    10. Originally land patent name 1667. Esperanza, village plat 1794, merged into
    Athens.
Athens Station, railroad placename, 1872.
Limestreet p.o. 1891-1903.
Prentiss, station of Athens p.o. 1891-1903. Location not yet identified; probably on Old
    King's Road near West Athens.
West Athens, locality.

CAIRO, formed as "Canton" Mar. 26, 1803 from Catskill, Coxsackie and "Freehold"
[now Durham], name changed Apr. 6, 1808.

Acra p.o. 1827-date.
Cairo p.o. 1804-date. Alternate name:
    Canton p.o. 1804-17.
Purling p.o. 1894-date. Previously:
    Forge [sometimes Cairo Forge]: business est. 1788.
Round Top p.o. 1879-87, 1910-date.
Sandy Plains, locality.
South Cairo p.o. 1837-date.
Woodstock, locality.

CATSKILL, formed Mar. 7, 1788 as a town of Albany co., annexed to Ulster co. Apr. 5,
1798, founding town of Greene co. Mar. 25, 1800. Ceded territory to Cairo 1803, Athens
1815; annexed territory from Woodstock Mar. 25, 1800.

Alsen p.o. 1902-47. Railroad stop and cement plant est. 1901.
Blivinville, locality. Now part of Catskill village.
Cairo Junction, railroad locality 1885-1917.
Catskill p.o. 1800. Incorp. village 1806. Previously:
    Catskill Landing.
Cauterskill, locality. Previously:
    Belfast Mills.

Cementon p.o. 1906-date. Previously:
  Smith's Landing p.o. 1875-1906.
Embought, farming district. Previously:
  Great Embought.
Hamburg on Hudson, fishing hamlet.
High Falls, locality. Previously:
  Great Falls p.o. 1887-91, station of Saxton, Ulster co.
Jefferson Heights, part of Catskill. Previously:
  Jefferson Flats. Previously:
  Jefferson.
Kiskatom, locality. See also Lawrenceville.
Lawrenceville. Previously:
  Kiskatom p.o. 1843-63, 1874-1902.
Leeds p.o. 1827-date. Previously:
  Mill Village p.o. 1827. Previously:
  Madison. Previously:
  [Old] Catskill.
Palenville p.o. 1826-date. Alternately:
  Irvingsville p.o. 1833-41.
West Catskill. Now part of Catskill village.

COXSACKIE, formed Mar. 7, 1788 as a town of Albany co. Freehold [Durham] taken off 1790. Original town of Greene co. 1800. Parts of Cairo and Greenville taken off 1803. New Baltimore taken off 1811. Part of Athens taken off 1815.

Climax p.o. 1892-date. Previously:
  Lime Rock. Previously:
  Guinea Hill.
Coxsackie p.o. 1805-date. Incorp. village 1867. Land patent name from 1662.
Earlton p.o. 1929-date. Previously:
  Urlton p.o. 1886-1929.
High Hill, locality.
Jacksonville, hamlet.
Loxea p.o. 1880-86, station of Coxsackie p.o. Location not yet identified; possibly at
  Climax.
Result p.o. 1890-1908.
West Coxsackie p.o. 1886-date.

DURHAM, formed as "Freehold" Mar. 8, 1790 as a town of Albany co. Original town of Greene co. 1800. Parts of Cairo and Greenville taken off 1803. Name changed Mar. 28, 1805. Called "New Durham" at time of settlement.

Broadway, rural district.
Cornwallville p.o. 1826-date.
Durham p.o. 1808-date. Previously:
  Freehold p.o. 1800-08.
Durham Center, hamlet.
East Durham p.o. 1839-date. Previously:
  Winansville p.o. 1832-39.
East Windham p.o. 1849-1979.
Hervey Street, hamlet.

Meetinghouse HIll, rural district
Oak Hill p.o. 1818-date. Previously:
    DeWittsburgh.
Saybrook HIll, rural district.
South Durham p.o. 1817-1942.
Sunside p.o. 1893-1945. Previously:
    Centreville.
West Durham, hamlet.
Wright Street, rural district.

GREENVILLE, formed as "Greenfield" Mar. 26, 1803. Name changed to "Freehold" 1808, to Greenville Mar. 17, 1809.

Freehold p.o. 1820-date (with gaps).
Gayhead p.o. 1831-1955.
Greenville p.o. 1812-date. Inc. village. Previously:
    Greenfield (cf. Coxsackie map 1797).
Greenville Center p.o. 1887-1960.
Newry, locality, on border of Albany co.
Norton Hill p.o. 1849-date.
O'Hara Corners, locality. Place Corners, locality.
Surprise p.o. 1889-1990.
West Greenville, hamlet.

HALCOTT, formed from Lexington, Nov. 19, 1851.

Halcott p.o. 1892. Probably same locality as West Lexington.
Halcott Center, p.o. 1862-date.
West Lexington p.o. 1840-59.

HUNTER, formed as "Greenland" Jan. 27, 1813. Name changed Apr. 15, 1814. Part of Saugerties taken off 1814. Part of Jewett taken off 1849.

Beechview p.o. 1919-38, station of Haines Falls p.o. Same as:
    Catskill Mountain House. Previously:
    Pine Orchard.
East Hunter p.o. 1826-42.
Edgewood p.o. 1881-1915 (factory opened Aug. 1881).
Elka Park p.o. 1893-date. Development began 1889.
Haines Falls p.o. 1883-date. Previously:
    Haines Corners.
Hunter p.o. 1818-date. Incorp. village 1894. Alternate name:
    Edwardsville, briefly c.1820.
Kaaterskill p.o. 1882-1925 (with gaps). Hotel built 1882.
Kaaterskill Junction, railroad locality, 1882-1940.
Kaaterskill Station p.o. 1914-17 as sta. of Haines Falls.
Lanesville p.o. 1871-date.
Maplecrest p.o. 1921-date. Previously:
    Big Hollow p.o. 1829-1921.

Onteora Park. Development began 1887.
Philadelphia Hill, private park.
Platte Clove p.o. 1875-1919.
Stoney Clove p.o. 1858-62.
Tannersville p.o. 1833-date. Incorp. village 1895.
Twilight Park. Development began 1887.

JEWETT, formed Nov. 14, 1849 from Hunter and Lexington.

Beaches Corner p.o. 1878-1910.
East Jewett p.o. 1854-date. Previously:
    East Kill p.o. 1829-1854.
Goshen Street, formerly a farming district.
Jewett p.o. 1850-date. Also Jewett Heights. Previously:
    Lexington Heights p.o. 1819-1850 (with gaps).
Jewett Center p.o. 1850-1902. Previously:
    East Lexington p.o. 1832-50.
South Jewett, locality.
West Jewett, locality.

LEXINGTON, formed as "New Goshen" Jan. 27, 1813 from Windham. Name changed
Mar. 19, 1813. Part of Jewett taken off 1849, a small part annexed back 1858. Part of
Halcott taken off 1851.

Broadstreet Hollow, locality. Also Forest Valley.
Bushnellsville p.o. 1844-1927.
Lexington p.o. 1815-date.
Mosquito Point, locality.
North Lexington, locality. Formerly:
    Barbertown.
Sportsville p.o. 1834-35. Identified as being in Lexington
    (then including Halcott andwest part of Jewett) by Disturnell, 382.
Spruceton p.o. 1879-1957.
West Kill p.o. 1833-date.

NEW BALTIMORE, formed Mar. 15, 1811 from Coxsackie. Shutters, Little and Willow
Islands annexed from Kinderhook Apr. 23, 1823.

Grapeville p.o. 1869-1920.
Hannacroix p.o. 1924-date. Previously:
    New Baltimore Station p.o. 1887-1924.
Medway p.o. 1847-1919. Previously:
    Four Corners.
New Baltimore p.o. 1823-date.
Staco, locality.
Stanton Hill p.o. 1873-1904.
Sylvandale p.o. 1898-1904, station of New Baltimore Station p.o.,
    near present Shady Lane and Sodom Road.
West Baltimore p.o. 1830-31.

PRATTSVILLE, formed Mar. 8, 1833 from Windham. Part of Ashland taken off 1848.

Huntersfield, farming district.
Little Westkill, farming district.
Prattsville p.o. 1833-date. Previously:
    Schoharie Kill p.o. 1821-1833. Previously:
    Batavia, pre-Revolutionary name.
Red Falls p.o. 1848-1904.

WINDHAM, formed from Woodstock Mar. 23, 1798 as a town of Ulster co. Original town of Greene co. 1800. Part of "Freehold" [Durham] annexed 1803. "Greenland" [Hunter] taken off 1813. Prattsville taken off 1833. Part of Ashland taken off 1848.

Brooksburg p.o. 1912-23. Also Brooklyn. Previously:
    Union Society p.o. 1850-68, 1870-1912. East Windham [see Durham town].
Hensonville p.o. 1853-date. Previously:
    Baileys Four Corners p.o. 1850-53. Previously:
    Union Society p.o. 1825-50.
Mitchell Hollow, locality.
Nauvoo, locality in 1905 census schedule.
North Settlement, (former) farming district.
Windham p.o. 1873-date. Previously:
    Windham Center p.o. 1837-73. Previously:
    Osbornville p.o. 1831-37.
Windham p.o. 1801-53. Alternate name:
    Batavia 1801-03.

Sources:

J.H. French, *Historical and Statistical Gazetteer of New York State* (Syracuse: R.P. Smith, 1860).

John L. Kay and Chester M. Smith, Jr., *New York Postal History: The Post Offices and First Postmasters from 1775 to 1980* (State College: American Philatelic Society, 1982).

POPULATION OF GREENE COUNTY

	1800	1810	1820	1830	1840	1850	1860	1870	1880	1890	1900	1910	1920	1930	1940	1950	1960	1970	1980	1990
Ashland						1290	1212	992	899	787	692	640	560	482	566	542	548	630	744	803
Athens			2030	2425	2593	2986	2791	2942	3065	2876	2891	2720	2361	2254	2375	2372	2894	2991	3462	3561
Cairo		2035	2353	2912	2812	2831	2479	2283	2287	2191	2176	1841	1487	1772	1905	1944	2825	3546	4729	5418
Catskill	2408	4245	3510	4861	3458	5454	6275	7677	8311	8263	8566	9066	7670	8200	8630	8575	9906	10432	11453	11965
Coxsackie	4676	4047	2353	3373	3799	3741	3661	3829	4009	3773	4102	3620	2994	3139	4146	4703	4794	4812	6018	7633
Durham*	3812	2944	2980	3039	2613	2600	2558	2257	2173	1925	1636	1475	1211	1104	1223	1233	1313	1650	2283	2324
Greenville		2304	2374	2565	2261	2242	2268	2084	2043	1951	1651	1556	1362	1276	1477	1613	1879	2279	2849	3135
Halcott							504	426	396	357	350	331	272	223	273	244	193	199	150	189
Hunter			1025	1960	2433	1849	1698	1524	1882	2436	2788	2699	2309	2299	2166	2028	1799	1742	2252	2116
Jewett						1452	1145	1105	1075	976	1028	1057	883	835	732	692	562	600	723	933
Lexington			1798	2548	2902	2263	1657	1371	1356	1229	1153	1054	1075	815	827	833	698	666	819	835
New Balto			2036	2370	2347	2831	2512	2617	2620	2455	2283	1936	1536	1434	1489	1781	1972	2068	3050	3371
Prattsville				2069	1989	1511	1240	1118	876	775	781	830	706	848	825	790	721	666	774
Windham	1688	3961	2536	3472	2670	2048	1659	1485	1461	1503	1387	1438	1246	1269	1269	1360	1289	1190	1663	1682
TOTAL	12584	19536	22996	29525	30446	33126	31930	31832	32695	31598	31478	30214	25796	25808	27926	28745	31372	33526	40861	44739

* 1800 statistic is for "Freehold"

The Catskill Mountain House, *America's Grandest Hotel*, by Roland Van Zandt. The classic study of the pursuit of the Romantic Ideal in America, personified in the birth, growth and fiery death of the nation's first mountain resort hotel, built in 1823 and perched "like the wish of a child on the very edge of an overhanging ledge of the mountains, commanding a view that was once the most famous in America." "**The Catskill Mountain House** *is the story of a love affair—love at first sight. Mr. Van Zandt follows the great days of the famous hostelry with pride and the days of its decay with heartbreak.*" (*The New York Times*) 448 pages, 94 illustrations, 9 maps, paper, $19.95.

Through A Woman's Eye, *Pioneering Photographers in Rural Upstate*, by Diane Galusha. Turn-of-the-century rural America as it was seen and experienced by three farmers' daughters who became pioneering photographers in the remote northwestern Catskill Mountains. They became the principal chroniclers of their communities, preserving for all time images of a bygone world, affording the modern viewer a window on the past through the unique perspective of a woman's eye. 200 pages, 61 full page photographs, paper, $29.95.

The Old Eagle-Nester, *The Lost Legends of the Catskills*, by Doris West Brooks. Nominated for a national story-telling award, **The Old Eagle-Nester** combines fiction and legend with a "pinch of magic and a smidgen of witchcraft." "*A beautifully designed and illustrated book,*" said the *Hudson Valley Literary Supplement. Dutchess Magazine* proclaimed, "*This is wonderful stuff, some of it funny, some of it frightening, all of it entertaining.*" 128 pages, illustrations, paper, $13.95.

The Mill on the Roeliff Jansen Kill, by The Roeliff Jansen Historical Society. From its founding in 1743 by the Livingston family, through 250 years of Hudson Valley history, the story of the oldest operating commercial mill in New York State, a collaborative work by seven historians, was recognized by a joint legislative resolution by the Senate and Assembly of New York State commemorating this publication. 144 pages, 36 photographs, 2 maps, paper, $15.00.

Chronicles of the Hudson, *Three Centuries of Travel and Adventure*, by Roland Van Zandt. From Robert Juet aboard the Half Moon in 1609, to Henry James's reflections as he viewed the Hudson through the windows of a steam engine train in 1905, Van Zandt captures 300 years of travelers' adventures and perspectives in this "journey through time." Hudson Riverkeeper John Cronin, in his introduction notes: "Each generation born to the Hudson is entitled to its own journey of discovery. Roland Van Zandt's legacy to us is as a friend and tour guide on that journey." 384 pages, 51 illustrations & maps, paper, $24.95.

Kaaterskill, *From the Catskill Mountain House to the Hudson River School*, by the Mountain Top Historical Society. The legendary Kaaterskill—synonymous with scenic beauty; inspiration for Thomas Cole and the Hudson River School; the birthplace of

American mountain resorts; immortalized by James Fenimore Cooper and William Cullen Bryant; and now the heart of the Catskill Park and Preserve—profiled from seven different perspectives by seven prominent authors. 120 pages, 30 illustrations, hiking map, paper, $13.95.

Big Hollow, *A Mountaintop History,* by Elwood Hitchcock. An intimate portrait of an isolated mountain valley community that witnessed the changing fortunes of the Catskills in microcosm; from wilderness to a scattering of family farms, through the "grand hotel" era, to the modern day—a return to quiet farms and country retreats in the shadow of a decaying resort, all amid the splendor of a hiker's paradise of thousands of acres of forest preserve. *"If there is such a thing as 'living history,' Mr. Hitchcock and his book are it." (The Advocate)* 128 pages, 25 illustrations, paper, $14.95.

A Catskills Boyhood, *My Life Along the Hudson,* by Philip H. DuBois. An octogenarian professor emeritus recalls a bucolic childhood growing up in one of the oldest villages along the banks of the Hudson River, watching the advent of the modern age as the horse and carriage gives way to the Model-T. *"This book is filled with fascinating tidbits of life in the early century." (Kingston Freeman)* 128 pages, illustrations, paper, $12.95.

Mountaintop & Valley, *Greene County Folk Arts Today,* by Field Horne. Forty-eight folk artists profiled and photographed—from quilters, fish net weavers and stone wall builders to the "cutting edge" of chain saw carvers. Artists profiled were selected for the dignity and quality that their art presents, and the resulting book was awarded the coveted Heritage Award from the Federation of Historic Services. 48 pages, 33 photographs, paper, $10.00.

Black Dome Press Corp.,
RR 1, Box 422, Hensonville, NY, 12439.
Tel: 518 734-6357.
Fax: 518 734- 5802.
Prices & availability subject to change.